T0369452

Hand Guns, Concealed Carry, Gun Laws, Other Concerns, and Things You Should Know

A Basic Companion for the Casual Handgun Owner
and Concealed Handgun Carry License Holder

THIRD EDITION

HAMMOND SATTERFIELD

iUniverse, LLC
Bloomington

Hand Guns, Concealed Carry, Gun Laws, Other Concerns, and Things
You Should Know
A Basic Companion for the Casual Handgun Owner and Concealed Handgun
Carry License Holder

iUniverse books may be ordered through booksellers or by contacting:

iUniverse LLC
1663 Liberty Drive
Bloomington, IN 47403
www.iuniverse.com
1-800-Authors (1-800-288-4677)

ISBN: 978-1-4759-8694-5 (sc)
ISBN: 978-1-4759-8695-2 (ebk)

Library of Congress Control Number: 2013907646

Printed in the United States of America

iUniverse rev. date: 06/10/2013

The Second Edition, published April 1, 2013, included updates in the Arkansas concealed Carry
Laws which are used to illustrate and guide the reader through those dangerous areas where one
can run afoul of legal statutes. This Third Edition is for electronic distribution and incorporates a
re-titling of the book to more clearly state its contents.

Originally registered under the title: A Basic Companion for the Casual Handgun Owner and
Concealed Handgun Carry License Holder.

A printed version of this book was originally published in association with Micro Business
Publications, Inc. 12533 Rivercrest Drive Little Rock, AR 72212 under the title Hand Guns or
Roses, Handle with Care.

Contents

Could You Benefit From Reading This Book? Some Questions

So, you have some doubts as to whether or not you could benefit from spending a little money and time on this *Companion*? Take the following test. If you pass, you probably know quite a bit already. If you do not answer as many questions as you would like, or you do not make a passing grade of twenty correct answers out of twenty-five questions (80 percent), then this book just might be one of the best investments that you will ever make. One new item of information might possibly save you from hundreds to thousands of dollars. Review the test, and then decide for yourself. But,

"You makes your choices and you takes your chances."

1. What occurs when you fire a handgun straight up into the air?
2. Name the three general categories of handguns.
3. Of the eight most common styles of on-body holsters, how many can you describe?
4. What are the two major concerns that dictate the type of gun safe that you should consider?
5. What is the primary distinction between the crimes of "Assault" and the crimes of "Battery?"
6. Between the crimes of "Assault" and the crimes of "Battery," which type of crime is the typical handgun owner **most likely** to commit?
7. Do you understand the **legal** concept: "Choice of Evils?" Please explain.
8. What actions are you **lawfully** authorized to perform with a CHCL that a non-CHCL holder cannot lawfully perform?
9. If you **have** a CHCL, can you lawfully make a "Citizen's Arrest?"
10. If you **do not have** a CHCL, can you lawfully make a "Citizen's Arrest?"
11. Under what circumstances can you lawfully fire a warning shot to diffuse a dangerous situation?

12. Explain the difference to a shooter between a SA and a DA handgun.
13. Explain why "mushrooming" is an important characteristic you should consider.
14. How often should you clean your handgun?
15. You are fighting with a criminal who has grabbed onto your semiautomatic pistol. In the struggle the magazine gets ejected. You successfully wrench the handgun free and press the trigger. What happens? Explain three scenarios.
16. You have finished loading your six shot Ruger *Bear Cat* .22-caliber revolver with .22-caliber long rifle ammunition. You close the cylinder's loading aperture. You aim at your target and you squeeze the trigger, but nothing happens. Please explain.
17. Explain the following two terms: RN-FMJ and JHP.
18. What is one of the benefits of a semi having a "tang?"
19. If you have a CHCL, can you lawfully carry your weapon into a restaurant that sells alcohol and/or beer for consumption on premises?
20. If you are involved in a shooting incident, what is the common legal advice concerning what you tell the police?
21. Name two of the **most inexpensive** handgun ammos to use for target shooting?
22. Can you list three reasons that support your obtaining a CHCL?
23. Does it make a difference if you qualify at your CHCL class by firing a revolver rather than a semiautomatic?
24. What is the key difference between "Aggravated Assault" and "Assault in the First Degree" with a firearm?
25. Can you describe the circumstances under which you can lawfully shoot another human being?

Thank you for your patience in taking the above exercise. Hopefully, it was helpful in assisting you to determine your knowledge of handguns and handgun-related concerns. Twenty correct out of twenty-five answers is a score of 80 percent. Does your score demonstrate that you possess an adequate knowledge of handguns, handgun-related issues, laws, self-defense scenarios sufficient for your mental comfort, and for the safety of your family and friends?

If you are not an experienced "shootist," or handgun owner, the following definitions may assist you with the above test. These were placed after the test intentionally. After all, if you did not know these common terms, that indicates something about your knowledge level.

1. CHCL = Concealed Handgun Carry License
2. DA = Double Action
3. JHP = Jacketed Hollow Point
4. RN-FMJ = Round Nose-Full Metal Jacket
5. SA = Single Action

If you wish to submit comments or corrections, the author can be contacted at *Handgunsorroses@gmail.com*.

Test answers are in *Appendix D.*

Preface to the Third Edition

The original title of this manuscript was: *A Basic Companion for the Casual Handgun Owner or New Purchaser of a Pistol, and Anyone Interested in the Laws and Issues Pertaining to Handgun Ownership and Concealed Handgun Carry Responsibilities.* My Significant Other opined that normally the titles of books are not a full paragraph long. I was surprised at her inability to appreciate my effort to fully inform the potential purchaser of the book's content and value by the title. I challenged her to come up with a better title. She thought briefly, and then she suggested "Guns and Roses." With a smile of superior comprehension of the manuscript's contents, I reminded her there was zero, nil, nada, nothing to do with roses in the entire manuscript.

She thought for a minute and then explained that I was being too **literal.** *"Both a handgun and a rose are beautiful objects in their own right and for their own purposes. Each demands proper handling and care. Abuse handling either and their respective 'thorns' will inflict pain for your carelessness,"* she said.

As Fate would have it, I was advised that an aging rock band might have some type of paranoid, possessive obsession with a similar name, thus "Guns and Roses" was not to be. After considerable debate and discussion (with some heat I might add) a new title was created.

Thus the original title, *Hand Guns or Roses, Handle with Care,* was born. (There is still no mention of roses in the book.) Although that is a fantastic title, many more sober minded and less creative minds have opined that the title makes one think the book is a murder mystery, or a rock music compendium, or a flower guide. Bowing to reader feedback, publisher pressure, and some sense of having been right in my original assessment of the book's title, the new title is now a comprehensive statement of content and purpose.

Acknowledgements

As with all writing, this manuscript would never have seen the light of day without the assistance, encouragement, and work of others. My list of people to thank is longer than I can remember and for those I omit, please forgive that failure. My son, Holt Satterfield, was the initial inspiration for my writing endeavors. My wife, Gwynne, has been my constant and most vocal encourager until I finally wore her out with this manuscript. My brother, "Bick" Satterfield, took her place and is still my most vocal supporter. Angie Martin has helped me assemble bound scripts for reviews. Dr. Joe Crow assisted in taking those pictures that turned out well. Unfortunately, he was not available for all sessions. *BULLSEYE Guns and Ammo* graciously allowed me to take pictures of some of their inventory as did *Don's Weaponry*. Then there were those friends who spent their time reading various versions of the manuscript: John Thomason, John Dickens, Larry Little, Sandra Fiser, Gaylon Boshears, Artie Murphey, and others. In addition there were several professionals who also reviewed the work and gave invaluable comments. Because of their employment and reputations, they desired to remain anonymous. Nevertheless, a grateful thanks to them too. My thanks to Ken Goosen who encouraged and assisted in the publishing of this work. And finally thanks to Grace Quay who did her best to wrestle this manuscript into some semblance of proper "Queen's English."

In spite of all their help, assistance, recommendations, and corrections you may still encounter the lurking error, confusion, or grammatical issue; they are mine, and mine alone to bear.

Introduction

Hand Guns, Concealed Carry, Gun Laws, Other Concerns, and Things You Should Know is written for you, the average citizen, not for the gun expert. What can you expect to learn from reading this *Companion*? First, you will not become sufficiently educated to work in a gun shop, or to teach a course on handguns. Then, how will you benefit from reading this book? It is the author's expectation that you will have enhanced your capabilities in the following:

1   You will understand the basics of handgun operation and the strengths and weaknesses of each of the three major categories of handguns.

2.   You will have sufficient knowledge to assess which type of handgun best meets your unique requirements.

3.   You will understand the differences in ammo types and which might be the best selection for your requirements, as well as the best buy.

4.   You will have a good idea of which caliber handgun might best suit your unique self.

5.   Arkansas statutes are used to point out and emphasize specific areas where you, the handgun owner, are most likely to run afoul of the law. With more knowledge you will be better prepared to avoid handgun related troubles.

6.   You will know the basics of safe handgun storage.

7.   You will be knowledgeable in the options of concealed carry, the holster tradeoffs, and you should be competent to decide which holster is the best option for you.

8.   You will read some scenarios of dangerous encounters and how you might avoid, or survive, such encounters.

9.   You will be exposed to some new ideas and concepts.

10.   Most critically, you will be better educated on safe handgun handling.

11.   You could pick up ideas that might save you hundreds, if not thousands, of dollars over the years.

12.   You will be shown many of those legal missteps that can sneak up on you. That knowledge should assist you in avoiding a

"police encounter of the worst kind." The potential savings from avoiding legal expenses are too great to even estimate. In this area, knowledge can equal wealth—yours.

13.   Finally, this *Companion* is written for the lay person, by a layman. This book is not designed to cover one or two subjects "an inch wide and a mile deep." It is written to cover a range of related handgun issues and topics. You will receive broad perspective and knowledge. Some areas you may wish to research further. But you will receive sufficient knowledge in other areas to enable you to make competent decisions without further research.

I have used Arkansas statutes to discuss laws and implications. There are obvious reasons for this. First, that is where I live. Second, the Arkansas Law Library is convenient. The differences in the wording and statutes of every state will vary, but the implications and concerns of the citizen do not. What may be a 1st degree infraction in Arkansas may be a 2nd degree, or vice-a-versa, in another state. I hope that this book will be of great benefit to the reader regardless of state of residency. Once you have an outline, it should be much easier for you to research your own state's legal differences. Some states, such as Ohio, have excellent books covering gun-related legal issues.

After obtaining my own Concealed Handgun Carry License (CHCL), I discovered, despite the training, I was woefully ignorant of handguns, of critical gun-related laws, and of my liabilities. I also spent a lot of money on guns and gun paraphernalia which, in hindsight, was probably not necessary.

True, the best teacher is experience. But only a fool refuses to learn from the experiences of others, especially if those experiences of others were mistakes. If from reading this *Companion*, you can avoid some of my missteps, and become better informed on some of the little details, then I have been successful. If through this knowledge, you avoid some unnecessary expenses, then you have been even more successful.

Remember, *"Officer, I didn't know that was against the law,"* is probably even less effective when applied to handgun violations than to traffic tickets. *"What? You've got to be kidding! That's a stupid law!"* is not much of a defense either.

Readers beware! I am not a lawyer. I am not a gun expert. I am not employed by or paid by any gun manufacturer or any other interested organization or expert. So, why am I qualified to write this *Companion?* Like many of you, I was enthusiastic, but somewhat uninformed and not very knowledgeable when first turned loose with handgun purchase decisions, gun ownership responsibilities, and concealed carry legalities. Recognizing these deficiencies, I have learned much of this the old tough way, through hard work and experience.

Since completing my own CHCL class, I have invested in further handgun education. I completed the NRA's *Basic Pistol Course* (for which I received a certificate suitable for framing) and the training to become an Arkansas Licensed Instructor for the Concealed Handgun Carry Class. Despite this training, unfortunately, I found no single source that covered all of the necessary, related topics. Therefore, I have tried to combine a lot of handgun areas into one volume. If I can save you a little time, a little money, and a lot of heartache and broken dreams, then it has been a good endeavor for us both. This book just might turn out to be the best money that you ever invested in a book.

This *Companion* is sequenced somewhat in the chronological order of the decisions that you will face or should consider. Although later chapters often incorporate information from earlier ones, it is not necessary to read this book from front to back. It is not a novel or a textbook. Therefore, feel perfectly at ease skipping to a chapter which corresponds to your immediate interest or concern, even if not in the sequence supplied.

A Letter to the Ladies

Let me be very blunt. You are the prey. Whether the crime is rape, sexual assault, purse snatching, carjacking, kidnapping, battery, robbery, or spousal abuse, you are the prime target. There is nothing you can do to change your being viewed that way by the criminal. He sees you as a weaker physical being that he can intimidate or physically overcome more easily than a potential male victim. In addition, you have appeal as a female, depending on the miscreant's intent. Therefore, you are the easier target, the desired target, and the prime target.

You may have taken lessons in various types of fighting skills and techniques, and if you practice frequently and laboriously, you just might be able to discourage that two hundred and twenty-five pound perp intent on taking you down. However, as Damon Runyon wrote, *"The race is not always to the swift, nor the fight to the strong, but that's the way to bet."* If a "Hulk Hogan" sized miscreant suddenly turns up in your face, can you react swiftly enough to take him down? Maybe, but I am not going to bet my wife's future on that happening.

In December, 2011, a newspaper article told of the local police trying to subdue a man who, as it turns out, was high on a drug concoction of PCP and cocaine. Desperate, one officer "tasered" the man; the man just pulled the barbs out of his body and kept on coming at them.

In November, 2011, in a Little Rock, Arkansas, movie theater parking lot, a woman was walking to her car. Suddenly, a car swooped in beside her and a man jumped out and tasered her. She fell to the pavement. Somehow, she was able to roll underneath her car. Another man jumped out of the perp's car. Only her having the presence of mind to roll to safety under her car and the intrusion of a Good Samaritan walking by preserved her life, as she knew it.

The CDC released a report in December, 2011, stating *"that almost one in five women in the U.S. were rape or sexual assault victims, and 35% of those women who were raped as minors were also raped again as adults."*

The world is not the same as it was just a short time ago. There are some people roaming the streets who are consumed with evil and have no conscience. There are people out there who are so drug crazy, your life means nothing to them if it stands in their way to obtaining their next fix. And then there are those who are just criminals; who want what is yours, or even worse, want you.

Yes, you can do something to make the criminal's assessment of you as an easy target turn out to be wrong—very, very wrong.

A pistol is not a perfect solution to an imperfect world. Neither is chemotherapy a perfect solution to cancer, nor is open-heart surgery a perfect solution to a heart defect. But sometimes an imperfect solution does push the odds of survival, the odds of not being a victim, in your favor.

My daughter was walking with her small boys along the dirt road in front of her farm. Her two dogs, about fifty yards in front, ran up the small hill over which the road was meandering. Suddenly, shots rang out, seemingly right by her. My daughter froze, quickly gathering her small boys around her. She was frightened and began to call for her dogs. They did not come. Fortuitously, a neighbor drove up, and she explained the situation and her fright to him. He drove ahead and in a moment called for her to join him. When she crested the hill, there was blood over the side of the road, no dogs in sight. The dogs' bodies were later found by the Game Warden in a neighbor's field hidden behind a woodpile. She filed a formal complaint, and two men, her neighbors, were arrested. They spread the word that if they went to jail, *"There would be hell to pay!"* The threat was repeated abroad by relatives of the two dog-killers. The implication of their threat toward my daughter, her family, and her farm was made very clear. Several times when driving, she would look into her rear view mirror and discover one or the other of the dog-killers stalking her in a pickup truck. She took out a restraining order.

My daughter was unable to sleep. She was frightened to leave the house. Shopping was an ordeal of terror. Sending her children to school was an ordeal of misery. She feared that something terrible might happen to them while they were absent from her. She feared just being alone when the children were at school. Finally, she took the Concealed Handgun Carry License (CHCL) class and obtained a pistol. The difference in her confidence is amazing.

Not only can she now function in her daily routine, she feels confident that she can protect herself and her small boys. Can she truly? Well, honestly, that would depend on the situation. But there are a few things that are certain: she is armed, alert, legal, and she has a renewed confidence. The odds, if not in her favor, have at least been improved. As often said out west, "*God made man; Samuel Colt made man equal.*" This is probably even more relevant when applied to a woman.

There is another reason to consider becoming armed;

> . . . *based on data covering 1979-87 supplied by the Department of Justice's National Crime Victimization Survey, Lawrence Southwick found: 'the probability of serious injury from an attack is 2.5 times greater for women offering no resistance than for women resisting with a gun. In contrast, the probability of women being seriously injured was almost four times greater when resisting without a gun than when resisting with a gun.*

So, **if you are armed, and you resist an attack by a rapist or assailant, you have a 400% better chance of escape without serious harm than if you are unarmed and resist**. Yes, you are correct; carrying a handgun, even purchasing one, is a major decision and lifestyle change. You have a choice: you can get armed and improve your odds of survival, or just put your trust in blind luck.

"*Lightning and violence have one thing in common; they both strike somewhere.*"

But,

"*You makes your choices and you takes your chances.*"

A Memo to the Men:
Husbands and Fathers

It is probably a good time to review the details of the major clause of that contract into which you entered. Remember the oath you swore in front of God and Country to uphold that contract? I am talking about the "Contract" into which you entered when you were married and its codicil that is invoked when you become a father. That is right, your marriage vow contract. There is one major clause that is germane to our discussion here. It is the clause under which you swore and promised to be "the shepherd." You know, like the "good shepherd" over your flock. In fact, it is Biblical. Go to Ephesians 5:25 and read it for yourself. *"Husbands, love your wives, just as Christ also loved the church and gave Himself up for her."* And just what did Christ give up for the Church? As you well know, He gave up His life to save us. Just so, as the shepherd of your own flock—your family—you are obligated to defend them with your life.

No, I do not imply that in a time of crisis, that you just lie down on the floor and whimperingly beg some perp to take you as the sacrifice and let your family go. I am asserting that you, just as a shepherd does, take precautions and obtain the tools necessary to protect your flock, as well as being mentally prepared to confront aggression toward your family from criminals of any variety, kith, or kin. I know that you are one of the good-guy husbands and fathers by the very fact that you are reading this. You see, if you had been guilty of domestic abuse, child molestation, or had a restraining order against you, you would not be eligible for a CHCL. *(Arkansas statute: 5-26-313. Notice. A person who is convicted of any misdemeanor of domestic violence shall be notified by the court that it is unlawful for the person to ship, transport, or possess a firearm or ammunition pursuant to 18 U.S.C. § 922(g)(8) and (9), as it existed on January 1, 2007.)* Ergo, since you are reading this you have not done any of those bad things.

Remember the movie *My Fair Lady* with Rex Harrison and Audrey Hepburn? Rex Harrison, playing Professor Higgins, made the comment, *"Why can't a woman be more like man?"* Well, they just were not made that way, and praise the Lord for that. Generally, women are weaker physically. Plus, they do not carry that same characteristic of aggressive behavior that comes with the male. Yes, I agree that if you threaten the cub of the mother bear, you should watch out, but you know what I mean. Men are the ones who more often engage in physical contact sports and are normally the hunters and providers. Women serve a different, but vital role in the family. As a man, husband, and father, your job is to provide shelter and protection to your entire family.

Some like to use the analogy of you being the "sheep dog" to protect your sheep. I can buy into that analogy when it pertains to the world at large; you can intervene aggressively and bring harm to an assailant, just as a sheep dog would do to protect or defend. But a sheep dog, once the attacker is neutralized or chased off, just licks its paws and tends to its own business. As a husband and father, you have greater and longer lasting responsibilities. Yes, you defend aggressively, but then you have to bind up the wounds, treat the scratches, kiss the "boo-boos" of life, salve life's traumas, be a good listener, a companion, a friend, a role model, sensitive to the needs and desires of those you love, a provider, and the list goes on and on. That is why I think your role is more like a shepherd than a sheep dog.

Your first step is to prepare yourself. How? Well, prepare yourself by obtaining the tools with which you can protect your family when you are present. Unfortunately, as your family's shepherd, you cannot be there 24/7. But you can do something for those times that you are absent. You can ensure that your helpmate takes the necessary steps to prepare her to be capable of defending herself and family when you are not present. Whether it is with a pistol and CHCL, or merely a *Taser* or "Mr. Pepper," or self defense classes, or better yet, all of them—do not let her become a victim for lack of your diligence and effort. To repeat, if your wife: "*is **armed and resists** an attack by a rapist or assailant, she has a 400% better chance of escape without serious harm than if she is **unarmed and resists**.*" (This was taken from the Department of Justice's *National Crime Victimization Survey*, Lawrence Southwick.)

Of course you cannot arm a child, and children cannot obtain a CHCL. However, you should consider training and teaching firearm safety and skills to a child from a very young age. No amount of self-defense training can enable a child to overcome a two hundred pound felon, but you can train your children to avoid danger. Teach them the "Three S Rules of Survival: Don't do stupid things; Don't go with stupid people; and Don't go to stupid places." Of course this implies that you do not do these stupid things yourself. Remember you are the role model.

A simple example: "*Sally, if a stranger approaches you and tells you that his little puppy dog is lost. That it is a timid little puppy and will come to children more readily than adults. That the puppy's name is Fifi. 'Can you say Fifi little girl? Good.' And then asks you to come with him to find the puppy. Do Not Go! Turn and start screaming 'Help! Police!' at the top of your voice and run toward an adult who you know will protect you. If you go with a stranger, that is a stupid thing to do, and you are not a stupid girl. You are a very smart and wise girl.*" Tell her to keep running and screaming until she is safe in those friendly arms. Take her outside and practice. When you see a dumb stunt on TV that endangers a child, point that out to your child and explain how it violated the "Three S Rule." (Yes, I know that using the word *stupid* is not politically correct.)

Teaching "safety-consciousness," whether using the "Three S Rule," or your own safety rules or guidelines, is a life-long training process. It is not a one-shot conversation. For example, "*Sally, no good things happen in bars after midnight. If that's where Fred wants you to hang out with him, don't! It can get you assaulted, raped, or murdered. If he wants you to do a stupid thing in a stupid place, that makes me think he is a stupid kind of guy and not trustworthy of protecting you outside of my sight.*" (Obviously, Sally has grown up a little from the previous example.) Think that Sally will object and counter that Fred is a big guy and can protect her? In the December 23, 2011, issue of the *Arkansas Democrat Gazette* an article read:

> *Tavern Owner struck in Head! A Little Rock business owner was struck in the head with a gun in the parking lot during a robbery late Tuesday night. The owner told the police he stepped out of his bar about 12:20 a.m. to get something from his car parked just outside. On the way back inside, he was struck in the back of the head. Someone told him to empty his pockets.*

The man survived, but what if it had been Sally's Fred and the perp was really after Sally, or perhaps Sally was just a target of opportunity after he knocked out Fred? OK, so you don't buy into that scenario, try this one from the August 18, 2012, paper of same name:

> *A woman was robbed Thursday night at gunpoint outside the* [name withheld] *tavern . . . about 11:10 p.m.* [She] *was walking through the parking lot . . . when she was approached by a man holding a handgun. The man told* [her] *not to run and she tossed him her purse. The gunman took the purse . . . got into the passenger side of a . . . sedan that fled east . . .*

This young lady was very fortunate, they only wanted her purse. For a woman, especially an unescorted woman—wrong place, wrong time.

Well, some of my personal bias may creep in now and then, but you get the drift. You be the **Shepherd**! But you must also prepare your flock to be capable of defending themselves while they roam "in the meadow of life" beyond your personal view, or reach, or protection.

Well, so much for the sermon.

"You makes your choices and you takes your chances."

Chapter 1

Why Do You Need to Possess, Much Less Carry, a Handgun?

The Political Climate

Aren't you being a little paranoid? After all, you have the local police, the county sheriff, the state police, and the FBI to protect you. Why do you need a weapon to protect yourself, much less a handgun and a Concealed Handgun Carry License (CHCL) that allows you to tote the thing around with you? Do you know how heavy a loaded handgun is? And besides, don't you know that "guns kill people?" You could really hurt yourself! Haven't you read what the Brady Gun Control Advocacy Group says about this? Don't you agree that the NRA just endangers all of us with their advocacy? Don't you think that after all is said and done, you are just being paranoid?

The Local City Environment

On Tuesday evening September 6, 2011, at a T.E.A. Party meeting at the Fletcher Library in Little Rock, Arkansas, City Director Lance Hines was citing an example of his perception of inadequate Police response times to support the need to pass the 1% sales tax increase to be voted on the next Tuesday. He stated that in his district in West Little Rock, the average response time for police on a "code one" call, (shot fired?), was a fifteen to twenty minute average versus the rest of the city's five to ten minute average response time by police. (His facts, not mine.) He was encouraging a "Yes" vote so that the tax increase would pass. That would allow additional police stations to be located in his district to bring the response time in line with the rest of the city's five to ten minute average response time.

The implication of that statement is that you, the average citizen, needing police assistance for an encounter with an armed and dangerous perpetrator intent on doing you harm, will, on average, need to "entertain" the "perp" for at least five minutes prior to police help arriving **once you notify 911**. If the police are already dispatched on another "code one," you may have an even longer wait. And if the police decide to arrive with overwhelming force, (think multiple cars with those blue "thingees" flashing on top), you may have a longer wait since the first car may just park and wait for back up. (Remember the Connecticut home invasion in 2009 where three females were raped and burned alive as the first responder waited down the block for overwhelming force and Command to arrive?) The police have learned the hard way that bad things can happen to officers who attempt to handle "code one" incidents all by their lonesome.

Now do not get me wrong. The police do a very effective job. Their mere presence in a community aids in maintaining the general peace and criminal intimidation. Once a violent crime is committed, they respond quickly, investigate thoroughly, and strive to apprehend and bring the miscreant to justice. Unfortunately, they cannot be in all places at the same time. Most will admit that they cannot protect you from a criminal intent on doing you harm. Ronald L. Cruit in his book *Intruder In Your Home* has this opening quote: *"Crime is so far out of hand, we can't protect the average citizen. He must protect himself.—former chief, Los Angeles Police Department."*

Let me give you an analogy. Think of a shepherd with approximately 3,000 to 4,000 sheep spread out over 2,000 to 3,000 acres. Our shepherd is very vigilant and loves his job and is dedicated to protecting his flock. But the wolf does not alert the shepherd as to where and when he will attack the flock. Suddenly, the shepherd hears the baaing and bleating of terror and pain. He determines the location of the cries and heads off at a full run. If the wolf attack is close, he might get there in a minute or two. If the wolf attack, as they often are, occurs at the far reaches of his protective responsibility, the shepherd may not reach that location, despite his running at full speed and wanting to save his sheep, for five to fifteen minutes. Even if he arrives within five minutes and sees the wolf and drives it off, subdues it, or even kills it, one or more of his flock are now probably already grievously injured or dead. That is what your typical police officer on night patrol faces: a very large geographic area containing thousands of people. The criminal typically will not commit a crime if he sees a patrol car; he waits until it is long gone.

Do not misunderstand any of my comments about the police; without them we would have anarchy. As George Orwell put it so well in an April 4, 1942 BBC broadcast:

> *"We sleep safe in our beds because rough men stand ready in the night to visit violence on those who would do us harm."*

Your New Statewide Environment

Early in 2011, the Arkansas State Legislature, under the leadership of Governor Beebe, passed a new law concerning the incarceration of criminals. They cited a Pew Center study asserting that the state would spend an additional one billion dollars incarcerating criminals over the next ten years if the state did not do something radically different. Well, the state's politicians did something radically different.

The State Legislature enacted a new law which no longer requires a felon to be sent to prison for a non-violent crime. The Pew Center study estimated that change would save from 6,000 to 10,000 additional prison beds from being built. Where will those 6,000 to 10,000 non-violent felons be housed under this new law? The answer is—wherever they want to live. They will be paroled onto the highways and byways of Arkansas. Even with best efforts, there will be, at time of this writing, several hundred parolees per Parole Officer. Even with ankle bracelets, and at this writing there is no publicly announced budget to purchase another 10,000 or so ankle bracelets, the felons are still free to practice the vocation of their choice.

Given such leniency and a second chance opportunity, let us hope few of these non-violent felons will return to their prior career of crime. And if they do, pray that it remains a crime of the non-violent kind. But with humans, being what we are, the odds favor a few of these additional thousands of felons crossing the line from non-violent to violent felons bent on *"makin' what's your'n, his'n,"* willing to harm or kill you in the process. After all, it has already been determined that they are "outlaws!"

When the word spreads nationally that in Arkansas you can "Commit the Crime and Pay No Time," there just might be an influx of additional criminals seeking a new "happy hunting ground." Let us hope that this does not happen and that these miscreants do not view our state as their new "Land of Opportunity," a "Wonder State" for their preferred profession.

3

Oh, I know; you think I am just being unnecessarily alarmist, but hear me out. According to the *Arkansas Democrat Gazette* on 26 December, 2011, there were two fatal stabbings in North Little Rock.

> *[Tracey] Mills* [first victim] *was leaning against a porch with one stab wound in the chest. She told deputies that Davis had stabbed her and Smith* [the second victim] *. . . Davis* [had been arrested] *Oct. 19 and charged with theft of property, theft of leased/rented property and obstructing governmental operations* [non-violent felonies] *according to . . . Pulaski County sheriff's office. Davis was* **released from jail Dec. 21, just two days before the stabbings.** *Since 2001, Davis* **has been arrested 13 times for various offenses** *including burglary, writing hot checks, theft by receiving, and failure to appear.*

(Emphasis is author's, but please note: an habitual, non-violent felon turned murderer.) So, Mr. Davis, after eleven years of "non-violent" crime, finally flipped to fatal criminal activities. "But this is just one instance," you retort. True, but to the two victims, it was one instance too many, and two fatal instances from which there is no recovery.

"A gun in the hand is better than a cop on the phone."

A National Perspective

On Wednesday, December 14, 2011, the National Center for Injury Prevention and Control at the CDC released results of a survey of 16,507 adults across the U.S. They stated: ***"nearly one in five women surveyed said they had been raped or experienced an attempted rape at some point."***

Further it was stated:

1. *One third of the 9,086 women surveyed said that they had been victims of a rape, beating, or stalking or a combination of assaults.*
2. *Almost half of female victims said they were raped before they turned 18.*

3. *About 80% of rape victims reported that they were raped before age 25.*
4. *35% of women who had been raped as minors were also raped as adults.*
5. *40% had been raped by an acquaintance.*

Young women under 25 and prior rape victims seem to be prime prospects for violent sexual assault.

Men, if you are married, there may already be three of the five women required to meet this statistical average in your life: mother, wife, mother-in-law. Add in sisters, sisters-in-law, and daughters, you probably have crossed the statistical threshold of "five." So the odds, per this survey, state that one of them, if not already, may become a rape or sexual assault victim.

Criminal justice statistics show that **79% of rapists are unarmed**, but nevertheless, there is a disparity of force present. They are armed with ferocious aggression, greater size or physical strength, or strength of numbers, as in a gang rape situation. Their statistics also note that 14% of rapists are armed with contact weapons (e.g., an edged weapon, a bludgeon, etc.), and only 7% of rapists tend to be armed with a gun. So, are you paranoid for wanting to acquire a handgun? I think probably not.

Hopefully, you are taking a carefully considered but sensible step to attempt to better protect yourself and your loved ones during that five to fifteen minute interval before the police can respond to your 911 call. Even more critical, a handgun provides you with the opportunity to protect yourself in those first fearful seconds or minutes prior to your even being able to call 911. Never forget, however, that along with this step to arm yourself, you have just committed yourself to a different lifestyle and a greater responsibility than you had before.

As an armed citizen, you now have the increased and readily available capability to harm another human being. If your actions with your handgun are not performed in strict accordance with the law, you could end up spending part of, or the rest of your life in jail. Your hasty, terror filled action, even though it is fully justified in your mind, must fall within the law. If not, then it falls "outside the law," and by definition that brands you—the perpetrator—as an "outlaw." So, read this *Companion* and perchance you will become a more knowledgeable protector of yourself and family.

Oh, and one other reason for you to become armed. In the book *More Guns, Less Crime* John Lott states on page 47:

The difference is quite striking: violent crimes are 81% higher in states without non—discretionary laws. For murder, states that ban the concealed carrying of guns have murder rates 127% higher than states with the most liberal concealed carry laws. For property crimes, the difference is much smaller: 24 %. States with non-discretionary laws have less crime, but the primary difference appears in terms of violent crimes.

Why would the citizens' ability to more easily (non-discretionary laws) obtain a concealed carry license reduce violent crime, you ask? It is answered in another book. David Kopel in *The Samurai, The Mountie, and The Cowboy,* page 127, note 254, states:

. . . a burglar's chance of being shot is about equal to his chance of being arrested. In a survey of felony convicts in state prisons, 73% of the convicts who had committed a burglary or violent crime agreed 'one reason burglars avoid houses when people are at home is that they fear being shot.'

By adding to the number of citizens who are armed and legally entitled to carry a concealed handgun, you are sheltering other citizens so that they are less likely to become victims themselves. You are being a "Good Samaritan" for all fellow citizens as well as protecting yourself and family.

So, get armed, get trained, get legal, be responsible, and help us all. And remember:

"When seconds count, the cops are just minutes away—after you call 911."

Chapter 2

Define Your Specific Requirements BEFORE You Purchase a Handgun

Tell me, why do you want to buy a handgun? Yes, I know the question is sort of nosy and none of my business, but I am trying to be helpful. You see, until you clearly define your needs and requirements, you could very well waste a lot of time and money until you give up in frustration or own more pistols than Custer's 7th Cavalry Troop.

What are Your Specific Requirements?

Your first responsibility is to define what your reasons, needs, and requirements are for wanting to purchase a pistol.

1. Just "Plinking,"
2. Home Defense,
3. Carry in car for protection on trips or just going to and from work,
4. Home and Car defense,
5. Carry concealed most of the time for personal protection,
6. Desire to become a competitive shooter,
7. All of the above.

That may not be an all-inclusive list, but it is a start. We will not spend any time on #6 as that is a separate subject beyond the scope of this author, which also eliminates #7.

Take the easiest requirement first.

Reason #1—Just "Plinking:"

"I just want a pistol to go shoot sometimes. You know, just go 'plinking' with my spouse, or kids, or someone. No real purpose or need, I just have this deep seated American Cowboy urge to fire a pistol like my ancestors did."

Response: A .22-caliber long rifle pistol (revolver or semiautomatic) is your best bet. It is a less expensive pistol, uses the least expensive ammo, has little recoil, less noise, and is fun to shoot. Also, you should get an Arkansas CHCL since you will be taking it around in a car quite a bit. True, you may not actually need a CHCL to lawfully transport an unloaded gun for recreation, but read *Chapter 14* before you decide to wear that idea as your shield of protection. By the way, if you purchase a revolver, it really does looks like a Cowboy's pistol.

Now, see how easy that was? It did not hurt one bit.

Reason #2—Home Defense:
This need brings up a series of questions that you need to consider. Who will be trained to shoot the pistol? Where will you keep it? How will you secure it? Do you live in an apartment or condo with thin walls and people living on the other side? Can you handle strong recoil? Will you practice until you are very, very good? Will you ever transport the pistol in a vehicle? Do you know your state's laws concerning transporting handguns and ammo? Will the pistol just sit for days, weeks, months, or years without being fired? Are you really fearful for your life in your surroundings or is this just a general precaution? Do you live in a rural area where you will use the weapon for potentially shooting at varmints of the four, as well as the two-legged kind?

Reason #3—Car Carry:
With "car carry" you will still be primarily keeping the handgun at home. Therefore, you can just begin by including those considerations listed under #2 above. Then you add in some considerations for car carry. Will you be crossing state boundaries? What are the laws of those states concerning transporting weapons if you do not have a Concealed Handgun Carry License (CHCL)? Are those states reciprocal with your state's CHCL holders? Where will you locate the pistol in the car? Do you know your state's laws concerning transporting firearms, "brandishing," and armed assault? How will you secure the pistol while in the car?

Reason #4—Home and Car Defense Carry:
This is a compilation of considerations for #2 and #3. Therefore just combine those two and you will have a great head start on the issues that you need to consider and resolve.

Reason #5—Concealed Carry:

To restate the obvious, since with concealed carry you will also have your handgun at home and in your car, you need to include the list of concerns to consider and resolve from #4. To that list of concerns and decisions, concealed carry adds a whole new dimension of concerns. How will you carry your pistol on your person? When will you take the CHCL class, if you have not already? Do you understand the reason to qualify with a semiautomatic pistol and not a revolver? Compare your normal daily dress with the types of holsters available for concealed carry; have you a preference? Is your spouse OK with this change in life-style? Are you aware of the liabilities if you conceal carry? Do you have insurance to cover you? Are you familiar with "The Plaxico Burress Incident?" No?

While at a New York city bar, Plaxico Burress, an accomplished professional football player, grabbed for his own handgun as it was sliding down the inside of his pant's leg. He accidentally pulled the trigger as he grabbed it, shooting himself in the leg. The result was a year in jail, tens of thousands of dollars in legal fees, and the loss of several millions of dollars income for the football season he missed. On top of that, he missed winning the Super Bowl. The Giants, who went on to win the 2012 Super Bowl, had already traded him to the Jets.

Point: if you carry, use a good holster and comply with the "concealed" portion of "concealed carry" as well.

Figure out your specific requirements

Home Defense only:

1. Do you live in an apartment or condo and have common walls with other families?
2. Do you live in a single family home but neighbors' houses are very close by?
3. Do you live in single family home and neighbors' houses **are not** close by.
4. Are there children in the house?
5. Will your spouse or younger children fire the weapon?
6. For home defense only, would a shotgun be a better solution than a handgun? A 12-gauge, short barrel, shotgun with "000" buckshot is a real defender of the home front.

7. Where will you keep the gun for ready access?
8. How will you secure the gun from unauthorized access?
9. How powerful a caliber can all your home shooters handle with **skill**?
10. Do you prefer a simpler or a more complex, additional function handgun?

Car plus At Home Defense:

1. All of the above under Home Defense.
2. Where will you put the pistol inside the car?
    a. Inside a crowded glove compartment?
    b. Inside a crowded center console?
    c. Loose on the seat?
    d. Loose on the floor?
    e. Holstered on your body?
3. How will you secure the pistol when there are passengers in the car?
4. If crossing state lines, find out their laws.

Concealed Carry:

1. All of the above under Home Defense and Car Carry.
2. Can you legally carry to your place of employment?
3. Does your employer's dress code eliminate certain concealment options? (E.g., if you wear a dress, an ankle holster just will not work.)
4. Can you change your everyday dress to accommodate a concealed carry weapon?
5. Does your daily work routine facilitate concealed carry? (E.g., if you are physically active, can you really carry so that the gun will not come out or be seen as your clothes fly around?)
6. Does your normal route to work pass through areas where weapons are illegal?
7. What method of concealed carry will you try first?

Some things to consider when deciding what handgun is appropriate for you:

1. Will you carry a concealed weapon?
2. How will you carry your weapon?
3. What is the largest caliber you are comfortable firing? After all, carrying a "cannon" will not do if you are too nervous or frightened to actually fire it; or you hit somewhere in Nebraska, when you do fire. If the pistol is not fun to shoot, then you probably will not practice. If you do not practice, you will not become proficient, and you may be dangerous with a weapon.
4. If money is a big issue, then ammo cost is a big consideration over a period of years. For example, saving $25.00 per one hundred rounds of practice shooting per month for 24 months is $600.00. Over ten years the savings is $3,000.00. Practice **a lot** with less expensive rounds. An excellent marksman with a .22-caliber is preferred over a poor marksman with a "cannon" left in the car or at home that is seldom fired.
5. Will you only leave your pistol at home for self-defense? If so, bigger is better. Well, bigger is always better, but if carry is not in the future, bigger is an easier choice.
6. If you want absolute certainty that the pistol will fire, then consider the very best semiautomatic or a revolver.
7. Do you want extreme safety? Demand thumb safety, hopefully along with magazine safety and grip safety and anything else on it that can add to safety. Do not forget a gun safe! Consider that the holster should have a thumb strap too.
8. Remember to carry in a good holster; avoid copying Plaxico Burress' experience.
9. You can probably add several other specifics for yourself.

A law enforcement officer, who is also an experienced instructor in CHCL classes and teaches advanced handgun protection classes, strongly disagrees with my "overly safe" attitude toward concealed carry. In his words, "*. . . active safety devices offer more disadvantage than advantage to a shooter. Under stress and fear of one's life, a safety is just one more step to accomplish that takes more time when time means life or death.*"

His advice is sound, experienced, and affords you the best chance of quick response in a terrifying encounter. Were I in law enforcement; a drug dealer; lived in an neighborhood where drive-by shootings are common occurrences; traveled in areas deemed unsafe; or had some other specific situation where I felt immediate draw was imperative; I would heed his advice completely.

The tradeoff: being overly safe on those hundreds or thousands of days when you will not need to draw and fire to save your life, versus a quick, unimpeded, simple response on that fateful day when you have a two or three second response window to save your life.

"You makes your choices and you takes your chances."

And keep in mind:

"Cheap is always an option,
but is it the option to pick when your life may be at risk?"

Chapter 3

Handgun Selection

This chapter is an overview of some handgun basics. If you are already a knowledgeable handgun enthusiast, this section may contain few new items. This section is for the new pistol person, or for the typical handgun owner who is relatively uninformed and who wishes to know more. It is also ideal for the first time purchaser of a pistol who is now interested in "packin' heat" or "pickin' a pistol," but is intimidated by all the terminology and options available. Some of you may be offended, as I will probably refer to hand-held firearms by a variety of names, all interchangeable to my mind, like: handgun, pistol, firearm, gun, etc.

Handguns come in three primary types or configurations: revolvers, semiautomatics (semis), and derringers. These categories are based on the mechanics of how the gun is initially loaded and each round subsequently positioned to be fired. Each type of handgun has its advantages and disadvantages. Each comes in a variety of calibers (diameter of its bullet in inches or millimeters), sizes (of the pistol itself), finishes (stainless, etc.), add-ons (safeties, etc.), and technical jargon. Determining which handgun is right for you will depend on your answers to the following questions. Why do you need a handgun? What does the handgun need to accomplish? Can you handle the weapon you need?

The state of Arkansas actually has two definitions for a *handgun*. Fortunately, the shorter one is encompassed in the longer definition. Arkansas defines a handgun as: "*any firearm, other than a fully automatic firearm, with a barrel length of less than twelve inches (12") that is designed, made, or adapted to be fired with one (1) hand; (SS 5-73-301)."* Since a rifle with a barrel length less than sixteen inches is unlawful, this sort of raises the question of what one calls a "one hand fired gun" with a barrel in excess of twelve-inches but less than sixteen-inches? Would you call it a "Hanriflgun," or perhaps a "Riflhangun?" Well, anyway, if you have a weapon other than the legally described handgun, we are not going to cover it in this chapter.

This chapter will describe each type of handgun using the classical method by which they operate. There are exceptions, but they are rare. For example, Arsenal Firearms has a **two barrel**, double stack semiautomatic. Dardick once manufactured a **magazine fed revolver** which shot "Trounds." They were made only from 1959-60. Mateba has a revolver with the cartridge cylinder forward of the trigger housing. Cobray has a *"Pocket Pal"* that is loaded similarly to a semiautomatic; you insert the bullets into a cylinder which is then inserted into the cylinder housing. It has two barrels: one for .380-caliber, the other for a .22-caliber bullet. Which caliber is fired is dependent on which cylinder you loaded and inserted. The cylinder operates like a revolver's; the firing mechanism is similar to a derringer's, as is the two barrel design. This book will not go into those types of different handgun designs. There is even a handgun that fires rocket projectiles and has no recoil. These are all interesting and have their uses, collectors or followers. This book will focus on the more standard handguns from which you can make a selection across many options at a reasonable price to meet your specific requirements. Why even discuss these rare handgun designs then? Because this book will state: "All semis have a magazine," or some other generalization, but you are now aware that there are exceptions. You will be more informed when discussing gun stuff with the experts, but it is very unlikely that any of the unusual or rare exceptions will ever come up. If they do, at least you can now say, "Oh yeah, I've heard of that."

Derringers

Let us begin with the simplest and then graduate to the more complex handguns. The simplest designed handgun is the derringer. Derringers are commonly referred to as "pocket pistols," "muff pistols," "belly guns," "palm pistols," etc.

Derringers are a class of handguns that, in my humble opinion, are a separate category of handgun distinct from revolvers and semiautomatics. A true derringer does not have a magazine and thus is not in the semiautomatic category. Second, a derringer does not have a cylinder that contains the bullets and rotates like a revolver's and thus is not a revolver. If you see a derringer with a magazine or a cylinder, it would be my assertion that it is not a derringer.

All that said, just what is a derringer? Originally, a derringer was a small pistol designed for pocket, purse, vest pocket, or muff carry that has from one to four bullets loaded directly into each of one to four barrels. There is no magazine and there is no cylinder. Whether the derringer has one, two, or four barrels, you load the cartridge into each individual barrel, one bullet per barrel.

Picture 3.1: *A Bond Arms derringer with a .45-caliber or .410 shotgun shell barrel configuration.*

Mentally, picture a double-barreled shotgun with a latch lever on top of the barrel, which, when pressed aside, drops the barrel down at a ninety-degree angle from the stock. You then load a shotgun shell directly into each barrel, snap the barrel back into place and you are ready to go. That is also the way that a real derringer operates, in my opinion.

Derringers have been so called since Henry Deringer of Philadelphia produced the first small, black-powder and ball pocket pistol in the mid-1800s. The whole class now carries his name, although slightly misspelled. All cartridge-loaded derringers have barrels that swing open, and you place the bullet directly into the barrel opening. Some barrels drop-down like a double-barreled shotgun. Others swing left or right away from the frame. Some flip upwards and do a back flip to expose the barrel for loading.

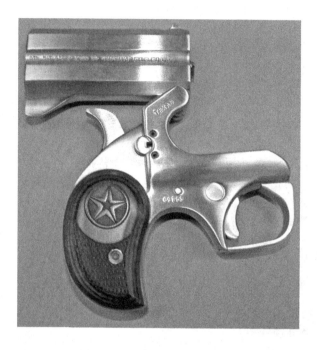

Picture 3.2: *A Bond Arms derringer with barrel opened in a flip-backward style for reloading.*

You literally place a bullet into each barrel. If you have a one-barrel derringer, you have a one shot derringer. If you have a two-barrel derringer, you have a two shot derringer. Some modern derringers have four barrels, which allows for four bullets and four shots. These tend to be larger and more bulky.

Derringers were designed for concealed carry in an era when all other pistols were rather large. We have all seen a derringer in western movies. The cute dancehall girl carried one stuck under her garter around her shapely thigh. The villainous card shark carried one in his vest pocket or in a contraption up his sleeve which, when released some special way, "snapped" the derringer down his arm, out of his sleeve, and into his hand before you could draw your own six-shooter or say "Dag-nab-it!"

Not only are derringers different in that they lack magazines and revolving cylinders, but their trigger mechanism operates differently.

A derringer of more than one barrel requires something or someone to tell the hammer over which barrel to strike the cartridge's primer. Some older derringers relied on the shooter to manually select which barrel by flipping a switch or pressing a pin. More modern designs normally handle this automatically for the shooter.

Originally, derringers were of the single action only (SAO) variety. Therefore, the shooter had to pull back the hammer before pressing the trigger to release the hammer to strike the primer. This was not as simple as it may sound because many of the models did not have a trigger guard. To hold the derringer sufficiently steady to cock the hammer, the shooter might be forced to place his finger on the trigger itself. If he pressed too hard on the trigger while simultaneously pulling back the hammer, guess what? Yep, the trigger releases the hammer as soon as the shooter removes his thumb from the hammer and "gun go boom." Hopefully, that was what the shooter intended; but as you and I will discuss, accidents do happen at the most inconvenient times, like trying to cock the hammer while the derringer is still in your pocket, purse, muff, or around your shapely thigh. Many modern derringers offer a trigger guard on specific models, often a removable one. Now, the modern derringers also offer double action with some models.

Derringers come in a wide selection of calibers; from .22-caliber all the way up to the reliable .45-caliber. One enterprising manufacturer even offers a model or two that emulates the Taurus *Judge.* It will fire both the .45-caliber and the .410 shotgun shell. A .410 shotgun shell of the "triple-ought" sized shot has five small marble-sized ball bearings; a real "perp" surprise from a small pistol.

The original concept of a derringer was to be a small, concealed carry handgun for close-up self-defense. The barrels were three inches or less. Good for hitting a target within five to maybe ten feet, but not for longer range shooting that required aiming. They were true "point and shoot" pistols. However, today you can purchase derringers with four barrels and some with barrels of six-inch length. They weigh as much as a standard sized semi but lack some of the benefits. Still, a derringer offers a fairly simple loading and firing mechanism for reliability.

One manufacturer even offers the ability to purchase a single derringer from them and then purchase interchangeable barrels to fit the same frame. This permits you to have the same frame and by replacing barrels, you can convert from a small sized .22-caliber all the way up to a large sized .45-caliber derringer. This conversion is quickly accomplished with a supplied "Allen wrench" to loosen a single screw, switch the barrels, and then retighten the screw. This is a really clever design.

What can we determine to be the derringer's strong points versus the revolver and the semiautomatic? The first advantage is the derringer's extremely simple operation. The only moving parts are the trigger and the hammer mechanism. No cylinder to revolve, no slide to rack, casing to eject, new round to load. Second, a traditional derringer is small and thus very appealing for concealed carry. Although a derringer does not have an advantage in smaller size over the smaller revolvers and semis, the derringer can provide a larger caliber in that small size. Do not overlook the benefit of the models that permit barrel exchange for different caliber shells. This flexibility allows the use of lower cost ammo for practice shooting and then a switch to a larger caliber for defensive carry.

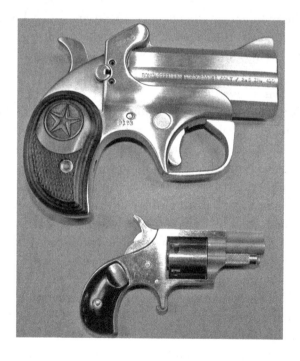

Picture 3.3: *Compare the sizes of a .45-caliber two-shot derringer to a .22-caliber five-shot mini revolver.*

The disadvantages of the derringer are quickly obvious. First, there is the limited number of rounds prior to a reload compared to the revolver or semi. The most rounds with a derringer are four and that requires a slightly larger frame with four barrels. A second disadvantage may be model type specific, but gripping and trigger-finger placement are sometimes an issue. For some models, the trigger movement is slightly different from the expected and may require that the trigger guard be removed in order for some to comfortably press the trigger rearward. Another disadvantage relates to the small size and the recoil from larger caliber ammo. A typical derringer may lack the recoil absorbing weight and mass of the other two types of handguns. The only practical way for you to determine this, is to actually test fire a model that you are considering purchasing. Another disadvantage for any small handgun is accuracy beyond ten to twenty feet. You would need to practice a lot with a derringer.

I have yet to purchase a derringer but I am just dying to do so. I think they are "neat," to use a technical "shootist" term. The smaller sized derringer would appear to be an excellent option for concealed carry, especially if you believe that any non-social interaction requiring you to draw, present, and shoot will require no more than two bullets within ten feet. I highly recommend the two shot, three inch barrel, .45-caliber and .410 combo, for dancehall girls, card sharks, and Mississippi river boat gamblers. In all truth and candor however, I have never fired one myself. Still, I am eager to acquire one. (Perhaps a derringer manufacturer will read this and just send me a free one—yeah, in my dreams.)

I have never owned nor shot a derringer; therefore, I feel completely qualified to give you my personal guidance for preferences on which is the best selection. (Observing politicians has convinced me that it is easier to take a position when unencumbered with facts or knowledge.) I cannot see any advantage to a SAO derringer. Second, a single-barrel, one-shot leaves me wanting. I would opt for a two-barrel, two-shot derringer. I would purchase a model with interchangeable barrels to allow for future modifications in caliber. Finally, I would start with a two-barrel, two-shot, DA, with removable trigger guard, with the barrel for the .410 and .45-caliber combination. (I wanted to ensure that any generous derringer manufacturer had the exact specs for my "gratis" gift. You think? Nope, not a chance of it happening.)

Revolvers

The next handgun in simplicity of operation is the revolver. Revolvers come in all sizes, from very small to very large. In fact, if one compares the sizes between revolvers and semiautomatics, revolvers can be smaller as well as larger than semis. Some revolvers are so small that they can fit into your shirt's top pocket. Others are huge; think "Dirty Harry's" .44-magnum revolver.

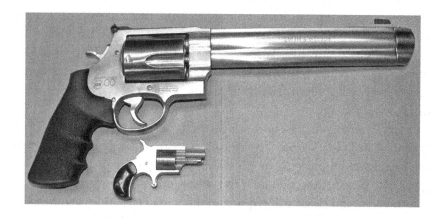

Picture 3.4: *Above is a very small .22-magnum revolver beneath a larger S&W .50-caliber revolver.*

Sizes aside, revolvers really come in three basic flavors: Single Action Only (SAO), Double Action Only (DAO), and Single and Double Action (SADA). The terms, single action and double action, refer to the *trigger's actions*. In other words, when the trigger is pressed backward, does it perform a *single* (one) action, or does it perform *double* (two) actions?

When the shooter presses backward on the trigger, the trigger can perform three actions: raise the hammer to a "half-cocked" position, raise the hammer to the "full-cocked" position, and finally release the hammer which then strikes the firing pin. (I know I said two actions, but think of it as ½, 1, and 2. Hey, give me a break. I did not invent this terminology.)

Revolvers have a cylinder that contains the bullets; it is located just above the trigger area. As the trigger is pulled, this cylinder "revolves" and positions the next bullet in position to be fired, hence the name "revolver." Peculiarly, some revolvers have cylinders that rotate counter-clockwise; others rotate clockwise. For our consideration, I cannot see a benefit either way, so just ignore this. (I know, why did I even include it then?)

Single Action Only (SAO) Revolvers

Single Action Only (SAO) is the least desirable revolver for concealed carry from my perspective because you **must** "cock" the hammer manually, all the way back, each time before pulling the trigger to fire each shot. When the hammer is pulled all the way back, this action also rotates the cylinder, placing the next round into the firing position. Again, the term "Single Action" refers to the trigger's work. In the case of a SAO revolver, the trigger does a single action: it releases the hammer to strike the firing pin. This was the revolver type available for most of the Old West era. But do not mentally picture what you have seen in a western movie. In the movies they are using revolvers, but unlike real life, they never ran out of bullets, they never reloaded, and they all had double action models.

A Single Action Only (SAO) revolver must have the "hammer" pulled back manually to a full cock. Then, when you pull the trigger, the hammer is released and hits the firing pin (if the firing pin is not on the end of the hammer) which strikes the bullet's primer which ignites the powder. The burning gases send the projectile down the barrel and also cause the recoil that you feel.

On SAO revolvers, you can manually pull the hammer back to a "half-cocked" position. That allows you to move the cylinder that contains the bullets. This is necessary for loading unfired bullets and unloading spent cartridges and checking each chamber. In the "half-cocked" position, the hammer should not release upon pulling the trigger, but strange things do happen; thus the old saying, *Going off half-cocked.* That is a bad thing, if you did not know it already. From the half-cocked position, squeezing the trigger of a SAO revolver should NOT pull the hammer all the way to the full-cocked position. The trigger will probably not move at all. To un-cock the half-cocked revolver, it is necessary to squeeze the trigger lightly and simultaneously hold the hammer with your thumb and carefully lower it. You might wish to practice this unloaded or outdoors.

One example of a SAO revolver is the Ruger *Bearcat* revolver shown in picture 3.5. In the half-cocked position, its trigger is frozen and will not move. One must manually pull the hammer to the full cocked position to fire, or manually lower the hammer to un-cock.

Picture 3.5: *The above is a .22-caliber Ruger Bear Cat* ***Single Action*** *(SAO) Revolver.*

Most modern revolvers are designed so that the cylinder swings away from the frame and has a rod that you can push backward toward the cylinder that will eject all the cartridges at one time. This makes unloading and reloading much easier than in those models with a cylinder that does not swing clear of the frame. With these types of revolvers, you have to open up a loading gate on the rear side of the cylinder and eject each bullet individually by pushing a rod down into the cylinder, one chamber at a time.

Double Action Only Revolvers (DAO)

Pressing the trigger fires a Double Action Only (DAO) revolver. You cannot manually pull the hammer back at all. The only way to fire a DAO revolver is to press the trigger. Again, the term "Double Action" refers to the trigger's work. Pressing the trigger both pulls the hammer back, action one, to the fully cocked position and then releases the hammer, action two, to strike the firing pin. When pulling the trigger back, there is usually stiffer resistance initially until you reach a point termed "staging position," at which point the trigger pull is easier. Two actions equal "double action," OK? Otherwise, it is the spitting image of the typical SAO revolver. The DAO revolver is often used for the smaller sized revolvers for concealed carry, as it allows the pistol's hammer mechanism to be concealed within the housing and not get hung up on clothing, etc.

Picture 3.6*: This is a Smith & Wesson .38 Special BODYGUARD revolver with laser light. A **Double Action Only** (DAO) revolver; notice absence of an external hammer.*

Single Action and Double Action Revolvers (SADA or SDA)

The "Single and Double Action" (SADA) revolver works as either a SA or a DA revolver—the best of both worlds, so to speak. You can pull back the hammer manually to cock the revolver, just like a SAO, and then pull the trigger to release it to fire the pistol. Or you can just press the trigger which will both force the hammer back into a cocked position and as you press the trigger farther the hammer is released which then strikes the firing pin, a regular DA operation. Again, other than having this dual capability, it is pretty much a spitting image of the other two.

Why would you want a SADA? So you can be just like the heroine in a cop show on TV. Like when the perp says to the lady cop, "You wouldn't really shoot me, would you?" Or, "Do you really know how to shoot that thing lady?" then you can pull the hammer back to the fully cocked position just to show the scumbag that you not only know how to operate it, but you are also willing to send him to Boot Hill.

In the fully cocked position the revolver has a shorter and easier trigger pull. Therefore, it fires quicker when you squeeze the trigger than when the hammer is not fully cocked. The amount of energy required to press the trigger is measured in pounds. Some pistols have trigger pulls with as little as four pounds while others may require two or three times that amount of trigger pressure poundage. It may be a consideration in your selection, since the stronger pull may cause your hand to wander "off target" compared to pulling the trigger on a pistol requiring a lighter pull. Thus, the advantage of the SADA with its staging point: you can actually feel this point in your trigger pull. You know that from that point till fired, the trigger action is going to happen much faster. When you manually cock the hammer, it operates from the fully cocked position and the trigger pull requires less poundage and is a shorter trigger pull. Thus, if you are fully cocked, a slight press on the trigger causes quick firing—an advantage, and a disadvantage. From a half-cocked position, squeezing the trigger rearward will fire the SADA. The trigger pull distance is shorter than when not cocked, but the trigger pull poundage is greater than when fully cocked.

Many models can have laser capability if the manufacturer allowed for their attachment in the revolver's design. For example, the Smith & Wesson *BODYGUARD 38 Special* (picture 3.6) is a DAO revolver that is available with S&W supplied laser already attached. I have never seen a revolver with a flashlight attached, but I am certain that some models probably have that capability. After-market gunsmiths and manufacturers are really clever in what they do with and to handguns.

***Picture 3.7**: This is a Taurus "Judge" five-shot **Single and Double Action Revolver** with a 2 ½ inch cylinder capable of holding .45-caliber Long Colt cartridges and 2 ½ inch long .410 shotgun shells. Note the presence of an external hammer.*

Hybrid Handgun "Shotgun"

Some experts will state that the optimum self-defense weapon is a short-barreled (sawed off) 12-gauge shotgun loaded with buckshot. Since any shotgun with a barrel under eighteen inches is illegal, this law presents a challenge.

In David Kopel's book *The Samurai, The Mountie, and The Cowboy*, on page 121, note 147 states:

> *At close range, the shotgun is the most formidable and destructive of all arms . . . Unlike bullets, shotgun pellets rarely exit the body. Therefore, the kinetic energy of wounding in shotguns is usually equal to the striking energy . . . all kinetic energy is transferred to the body as wounding effects. Shotgun injuries have not been compared with other bullet wounds of the abdomen as they are a thing apart . . . At close range, they are as deadly as a cannon.*

Shotguns come in a variety of shell sizes: .410-caliber, plus 28, 20, 16, 12, and 10-gauge. However, the most popular sized shotguns are the 12-gauge and the 20-gauge. The 12 and 20-gauge buckshot shells contain from nine to thirteen slugs per shell, depending on the slug sizes. The .410 has four to five slugs per buckshot shell, so the .410 shells obviously produce less damage and are probably not the size of the shotgun shells doing the damage noted by David Kopel. That said, four or five .410 buckshot slugs to the torso per round is still darn destructive and gives the person under attack a real burst of defensive firepower.

Wielding a shotgun with a barrel length of twenty or more inches inside a house can be just a little bit awkward. Also, a long barreled shotgun is rather impractical for carrying, even if only in an automobile. The Taurus Arms Company solves these problems with their *Judge* revolver (picture 3.7). This revolver is a five-shot dandy that will fire .45-caliber Long Colt (Cowboy) or .410 shotgun shells. Some more recent competitors have come out with similar revolvers that include the .45-caliber ACP (Automatic Colt Pistol) round, which is shorter than the .45-caliber Long Colt and, more important, usually less expensive and more readily available. Thus, in these models you have the option of three types of cartridges: .45-caliber ACP, .45-caliber Long Colt, and .410 shotgun shell.

Another variation of the Taurus *Judge*-type revolver is cylinder length. The shorter length cylinder accommodates the 2 ½-inch .410 shell only, while the 3-inch cylinder accommodates the 2 ½-inch or the 3-inch .410 shell. So, in one single revolver you could have the option to load .45-ACP, .45-Colt, 2 ½-inch .410 and 3-inch .410 shells. Moreover, one of the *Judge*-type revolver's interesting wrinkles is that being a revolver, you can mix and match cartridges in the same cylinder. For example, you could have a .45-ACP, followed by a 2 1/2-inch .410, followed by a .45-Colt, etc. The three-inch size .410 "000" buckshot has four or five slugs. This is pretty damaging when all of them hit the torso of the miscreant trying to take you down.

Several munitions manufactures have developed special .410 rounds for the *Judge*-type handguns. The rounds are for "personal defense." What makes them special is they have three slugs (copper discs) followed by twelve BBs in each 2 ½-inch shell or four slugs and sixteen BBs in the 3-inch shell. That's a lot of "shock" power for one round. Plus, since there is a natural spreading to the shot's pattern, exact aiming is less critical. This is an excellent choice for a carry or a home defense weapon. It contains some of the additional firepower advantage of the semi, plus it reduces exact aiming requirement for a perfect hit on target when under duress. A key safety consideration is that the .410 rounds are less likely to penetrate multiple walls and harm innocent neighbors. Pass-through is a major consideration if living in an apartment, or your house has other occupants who might be in harm's way if a round misses the target and continues through the wall and strikes an unintended target. One caveat: the .410 PDX round has a very wide pattern at twenty feet; you would get hits on the target but also, potentially, some collateral damage. Therefore, for carry outside of the home, the regular buckshot shells might be a better choice as they have a tighter pattern at twenty feet and thus less chance for collateral damage.

Some Summary Thoughts on Revolvers

The DAO revolver is good for concealed carry, as it can be manufactured to eliminate the external hammer sticking out. This eliminates the possibility of the hammer's end becoming hung on your clothing, thumb straps, etc.

The SADA is useful because it allows you to actually cock the hammer. When the hammer is already cocked, the pistol actually fires slightly faster, as the hammer is already back, and the trigger pull is shorter and quicker. Often, it also requires less pressure on the trigger to fire. Whether it is desirable to have a super-light trigger pull in a self-defense situation when your body is not functioning normally is questionable. It would probably be wise to not cock the hammer with a SADA revolver when pointing it at someone, as just a small finger twitch might shoot the pistol when you are not ready to do so. Of course, one of the cardinal rules of gun control is to never place your finger on the trigger until you are ready to press it and fire.

There are three designs of revolver hammers related to concealed carry ideal requirements. From least to most desirable they are: those with traditional exposed hammer with sharp edge, those with exposed but rounded hammer edges, and those, like the S&W .38 revolver (picture 3.6), that have a concealed hammer. The latter is obviously the best for concealed carry, all else being equal.

Revolvers, like derringers, operate simply because there are few moving parts. Revolvers have a couple of limitations compared to most semiautomatics, but they also offer a few advantages.

A couple of disadvantages: most revolvers are limited to a maximum of five or six bullets in the cylinder, a few have eight. Also unloading a cylinder of fired cartridges and **reloading unfired bullets is cumbersome and time consuming.** (That is why you never see that in most cowboy movies.) In addition, for a larger caliber revolver, the cylinder has a wider profile than a comparable caliber semiautomatic and thus makes it slightly more bulky for concealed carry.

You will search a long time to find a revolver with an external "thumb safety." I just do not think they come that way. You load them up, and they are ready to shoot—**no safety** to release, no magazine to push up inside the grip, no slide to pull back to chamber a round, no magazine release button to avoid accidentally pressing. Revolvers are simple, reliable, and designed to be drawn and fired, just like "Marshall Dillon" of *Gunsmoke* used to do so effectively.

Revolvers were so simple that older models often had the hammer resting directly on the bullet primer, or on the firing pen that rested on the bullet primer. If dropped just right, the blow on the hammer could actually force it to strike the bullet's primer and—guess what—yep, the gun goes bang, to everyone's shock and dismay. If you already own a revolver or have been "gifted" with one from a relative or friend, ensure that yours does not permit this to occur. You see, we only want the gun to "go boom" when we pull the trigger, not at some unexpected time or location due to chance and bad luck! The good news is that most modern revolvers have a hammer-block safety to prevent this; just be certain to confirm yours has this feature. If you are purchasing a new revolver, it should be OK, but please confirm just to be absolutely certain. The Ruger *Bear Cat* (picture 3.5) was originally made without the hammer-block safety. Ruger modifies the revolver at no charge to bring it up to current safety standards. If you have an older revolver, contact the manufacturer and determine if your model is safe or requires modification.

A revolver has a tremendous advantage in that the whole firing mechanism is less complicated than the typical semiautomatic when it comes to feeding a round into the firing chamber. With a revolver, if a round fails to fire, you pull the trigger again and the cylinder rotates. If the next bullet has not already been fired, it is ready to go and probably will go bang. With a semi, it is not that easy to correct a misfeed or misfire, and depending on the type of misfeed or misfire, it can be just a bit disconcerting and time consuming to clear and fire again. Revolvers, by their design, are extremely reliable "messengers of death."

One last item of interest for a revolver versus a semiautomatic handgun is from an article by R. K. Campbell, a peace officer, in the November/December, 2011, *Concealed Carry Magazine* in which he was discussing holsters for "snubby" .38 Special revolvers. He states:

> *In an intimate-range struggle the revolver may be pressed against an opponent's body and fired more than once. A semi-auto would jam at the first shot. This makes the revolver a top choice for backup use.*

Not having been forced to try this, or wanting to test it out, a logical review of the two firing and chambering systems gives some validity to his statement. The revolver positions the next round to be fired by the mechanical action of revolving the cylinder by pressing on the trigger. There is no ejection cycle, and chambering the next round to be fired is purely mechanical. A revolver has zero dependency on the back blast from burning gases, as the semi requires, to extract the fired bullet's casing and load the next round into the firing chamber. Exactly why pressing the barrel of a semi against a perp causes a jam, well, I will just accept it as a "truth" based on Mr. Campbell's assertion. (Several reviewers believe that this whole scenario is a little farfetched. I will leave that decision up to you. You will often receive conflicting views and opinions from experts; that is why the ultimate choice of your handgun must be yours, not someone else's opinion.)

While we are discussing concepts that I am unable to state with conviction or absolute truth, let us review another. If you are forced to fire a handgun still inside your pocket, the revolver will probably rotate the cylinder and position the next round to be fired without major issues. A semi just might have the slide become entangled in the lining of the pocket causing a misfeed on the next round. Since the fired round must be ejected inside your pocket, it just might become lodged against the side of the pocket and also cause a misfeed. In either case, you have probably ruined your jacket. (Again, an expert thinks that firing a weapon while still in your pocket is a very bad idea. In his opinion, "You would likely shoot yourself.")

There are many excellent books, videos, etc. on handguns. Your local gun shop is staffed with folks who can explain more about each type and model of handgun than my brain can comprehend or that you may really need to know. But nothing surpasses the actual handling of a handgun in person to get the feel, weight, trigger pull, and friendliness, or lack thereof, of the grip and trigger guard to your specifically and uniquely configured hand. Visit your local gun shop where some handgun guru will actually spend time with you and help make you more knowledgeable.

Just to provide you with further insight into my own preferences, here are my revolver specs for that manufacturer wishing to grace me with a freebie. (OK, I know.) I would prefer a small or compact sized DAO with internal hammer or striker for concealed carry, like the Smith & Wesson BODYGUARD discussed previously. If I could use an OWB holster, this would change to at least a compact size and maybe even a standard sized pistol. If carrying a standard size, and ignoring semis, the hybrid-revolver, with .410 buckshot and .45-caliber cartridges offers a lot of flexibility and stopping power. The 3-inch cylinder is preferable, but does add size and weight for concealed carry. Either size would work for me. I see very little reason for a SAO revolver, unless you are a collector.

Semiautomatics

Semiautomatics typically come in three basic flavors: small, compact, and standard. Think Poodle dogs that are sized from Toy all the way up to Standard. Semis come the same way: Small: four to seven bullets; Compact: eight to thirteen bullets; and Standard: thirteen to eighteen bullets. More bullets require a larger grip (handle) to hold the larger capacity. Usually, that also results in a longer barrel and an overall larger sized pistol. However, there are some tiny semiautomatics and perhaps there is a very large one lurking out there somewhere.

Picture 3.8: Above are a very small .22-magnum revolver and a very small .380 semiautomatic.

The larger the semi's ammunition's caliber, the greater its recoil will be when fired, all other thing being equal. As you can see in picture 3.8, some semiautomatics are small and might fit into your shirt pocket. The very small and very large sizes are the exception. Some makes and models actually offer three sizes in the same model and caliber, sometimes just two. Glock has so many options that they just number them. Smith & Wesson has a series called "M&P" that comes in Standard and Compact sizes for each caliber.

Why the different sizes? Good question. One reason is to appeal to those folks who want to pack identical pistols of different sizes based on changing circumstances. The owner can carry the "Standard" size that can hold fifteen or more rounds as well as having the option of a "Compact" size for easier concealed carry that offers 8-10 rounds. If there is a "Small" size available in the same line, it is a good choice for pocket or purse concealed carry.

There is good logic to carrying the same type, caliber, and model of pistol when you step down from the larger to a smaller size based on the demands of your day's dress code, planned activities, or destinations. Since the different sizes of the same model all operate identically, you will not get confused or fumble when under pressure because you have pulled out a handgun under extreme duress that you have not carried or fired for nine months, and it is slightly different from your normal carry. For example, one has a thumb safety, the other does not, or the grips feel different, or are a different size, or one has a de-cocker and the other does not, etc.

Picture 3.9*: For comparison purposes: A Standard sized 9mm semi along side a Small sized .380 semi. The standard size has a capacity of 17+1 versus the small's capacity of 6+1. The caliber is not the same but this provides you with a bird's eye view of the size difference if considering Concealed Carry.*

Besides the number of bullets permitted, another characteristic of the same model handgun offered in different sizes is weight. Weight impacts recoil. The smaller handgun usually weighs less. This generalization is not totally valid as the construction materials can vary from stainless steel to composites, and that impacts weight. But within the same make and model, smaller is generally lighter. Lighter may have more appeal to females who are less likely to enjoy an extra two to three pounds of a Standard size in their purse, bra, or around their waist. A trade-off is that the smaller size and lighter gun will result in greater recoil within the same model and caliber. Moreover, the larger handgun has more grip surface area. This translates into better control for the shooter because the grip better fills the shooter's hand. Recoil is also distributed over a larger grip surface area so the felt recoil may actually be perceived as reduced.

Picture 3.10*: This is a Sig Sauer P238 .380 caliber semiautomatic. It has a 6+1 capacity and is a **Single Action** semiautomatic. You can just see the round end of the hammer at top right. This is a Small sized semi: 5.5 inches long, about 1 inch wide and 15.5 ounces in weight.*

Just to complicate things, semis can also be Single Action Only, Double Action Only, or Single and Double Action. For example, the Sig P238 (picture 3.10) is termed a SAO. Why? If you load the magazine with six rounds and slap it up into the grip and then pull the trigger to fire, it will not fire. The trigger moves but nothing happens. Once you pull back the slide and release the slide, it will zoom forward and strip the top bullet in the magazine and place it into the firing chamber. The motion of pulling back the slide also "cocks" the hammer to the rear. This is considered a "manual cocking," just like the old cowboy SAO revolver, except in this case, it is the slide doing the cocking, not your thumb. You can manually release the hammer from the cocked position with very careful thumb and trigger finger coordination, but that is how many weapons go off accidentally. Once you have a round in the chamber and the hammer cocked, the SAO semi will continue to fire automatically each time you pull the trigger until the magazine is empty, (acting just like a double action semiautomatic). How does it do that when a SAO revolver must be manually cocked prior to each trigger pull? It is the slide moving rearward to eject the casing and pushing the hammer back into the cocked position at the same time. It does the "manual" cocking "automatically" for you, using the recoil of the fired bullet. This type of semi has an external hammer and is called "hammer fired" because the hammer strikes the firing pin. Because the trigger's action only releases the hammer, it has only a "single action."

Beretta manufactures a *3032 Tomcat* semi that has a tilt-up barrel. With the *Tomcat,* you do not slap the magazine into the grip and pull back the slide to chamber a round and cock the hammer. With the Beretta *Tomcat,* you slap the magazine into the grip, and then the Beretta Tomcat's barrel can be tilted up and a round manually placed into the firing chamber (just like a derringer) and the barrel pushed back down into the firing position. No hammer has been cocked by this action or by loading of the magazine. When the Beretta *3032 Tomcat's* trigger is pressed, the hammer is pulled back; trigger action one. As the trigger is pressed further, the hammer is released (trigger action two), and strikes the firing pin. This is a true Double Action type of action.

Confusing? Yes, you probably read all the above correctly, and are still confused. Forget the *Tomcat* for a minute, as its tilt-up barrel is somewhat unusual. Here are the steps to load and fire both a SAO and a DAO semi: load the magazine, slap the magazine into the grip, rack the slide and release it, press the trigger and each semi goes boom. You execute the exact same actions whether the semi is a single or double action. If it is a *Tomcat* style, then, after loading the magazine, you must lift up the barrel and shove a round into the firing chamber and press the barrel back down into place. With the *Tomcat* style, this does not "cock" the pistol. This step does provide you with the extra round in the firing chamber plus the full capacity of the magazine. To gain that with the other styles is a longer process.

Both the SAO and the DAO semiautomatics are loaded and "racked" the same way. When you "rack" the SAO, you are also "cocking" the hammer. When you "rack" the DAO, you are not cocking the hammer;

that is accomplished by the trigger pull when you fire the pistol. Both of these styles of action are ready to go without requiring that you tilt up the barrel, place a round into the firing chamber, and press the barrel back down. This is required for the *Tomcat*. It requires manually inserting the bullet into the firing chamber in order to have a round ready to fire. Why would one prefer a pistol with a tilt-up barrel? Good question. Believe it or not, racking the slide on a semi requires just a little bit of strength. Some people find that a challenge and prefer the tilt-up barrel. Also, if you are careless when racking the slide and releasing it, the fast movement of the slide forward sometimes catches part of a finger and can cut you. This painful event should only happen once per person unless you have a high tolerance for pain.

This was a lot of discussion about "racking" the slide back and releasing it to load a round into the chamber, but it is important. Under stress, even experienced felons have been known to forget to do this. Remember Annette "Squeaky" Fromme, one of the Manson molls? Somehow, she missed going to jail for murder with the rest of the gang, but she did do her own three decade stretch for attempted murder. Fromme was convicted in 1975 of pointing a gun at then President Gerald Ford in Sacramento, California. Despite being a longtime, dedicated follower of Charles Manson, when she pointed a gun at Ford a year after he became President, there was no bullet in the chamber. There was a magazine with ammunition inserted into the grip of the .45 Colt semi, but no round in the chamber. Fortunately, Secret Service agents prevented her from racking the slide and re-firing, or else she would have been successful in her assassination attempt. Lucky for President Ford, she was too agitated to remember that she had ejected the round from the chamber back at her apartment, or at least she so claimed later in her defense. (Unless there was no loaded magazine in the gun, her "racking" at the apartment to eject the chambered round would just have loaded another round into the firing chamber. My opinion, she just forgot to ever "rack," period.)

What do we learn from this? Well, first to avoid Annette "Squeaky" Fromme. She was released from prison in August, 2009, and now probably better comprehends how a semi works than she did previously. Second, even with an excellent weapon like a Colt .45 semiautomatic, if you **do not** rack the slide to chamber a round, when you pull the trigger, the gun goes "click," not "bang." (Actually, the trigger probably does not move at all so there really isn't a "click" noise.)

All semiautomatics have magazines. All magazines must be loaded with their bullets out-side of the handgun, unlike the revolver. With a revolver, you load bullets into the cylinder one chamber at a time; then you close the cylinder, and you are "good to go." With a semi, you load the magazine and then carry it over to the handgun and shove the magazine up inside the grip till it clicks into position.

Then, for most semis, you pull the slide (it rides over the barrel) all the way back and release it. This has "cocked" the hammer, or striker, in a SAO and a SADA. When you release the slide, a spring drives the slide forward and as it does so, the slide strips the top round from the magazine and loads that round into the firing chamber.

While we are discussing magazines, let us look at the Sig P238 (picture 3.10). It is difficult to have a good perspective from a picture, but when a normal-sized hand grips a small semi like this Sig, the "pinkie" finger hangs just below the grip. Unless you have very small hands, there just is not room on the grip for the last finger. Some folks just curl the "pinkie" and fold it back, fist-like, into their palm. Others will hold it underneath the magazine, like it is helping to hold the magazine in place or something. This was my wife's dilemma—the "floating pinkie"—and she found it too distracting to be comfortable with her pistol. Some handgun models offer an "extended magazine." This has two advantages: a place to rest the "pinkie" finger, plus one or more extra rounds of ammunition in the magazine. The only disadvantage is that the larger magazine sticks out farther and might be a little more of an issue with concealed carry. All in all, it is a very nice solution to the problem of the "floating pinkie." (See pictures 3.11 and 3.12.)

Picture 3.11: *Comparison of standard magazine (6 rounds) on left and an extended magazine (7 rounds) on right; both for the .380 semi shown above.*

Picture 3.12: *A .380 small semi loaded with the extended magazine. Increases ammo capacity to 7+1 plus provides a location for the "floating pinkie."*

Let us address the "+1" notation for ammo capacity. To obtain this +1 capacity in the typical semi is a little cumbersome. The *Tomcat* addresses this by requiring that the extra round be placed into the tilt-up barrel before it will fire. Other semis can provide this additional capacity, but in a more cumbersome manner. To obtain that +1 round, one must first rack a round into the firing chamber, and then release the magazine. Next, place another round into the magazine to replace the round that was loaded into the firing chamber by racking. This replenishment takes full advantage of the magazine's capacity. That is why you see a semi's bullet capacity always listed as 17+1 or some such two number set. In this example, the magazine can hold 17; the firing chamber 1. But to obtain that bullet capacity requires these extra steps. You have to load the magazine with 17 rounds, insert it into the grip, rack a round into the firing chamber and then eject the magazine. Then you add one additional shell to the 16 left in the magazine to increase it back to 17 and then reinsert the magazine into the grip of the semi. If you have one of those semis that allow the barrel to flip-up, you can load the firing chamber without using the slide, such as with the Beretta *Tomcat*. You avoid the magazine exercise, but you still have the extra step of flipping the barrel up, inserting a bullet into the firing chamber, and lowering the barrel down into place.

Regardless of whether the barrel flips up or you have to use the slide to chamber the first round, it still is an extra step to gain the full capacity of 17+1, or whatever the semi's capacity happens to be. Just how important is bullet capacity to self-defense and concealed carry? That is a very good question. I would guess that most of us will never get involved in some type of drawn-out gunfight. Most self-defense situations, as per the experts, are over within 3-5 seconds. If that is the case, the capacity addition gained by releasing the magazine to reload the round that was chambered seems to be of minimal value. However, it takes just a few seconds of extra effort, so why not do it. Of far greater significance is having the handgun with you, whether with six or seven rounds, than to not be armed at all. Do not think that you must carry large firepower, such as with a standard size with 17+1, and then fail to actually carry it because of weight, bulk, or lack of good "conceal-ability" for your dress. If the number of rounds really worries you, you can augment the smaller capacity by carrying an extra, fully loaded magazine or two. My two CHC pistols have five or six rounds and I am comfortable with that, but I am inexperienced, have no special training, and probably lack a good perspective. I also plan to avoid engaging in gun fights if a hasty retreat can be executed safely.

After chambering the first round with either technique, each time you pull the trigger the semi fires the bullet and the gas from the powder's explosion (really controlled burning) drives the slide rearward. As the slide goes rearward it extracts the empty shell casing and tosses it in the general direction of your face (just kidding, unless you are firing left handed), and then the spring takes command and drives the slide forward. As the slide moves forward, it picks up the top round in the magazine and positions it into the firing chamber. The semi "automatically" continues firing each time you pull the trigger and there are bullets in the magazine.

The reason these are named "**semi-automatics**" is that you must pull the trigger each time you wish to fire the weapon. A fully automatic weapon will fire continually as long as you hold the trigger back, and will stop firing only when you release the trigger or run out of ammunition.

When you watch the TV cop shows, you will notice that they all carry semiautomatics. They draw them from their holster, grasp the grip with two hands, and point them at the "perp." These semis are all Standard size and look large, black, and menacing. The perp usually gives up, but would probably do the same if the cop were pointing "Dirty Harry's" .44-magnum revolver at them. Most law enforcement agencies have adopted semis as their standard because of the increased capacity over the revolver. Semis are also more readily adaptable to having additional things hung onto them, such as a flashlight.

Picture 3.13: *This is a **Standard** size Smith & Wesson 9mm "M&P" semiautomatic with 17+1 capacity. This is a Double Action Only (DAO) semiautomatic; there is no external hammer.*

Just to keep my promise on keeping the SAO and DAO discussion from being confusing, let us review the Smith & Wesson *M&P* model (picture 3.13). It is a Double Action Only semi. It has no external hammer. In fact, it has no hammer at all; it has what is termed an internal "striker." For our purposes, a hammer and striker have the same function. Remember, the term "Double Action" or "Single Action" refers to the trigger's work. With the *M&P*, after you insert the magazine, just like the Sig, you must "rack" the slide rearward and release it to chamber a round. But the *M&P* action does not push back a hammer/striker into a cocked position. After a round is chambered, pulling the trigger does two works: it pulls back the "striker" and then releases the "striker" which strikes the primer, which ignites the powder, etc. To you and to me, we have taken the same action: inserted a magazine, chambered a round, pulled the trigger, and the gun fired. But because of internal design, one is a SAO and one is a DAO. Point: the action may or may not be that important to you in a semi as it is in a revolver. It is a critical feature in a revolver. As far as the way you operate and fire the semi, the actions you take may well be identical. Still, there must be some known tradeoffs best covered by your local gun store expert. For example, trigger pull distance and required pounds of pressure may be less with a SAO since the hammer is already cocked.

The semi has several advantages over a derringer and revolver

One advantage of the semi is the much larger capacity for bullets prior to reloading. A derringer has at most four rounds and a revolver has five to eight rounds versus up to seventeen or more rounds for the standard sized semi. Two or more time-consuming reloads are needed for a revolver to have the same firepower as a Standard semi. Not only does the semi provide a significant advantage in the number of bullets going "down range," the semi does not require two dangerous reload times as required by a revolver. Also, reloading a semi is much, much faster than a revolver, assuming that you are reloading with a spare magazine that is already fully loaded with bullets. If you must first stuff up to seventeen bullets into the magazine, then there is no reload advantage over a revolver and perhaps even a slight disadvantage time-wise. But, once you have the magazine fully loaded and reinserted into the semi, you would have more firepower. Most police carry two or three extra fully-loaded magazines, giving them almost sixty rounds of firepower to be quickly loaded and fired. This far exceeds the best, most adroit revolver expert's firepower. With a little practice, you can eject, grab an extra loaded magazine from the belt holster, insert it, rack the slide, and fire within four-to-five seconds. Also, an extra loaded magazine is a very small item to carry by itself; think cell phone size.

There are revolver "Speed Loaders" and "Speed Strips" that can materially assist the revolver reload time. But "Speed Loaders" are the size of a small tennis ball sticking out on the side of your belt, or wherever you would carry it. This is an issue to consider if you are going to carry concealed. Reloading a derringer is also a little time consuming, and you must do it every one to four rounds, not a desirable action in an extended fire fight.

The major disadvantage for a semi is the more complex shell extracting and reloading mechanics. Even the best semis have been known to misfeed or misfire. The less well made semis can almost make a habit of it. When you are facing a perp who has you in his sights, you want a pistol that, when you draw and pull the trigger, will go bang! It will go bang 9,999 times out of a 10,000. If you buy a semi, invest in a very good one; this is not the area to go cheap!

Semis can also be more sensitive to specific ammunition brands and bullet shape. Semiautomatics were originally designed to feed round-nose (ball) ammunition. Hollow point ammunition has a flat nose and has the potential to not feed as well. Most modern designs of both ammunition and feed ramps on semis have vastly decreased this problem. I had the personal experience of a semi having misfeed problems "out of the box." Since I buy the cheaper ammo to save money, my first thought was that it might be the ammo causing the problem. I next tried three brands of ammo and discovered that all three had misfeeds, but that the cheaper ammo had slightly more. I called the pistol manufacturer who immediately emailed me the UPS prepaid mailer and said to send in the semi. Within two weeks I had it back with comments on the specific "actions" by the gunsmith. No more misfeeds, but I now purchase the more expensive ammo. Since this is my wife's concealed carry semi, I will take no chances on her safety by buying the cheaper ammo; nor should you.

Another potential issue with a semi is to hold the grip in such a manner that **your thumb accidentally presses the magazine release button while you are firing**. It can be embarrassing to have the magazine release or eject and the pistol stop firing while you do not have a clue to just what is going on. However, live fire practice, correct gripping, and self-awareness will overcome this problem most of the time. Some semis have the magazine eject "button" on the bottom of the grip at the point where the magazine is inserted. Some of the Sig Sauer models that I have fired have this feature. It overcomes the accidental magazine ejection, but it makes a quick magazine change more cumbersome and time consuming and requires both hands to accomplish. Just remember:

"The loudest sound in the world is a click when you need a bang."

Many semis are designed to **not fire** if the magazine has been released or removed, even though a round is chambered in the gun. This safety feature is usually termed a "magazine disconnect" or a "magazine safety." It is a very desirable feature in my perspective, but not all semis come with it. Without it, a semi **will still fire a chambered round,** even though the magazine has been removed. The point is that a semi is not unloaded just because the magazine has been removed. Tragic accidents have occurred because people have mistakenly believed that releasing the magazine was equivalent to unloading the semi. That said, here is the opinion of a law enforcement office: *"In a physical struggle with an attacker, the magazine could be accidentally released from the gun. I would want to be able to fire the chambered round at the attacker. This would not be possible with a magazine disconnect."* So what should you do? You are faced with a trade-off: a safety device to help prevent a careless accident versus being able to still fire one round when in a fight for your life.

"You makes your choices and you take your chances."

There is another semiautomatic handgun feature that can be a **sometimes, one-time disadvantage**. Look back at picture 3.12 of the *Sig P238* semi. Notice the "structure" just below the hammer that protrudes outward from the back of the grip? Many experts refer to this as a "tang," which sounds to me like an oriental fruit juice or a colloquial pronunciation of "thing." Like in a movie when one of the good old boys turns and says to his buddy, "Bubba, hand me dat der tang." So, to avoid confusion, we will refer to this as the *thumb not being lacerated block*. This "thumb not being lacerated block" serves several functions. First, it functions to position your shooting hand and grip properly on the gun. Second, it protrudes out to such an extent that it should prevent your hand from gripping too high up the pistol's grip.

The slide is driven rearward by the fired bullet's gases at over 200 feet per second. If you have your grip up too high, the bottom of the slide, which has nice, clean, sharp edges, will slice open your hand between the thumb and index finger. Just how much too high you were gripping determines just how many stitches you might require. If you were really unlucky, it will cut you on both sides of your hand. This very accident happened to my son. He did not want to shoot any longer. Sort of ruined his whole day, I guess.

This is not a major disadvantage to selecting a semi as your weapon of choice. It is just that no one ever tells you these kind of things until

43

they happen, and then they say, "Oh, yeah, that happened to Betty Bop, too." Then, they may actually go ahead and explain what you did wrong as you wrap a hankie around your hand to stem the blood flow. Well, now you have been told! (Aren't you glad that you read this first?) Maybe the experts just do not conceive that anyone is that, well, unknowledgeable. Maybe it is thought of as a "rite of passage" in becoming a "shootist." If you are gripping with two hands, the weak-side hand is the one most likely to get into "harm's way" because it does not have the "thumb block" to protect it. This does not happen to every person who fires a semi; just to some of us. It also seems **to occur only one time per person.** At least I have never had anyone confess to me that they experienced it twice, or more. Therefore, I have termed this a *sometimes, one time* disadvantage because you will not repeat it if you ever have the misfortune to experience it.

It takes a bit of strength to "rack" the slide on a semiautomatic. The larger the caliber and size of the gun, the more strength it may require. If this is a problem for you due to age, injury, or lack of muscle strength, there are several alternatives to pursue. First, try a smaller caliber or a smaller sized semi. Both options may reduce the spring tension on the slide and may make it easier for you to "rack" the slide. Second, consider a small revolver. Third, a derringer is easy to load. A two barrel model shooting .410 PDX rounds will give you eight copper discs (slugs) and up to thirty-two BBs hitting a miscreant intent on doing you harm. I can almost guarantee that at close range, you will have plenty of time to get away or reload while he is counting the holes in his torso. And do not forget the *Tomcat* style of semi with a tilt-up barrel in lieu of requiring the slide to be racked.

OK, one last time I'll bore you with my own preferences. Since a SAO, DAO, and a DASA semi all require the slide to be racked to load a cartridge into the firing chamber, then the real preference comes from the difference between the trigger pull length, required trigger pull pressure or poundage, and safety. That said, the SAO semi should have a much shorter, lighter trigger pull which is nice for us "flinchers." For concealed carry, lack of an external hammer (DAO) seems preferable, but not critical. I value the thumb safety more than the magazine safety. If I could use an OWB holster, a 9mm semi with 17+1 capacity with thumb safety would be just fine for me should anyone be caring. If anyone really cares about my concealed carry "wants," the previously discussed Sig P238 with a thumb safety is a nice solution for ankle or pocket carry. Unlike revolvers, semis are more difficult to pin down as to exact preference based on trigger action.

Magazines

We need to cover this first; the device that you load and push up into the grip of a semi is called a "Magazine." It is not a "Clip." A clip is what girls put into their hair. If you go into a gun store and ask about "Clips," they will point you toward the women's department. OK, they probably do not have a women's department, but you will have just identified yourself as a "Greenhorn."

While we are on the subject of magazines, here are a couple of additional things you should know. All semiautomatics have a magazine to hold the pistol's ammo. Magazines have two basic designs: "single stack" or "double stack." A single stack magazine is constructed so that each round sits directly on top of the round underneath it. Therefore, the width of the magazine is only slightly wider than the width of a single bullet. A double stack magazine is designed so that each round sits about half off to the side of the round underneath it. The result is that for the same caliber the double stack magazine holds more rounds, in the same vertical space (height), than a single stack magazine holds. Assuming the same caliber handgun, the trade-off is more rounds and a wider pistol grip per double stack magazine versus fewer rounds and a slimmer handgun grip with a single stack magazine pistol. This wider grip size may be a consideration for concealed carry, depending on how and where you plan to carry. In addition, to obtain the double stack magazine semi, you may be forced to select a larger sized handgun. After all, to have a 9mm pistol with a 17+1 capacity in a single stack configuration would require a grip length approaching eight to ten inches in length. Therefore, most single stack semis will probably be small or compact size and most standard sized semis will be double stacked.

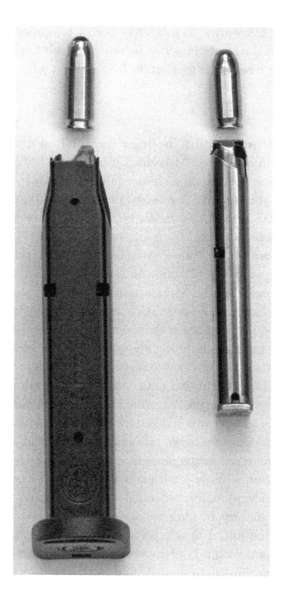

Picture 3.14*: Compare the 9mm double stack magazine (17 rounds) on left to a .380 single stack magazine (6 rounds) on right. The .380 is called a 9mm "kurtz" (short) in Germany. It is shorter, but the same diameter as the 9mm. The double stack above offers about three times the capacity but is only about 1/3 longer.*

A new semi comes with one or sometimes two magazines. Experts will tell you that you should have at least three magazines. There is some logic behind this assertion. If you carry, many encourage you to also carry at least one additional loaded magazine. If one of the two magazines with you gets lost or broken, you have a readily available backup at home without an on-line order or trip to the gun store. Plus, some magazines are harder to come by and you just might have to wait weeks for a new one. There is also another reason for having at least three magazines. If you engage in training that has you moving, shooting, ejecting empty magazines and loading full ones, the ejected, empty magazine may frequently hit the ground. Over time, these roughly handled magazines may become slightly askew, bent, or even cracked. These conditions will probably first come to your attention when you begin to experience misfeeds and or misfires. When a magazine causes this type of malfunction, it is time to give it a funeral with full honors and never use it again. I have read of one "shootist" who paints numbers on the bottom of each of his magazines. This helps to identify which are his, if engaged in a class with students moving, shooting, and ejecting magazines all over the place. It also allows him to identify the miscreant magazine. When he suddenly experiences a series of misfeeds or misfires, he then replaces the malfunctioning magazine with another. Since they are numbered, he can more easily ascertain which, if any, of the magazines might be the culprit. A final reason to own at least three magazines: if you accidentally eject or drop a fully loaded magazine and it hits a hard surface, you will probably be picking up pieces of the magazine and loose bullets. Magazines are not designed nor manufactured to withstand abuse. They are probably the most fragile part of the semi system.

One last item: magazines are a little difficult to load, and as the spring gets pressed down toward the bottom of the base, the effort to load the last few rounds increases. There are several devices that will make the loading of a magazine very, very easy. I own one called an *UpLULA*. (No, I haven't a clue as to what the name means. I would have suggested "Fingernail Saver.") It will work with multiple calibers, 9mm to .45-caliber, so I do not need to buy one for each different caliber semi. Your local gun store sells these; they are worth the price!

So, derringer, revolver or semiautomatic, either one of the three might be a good choice and do a fine job. There are trade-offs. Just ensure that you know them and then decide which type best meets your most important requirements. A semi of same caliber is usually of slimmer profile for concealed carry than a revolver. A revolver is just like *Old Faithful*; it is always on time and "spews hotly" as instructed. A derringer can offer a larger caliber in the smaller frame but with fewer rounds.

Do not assume that I have covered all that you should know. For example, we have not discussed grip safeties or de-cocker variables or a whole bunch of stuff. Go to a gun shop and touch, feel, dry fire if they permit, and ask at least a hundred and seven questions. No, they will not mind. They like to display their knowledge, and most important, they do not want you to buy a handgun that will not be satisfactory for you. See, they know that you will blame them if you are unhappy. After all, none of us take responsibility for our own mistakes. Once you buy a handgun; well, it is a little bit like eating peanuts, one is just never enough. Plus you will need to buy ammo and holsters, etc. and you will become their customer for years to come, if you are pleased with their help.

Which Caliber Handgun Is Right For You?

Recoil: *"For every action, there is an equal and opposite reaction."*
Based upon the above law of physics, as soon as a gun is fired, the hot gases that propel the missile down the barrel also push the weapon backward toward the shooter. This push-back is called *recoil*. Some people may find recoil discomforting and distracting, a response that can generate a "flinch" which adversely affects accuracy and just how quickly the shooter can re-aim the handgun back onto the target for a second shot.

Recoil is minimized by two choices over which you have complete control: heaviness or weight of the gun and caliber or size of the cartridge for which the gun is designed. Handguns come in a variety of materials: stainless steel, composite, aluminum, titanium, etc. This weight difference usually impacts recoil; the heavier the handgun, the less recoil felt by the shooter. The caliber of ammunition also adds to recoil. A .22-caliber has tiny recoil and shoots a tiny projectile. A .45-caliber has greater recoil and shoots a large projectile. The caliber you select will impact the recoil you feel. In addition to the weight of the handgun, the actual size of the handgun as well as the size of the grip may reduce the perceived recoil. The larger the handgun's grip, the greater is the surface area that the shooter's hand has to spread the recoil. Some manufacturers supply three grip sizes—small, medium, large—with certain models. This allows you to "tailor" the grip's size to your unique hand.

Some manufacturers offer models with *porting* as a feature to reduce recoil. "Porting" is the use of small holes (ports) along the top of the barrel to allow the gas to escape. Since some of the gas goes upward, there is less gas going out the barrel front pushing the projectile so there is less backward recoil. There are a couple of disadvantages of a "ported" handgun, in my opinion. If the gun is held close to the torso and fired, the shooter will probably be surprised and maybe a little stunned or even temporarily blinded by the hot gasses and powder debris escaping upward through the holes (ports) in the top of the barrel. If shooting at night, the hot gases escaping through the ports may temporarily cause night blindness until your eyes again adjust to darkness. Hence, it is probably a poor idea to purchase a "ported" handgun for personal defense. It is better to vary material and caliber to reduce recoil—or to "man-up" and practice until you are comfortable.

Caliber of Handgun

Handguns range in caliber or bullet size from .22 to over .50-caliber. All can effectively harm you, a loved one, an innocent bystander, or a malicious miscreant. Within each caliber size, the number of powder grains can vary, especially for those who load their own ammo. So the bullet's power can be changed. Also, the bullet's projectile size in weight (grains) can be manipulated in the same caliber. *Caliber* is the term for the diameter of the bullet in either inches or millimeters.

The smaller caliber handgun requires more accuracy of aim and more precise shot placement to inflict a "stopping shot" on a perp. A .22-caliber, .25-caliber, or .32-caliber can all be considered for self-defense and probably have some merit due to small size and low recoil. Plus, these caliber handguns can be augmented with "personal defense" (PD) ammo which helps compensate for the smaller caliber ammunition's lower penetration and shock force.

However, the general school of thought is that the smallest caliber size that is suitable for self-defense concealed carry is the .380-caliber cartridge, and this accommodation to a smaller caliber than a 9mm or .40-caliber is given grudgingly. The .380-caliber ammunition is available as Full Metal Jacket (FMJ) rounds as well as in other types of personal defense rounds, such as Jacketed Hollow Point (JHP). These personal defense rounds are designed to spread on impact and thus to create more force and damage inside the target. Yes, I know; very unpleasant to talk about, but that is what these rounds do and what handguns are designed to accomplish.

At one time, the .38 Special revolver was the favorite of the police (picture 3.15). Since these were revolvers and the perps switched to semis with three times the firepower before a reload, most police forces switched to semi 9mm and many now carry .40-cal semis for greater impact.

Picture 3.15*: A S&W .38 Special 6 shot policeman's Revolver shown beside a 9mm semi with 17+1 or as a .40-caliber with a capacity of 15+1. Bullets from top down: 38 Special flat nose FMJ; .38 Special JHP; .40-caliber JHP.*

The granddaddy of them all is the .45-caliber. If you want a "one shot stopper," this is your best bet; however, most experts will assert that there is not a "one shot stopper" caliber handgun. Thus, even this powerful caliber may have less power than desired to stop some of the "hopped-up" miscreants out there today. The .45-caliber does have a lot of recoil compared to, say a 9mm, but honestly, it can vary greatly by type and model. My Taurus *Judge*, at least to my mind, has surprisingly light recoil for a .45-caliber, at least when firing the .45-caliber Long Colt.

The most popular larger caliber is the 9mm. It is the same ammunition used by the WWII Germans in their funny looking "Lugers," and the ammo is still often called 9mm Luger. Since this is a very popular size, it is the most economical ammo, other than .22-caliber, to purchase at this time. It is about half the cost of a .45-caliber round. So if you are firing one hundred rounds per month and the difference is $25.00, you save about $300.00 per year. That is enough to allow you to go buy a safe or another gun. See how great these things work out?

Safety Features

There are a variety of safety features that are available on handguns; well, primarily on semis. Not all are available on any one handgun. You have to decide which are "nice to have" and which are "critical to have" for your carry or home defense handgun.

Here is a list of a majority of handgun safety features:

1. Thumb Safety*
2. Trigger Safety
3. Grip Safety
4. Magazine Safety (Disconnect)
5. Manual Safety* De-cocking Lever
6. Loaded Chamber Indicator
7. Cocked Status Indicator
8. Firing Pin Block
9. Automatic Firing Pin Safety
10. Half-Cock Position

11. Gun Safety Lock* (This feature actually locks the pistol from being fired by special key. Think of this more as an alternative to a gun safe rather than a safety feature being used while carrying.)

* Per my LEO reviewer, these active safety features require the shooter to de-activate them to fire. Therefore, their inclusion should be carefully considered against the scenario of trying to de-activate them under severe stress in a self-defense situation; i.e., greater safety versus faster shooting response.

Remember: ***"Don't do things that you do not want to explain to the paramedics!"***

Sights

Most handguns come with front and rear sights. Revolvers often have sort of a "half-moon" shaped front sight that sticks up like a shark's fin. (Go back and review the *Bearcat* revolver in picture 3.5.) It may or may not have a conventional rear sight. Often the rear sight is a slotted groove along the top of the barrel for you to view and center the front sight. After all, Cowboys just drew fast and fired; most did not bring the revolver up to eye level and aim. (Don't believe me? Then go watch a *Gunsmoke* episode. TV would not lie, would it?) Derringers are designed to be close encounter type responders. They may not be burdened with good sights. If you need to aim to hit a perp at one-to-five feet, then at least purchase the derringer model that fires the .410 shell.

Semis are more likely to have a set of conventional sights. The rear sight will have a notch or groove in its middle through which you view the front sight which is likely to be square shaped to fit nicely into the viewing slot in the rear sights. Some will have white dots to assist in viewing and aligning the front and rear. These dots may even be "night sights" which will glow in the dark and can be very useful if you are forced to fire in the darkness. Others may just have a red spot in the front sight for visual assistance.

The objective when using sights is to align the front sight in the groove or center cut of the rear sight. The top of the front and rear sights should be level across the top and the front sight centered in the rear sight's opening. Then you focus on the front sight and your target. Carefully squeeze the trigger straight back by using consistent pressure with your trigger finger. Do not jerk your finger quickly or jerk the pistol when you think it is set to fire. Follow these instructions, and you will hit the bull's eye every time. (Have I mentioned my own prowess as a "shootist"?)

Trigger Action and Concealed Carry

Just when you thought that you were finished with the Single Action versus Double Action discussion, here it comes again. A SAO (Single Action Only) derringer and revolver operate identically—you manually cock the hammer and then pull the trigger to drop the hammer onto the firing pin or primer. The trigger pull in this action is generally shorter—actual travel distance—and requires fewer pounds of finger pressure to squeeze the trigger reward. The reason for the shorter length pull is that the hammer is already back and thus there is no need for the longer pull to allow you to force the hammer rearward. The reason for the fewer pounds of finger pressure is due to the fact that the hammer is already rearward and no effort is required to move the hammer rearward using a drawbar or something. Thus, it only requires a slight pressure to release the hammer. This "quick" trigger action—short travel and light pull poundage—can come as a surprise and gun go "Boom!" before one expects it.

Therefore, if using a SAO derringer or revolver for concealed carry, you must first manually pull the external hammer rearward prior to squeezing the trigger to fire each shot. A slightly cumbersome action when seconds are critical. An option is to walk around with the derringer or revolver already fully cocked so that all that is required is for you to draw, present, aim, and lightly squeeze the trigger. A very dangerous method as the short, little poundage, trigger-squeeze will almost surely result in a "BOOM!" prior to your being ready. (Employing this carry technique is an excellent way to meet your neighborhood paramedics and the local police.) SAO derringers and revolvers **would not seem** an optimum choice for concealed carry.

The DAO derringer and revolver will have a longer trigger pull and require more pounds of finger-strength as the hammer is being forced rearward with a drawbar or something, by the trigger squeeze. When the hammer reaches the end of the pull, it is released and a spring pulls the hammer forward and the hammer strikes the bullet. Whether the derringer is a one shot to four shot, the trigger distance and poundage of pull required will be the same for each bullet fired. This is also true with a revolver—to rotate the cylinder requires the same trigger poundage and travel length for the first through the last round fired. Since there is no option for manually cocking the DAO revolver, you will have a longer and harder trigger squeeze for every shot fired than with a SAO. Still, in my opinion, a better option than a SAO for concealed carry, but the longer trigger pull and more finger squeeze pressure may cause the pistol to come "off target." Therefore, practice more to overcome this tendency, if you have it. (If you do not have this tendency, please let me know how you overcame it.)

Just like the SAO, the SADA derringer and revolver gives **the option** of having the first round "red-hot" with the hammer already manually cocked—a poor safety option—resting in your holster. When you draw and present the pistol toward a perp, a slight trigger squeeze will fire the thing since the hammer is in the cocked position and very little trigger pull is necessary to release the hammer. (Carrying your SADA in a fully cocked but holstered manner is an outstanding way to meet your criminal defense attorney, bail bondsman, emergency room staff, plus other local officials.) With the SADA **revolver**, all shots will require the harder, longer trigger pull, unless you use the option to manually cock the hammer prior to each shot. So, an unsolicited opinion, for derringer or revolver concealed carry, the best option is a derringer or revolver that is a DA; SADA is OK too, but second choice for me since they have the hammer thing sticking out. Should you purchase a SADA revolver or derringer, it is strongly advised to carry with the hammer down—requiring the long and strong trigger squeeze for the first shot. Never, ever carry a derringer or revolver with the hammer cocked is my advice.

Why drag you kicking and screaming through all of that you ask? Because of the confusion of this trigger action, etc. when semiautomatics are concerned. Remember, whether a SAO, a DAO, or a SADA semi, all must have the slide racked rearward to load the initial round into the firing chamber. (Yes, I know that I am overlooking the tilt-up barrel types such as the *Tomcat*.)

A SAO semi that has a round in the firing chamber also has the hammer cocked, accomplished by the same action of racking the slide to chamber the first round into firing position. Now, you have a "hot" pistol. All that is necessary for you to have a quick response—or an unexpected event—is a very slight squeeze on the trigger and your semi goes "Boom!" To repeat, being a SAO, once you rack the slide—which cocks the hammer—the trigger's travel distance is short and the trigger pull poundage required to squeeze the trigger is much reduced. Again, you have a cocked, ready-to-fire semi, and a very slight pull on the trigger might accidentally fire your pistol. If you have a thumb safety, this provides some degree of prevention of an unexpected event. It must be released before the semi will fire; a minimally time-consuming act that just might slip your mind in the heat of a dangerous encounter. Some SAO semis have a grip safety which requires pressure to release the safety in order to fire the pistol. Thus, even if the trigger is pressed rearward, unless the grip is squeezed simultaneously, it will not fire. A semi with both a thumb safety and a grip safety would seem safe to carry with the round chambered and the hammer cocked. The traditional "1911" designed semi has both features, as an example. You could also reduce the risk of having the SAO semiautomatic "hot" by walking around with an un-chambered round, but that will require you to rack the slide to both load a round into the firing chamber and cock the hammer before you can respond to any threat. This is generally a two handed, time-consuming, cumbersome act to be performed under stress. Remember the Squeaky Fromme episode? With a SAO, since every round fired will automatically send the slide rearward to eject the fired casing, then load another round into the firing chamber, and also cock the hammer; every shot will have the same feel for trigger travel length and poundage. Every trigger pull from first to last will be short and require light poundage. A SAO semi needs a thumb safety as a minimum, in my opinion

The DAO semi has the same action to load a round into the firing chamber as a SAO, but that action does not cock the hammer. Since the hammer is not cocked upon loading a round into the firing chamber, the first round to be fired might require a long trigger pull to move the hammer rearward with a drawbar or something; this might also require a trigger pull of greater poundage. When each round is fired, the slide's rearward movement not only ejects the expended casing, it also strips the next round from the magazine and loads it into the firing chamber. It does NOT cock the hammer. After the first round, all the remaining rounds will fire with the same long trigger pull and high pressure poundage. That said, my Smith and Wesson *M&P* is a DAO with only a four pound trigger poundage and a normal length trigger pull distance. Its trigger experience is exactly like a SAO semi. Why? Well, the official explanation is twofold: it was designed that way and it uses a firing sear rather than a hammer. (I think Mr. S&W just made an advertising mistake initially and is now too embarrassed to admit that the *M&P* is really a SAO; or if really a DAO, it cocks the striker about 90% when the slide is racked. They won't admit this though.) My point, SAO or DAO or SADA, even though the trigger is doing different steps, your feel as the shooter may not be exactly what you would expect. Therefore, dry fire and test fire before you buy.

A semi that is SADA offers a more complex environment than a SAO or a DAO semi. When the slide is racked to load a round into the firing chamber, the SADA is also cocked, just like the SAO. You can un-cock it either by using a de-cocker, if it has one, or by careful thumb and trigger coordination to release the hammer—a maneuver slightly subject to unexpected discharge until mastered. On some, perhaps the majority, if the de-cocker can be "active" during the racking process, then the hammer is not cocked and then the pistol will have the same trigger action on the first shot as a DA. Point of all of this: if you have a SADA, when it is initially racked and cocked, you have, for all practical purposes, a SAO semi. It only requires slight trigger pull poundage and trigger pull distance to fire. You have a "hot" pistol. As with the SAO, you have some options to eliminate or control this "hot" status. A thumb safety is such a device to add comfort and safety to your carry. Another is a de-cocker.

If you have a de-cocker, you can depress it and that will drop the hammer while simultaneously sealing off the firing pin so that the chambered round is not fired. Some pistols have de-cockers that drop the hammer completely. Others, like the Sig Sauer P230SL, only drop the hammer to the half-cocked position. To fire from a half-cocked position requires a somewhat shorter trigger pull distance than when the hammer is completely down, but requires the same high poundage pull as a DAO. Once de-cocked, it is extremely safe for you to eject the magazine and add that extra round to replace the one you just racked into the firing chamber to gain the weapon's full 17+1 or whatever its capacity. Since you have de-cocked the hammer, to fire the first round you will have the DA trigger pull experience—long and hard. All subsequent rounds fired will have the SAO experience, short pull and light poundage since the slide cocks the hammer during the eject—reload cycle. Thus, if you use the de-cocker to drop the hammer, the first round fired experience is very different from all the rest of the rounds fired in that magazine's load, assuming you do not again employ the de-cocker between rounds fired. The Beretta 92FS 9mm semi has a clever "de-cocker/thumb safety" combination. Depressing the de-cocker not only drops the hammer it also locks the trigger. Well, it doesn't lock it from moving, just from firing. The trigger can be moved back and forth till next week, but nothing happens. Push the "de-cocker/thumb safety" off and then the trigger action is DA with a longer, higher pressure squeeze for the first round and then the SA trigger squeeze for all subsequent rounds. (Point of this; be knowledgeable that not all de-cockers operate identically.)

If using a de-cocker, this difference in trigger action is fantastic and terrible, depending on your point of view, experience, and perspective. Since the initial trigger pull will be long—relatively speaking—and require more pressure if the de-cocker has been employed, you should not be surprised by a quick "Boom!" when you are firing the first round. Some think just the opposite, that it takes three days and Hercules to squeeze off the first round. Then, having adjusted to that, the next round fires with a short—compared to the first round—trigger pull and less squeeze pressure, sometimes surprising the shooter with an early shot. This boom, boom inconsistency is a concern to some and a boon to others. "Why?" you ask. "Good question," I respond.

First, what some dislike about this inconsistence. One, after de-cocking, the long trigger pull and high poundage required often pull the aim away from the bulls-eye and toward Oklahoma, or somewhere. Result, first shot is off-target. Two, the totally different trigger travel length and poundage for the second and subsequent shots can be disconcerting and confusing. For example, a surprise second shot too early as shooter expects a longer trigger squeeze. Three, it takes some practice—which you should do anyway—to become accustomed to differing trigger actions, one immediately following the other.

Next, what some love and adore about this inconsistency. After de-cocking, the required longer pull and Herculean first shot's trigger poundage offer some additional safety from an accidental discharge compared to the fully cocked—"hot"—status. If it takes until next Tuesday before the pistol fires—a slight exaggeration—after a Herculean squeeze effort—another slight exaggeration—, then you reduce the opportunity for a quick, unintentional discharge. For concealed carry, this might convince you that it is "safe" to carry the SADA semi "semi-hot:" round chambered, semi un-cocked, but ready to be fired with a DA trigger sequence. Add a thumb safety and you just might convince yourself that you are good to go under the clothing, so to speak.

Was this worth all of the above time and words? Well, it would have been worth over $550.00 to me. Personal experience: I was testing various handguns under the rental approach at the local pistol range. Apparently, all of them were DA. I complained to the range officer that the trigger pull took two hours and three strong hands to work. He suggested I try a SA semi. I did. I loved the short trigger travel and low pull poundage. At least I was now hitting the target and not Tulsa. I ran out and purchased same: a S&W *M&P* 9mm standard. (As confessed above, it is really a DAO disguised as a SAO semi.) It was love at first shot and still an adored and venerated object of my shooting affection. However, knowing even less then than I do now, I purchased it without a thumb safety. So, to carry concealed, do I carry it "hot:" chambered round, cocked with a short, light trigger pull, to make it go "Boom?" Or do I carry "cold:" no chambered round, hammer un-cocked requiring me to rack the slide to chamber a round quickly and cock the hammer when faced with an unsocial encounter of the worst kind? My solution was to purchase the same pistol, but with a thumb safety, thus the extra $550.00.

I just can't seem to hit the target with a traditional DAO trigger pull. (I explain to other "Shootists" that this is the result of a brilliant mind that has so much time to solve differential equations during the traditionally long DA trigger pull time, that I become distracted. They probably don't believe it, but it gives me some cover. Fortunately, no one has yet asked me what a differential equation is.) I want a SAO trigger experience, so I had to go for a SAO-type trigger experience, but with a Thumb safety for concealed carry. I justified to my inner child that even though the gun is "hot"—chambered round and hammer cocked—the thumb safety makes it OK. So, an additional $550.00 later, I have two semis rather than one. (I wish that I had read all about this here first.) Of course a SADA semi with a de-cocker would come close to accomplishing increased safety, but I would still be out the $550.00 bucks.

How about a quick summary of the appeal of the various trigger actions for concealed carry, per my opinion?

1.   Derringers: SAO, **not** for concealed carry.
2.   Derringers: DAO and SADA, OK, but two barrels with trigger guard and the .410 and .45-caliber option seems preferable. Just man-up and learn to shoot with the trigger guard.
3.   Revolvers: SAO, **not** for concealed carry.
4.   Revolvers: DAO and SADA, OK, but DAO with no external hammer would seem best option.
5.   Semiautomatics: SAO, OK with a thumb safety and a grip safety if available.
6.   Semiautomatics: DAO, OK with a thumb safety.
7.   Semiautomatics: SADA, OK with a thumb safety; a de-cocker is desirable—just ensure you understand exactly how it functions.

Of course with the semis, the magazine safety should be considered.

So which handgun for you?
Depends on your need, so let us repeat:

1.   Will you carry?
2.   How will you carry?
3.   What is the largest caliber you are comfortable firing? After all, carrying a "cannon" will not do if you are too nervous or frightened to actually fire it or if fired, you hit somewhere in Nebraska. If it is not fun to shoot, you will not want to practice and probably will not practice. Thus, you will not become proficient, and you may be dangerous with a weapon.
4.   If money is a big issue, then ammo cost is a big consideration over a couple of years. Saving $25.00 per 100 rounds practice per month for twenty-four months is $600.00. Over ten years, that is $3,000.00.
5.   If all you can afford is a .22-caliber, then go with it, but carry Hollow Points or PDX rounds. Practice a **lot** with less expensive rounds. An excellent marksman with a .22 is preferred over a poor marksman with a "cannon" left in the car

or at home that is seldom fired. You might find a .22 Magnum Revolver that would accept .22 Long Rifle bullets. That would permit a fair compromise: practice with .22-caliber ammo, but carry the .22-Magnum HP or PDX ammo.

6. If your plan is to leave your pistol at home for self-defense, then larger caliber and a larger-size handgun is better. Well, larger caliber and size are always better, but if carrying is not in the future, it becomes an easier choice.

7. If you want absolute certainty the pistol will fire, then consider purchasing the very best semi or a good quality revolver.

8. Do you want extreme safety? Demand thumb safety, along with magazine safety and grip safety and anything else on it that can add to safety. Do not forget a gun safe! (See *Chapter 7.*) The holster should also have a thumb strap (my personal opinion), even though it impedes a quick draw when you are making a two-second decision.

9. "Remember Plaxico Burress."

10. You can probably add several other specific features for yourself.

11. Oh, yeah, SAO or SADA can make a difference to your ability to carry safely and be safe when meeting an unsocial encounter of the worst kind.

And keep in mind:

**"Cheap is always an option,
but is it the option to pick when your life may be at risk?"**

Chapter 4

There Are No Good Surprises or Acceptable Excuses When Mishandling Firearms

When handling or messing with firearms, there are just not any good surprises with felicitous outcomes when an unexpected event (pistol discharge) occurs. All unintentional or accidental events are embarrassing, and may also be harmful, painful, deadly, costly, or all of the above. In addition, whether you intended for something to happen or not, you are still responsible for the outcome. Read that to mean morally, legally, and financially responsible. That responsibility may just be medical bills for you, and if so, count yourself fortunate. To back up my assertion, review some of the most frequently heard excuses or explanations following a surprise discharge event from mishandling a firearm. These are not invented, or intended to be humorous. I can assure you, for those who uttered them they were not humorous. These are all taken from newspapers, magazines, and a few "confessed" experiences of others. Even the one about the dog stepping on the trigger of the long gun placed on the deck of a boat is right out of the newspaper.

Judge: "Please explain just how the gun was fired."

Excuse #1a: "Judge, I didn't know that the gun was loaded."
Excuse #1b: "Judge, he told me the gun was unloaded."
Excuse #1c: "Judge, I remembered unloading the gun the last time I used it."
Excuse #2:   "Judge, I ejected the magazine and thought that the gun was unloaded."
Excuse #3:   "Judge, I told him a thousand times that he was too young to handle a gun and to never touch it."
Excuse #4:   "Judge, I never leave a loaded gun around the house. I don't know where he found the ammunition."

Excuse #5: "Judge, I always keep the gun locked up, but there had been a series of robberies in the neighborhood and so I was leaving the safe unlocked for quick access just in case a robber struck our house."

Excuse #6: "Judge, I keep the gun well hidden and out of his reach. I just can't understand how he found it."

Excuse #7: "Judge, when the gun went off with a small 'pop' sound, he looked down the barrel to see if the bullet was lodged in the barrel."

Excuse #8: "Judge, when the gun went off with a 'pop' sound, I just pulled the trigger and fired the next round, like I always do with my revolver."

Excuse #9: "Judge, we both leaned our rifles against the fence and as we crawled through the wire, one of them slipped and fell and it just went off."

Excuse #10: "Judge, the gun was tucked inside my belt and as it started to slide down the inside of my pants I grabbed at it and it just went off." (Remember Plaxico Burress.)

Excuse #11: "Judge, I placed the gun on the boat's deck and my dog must have stepped on the trigger."

Excuse #12: "Judge, when I was practicing my 'fast draw,' the gun just went off."

Excuse #13: "Judge, I was showing my gun when I dropped it and it went off."

Excuse #14: (Please feel free to add your own here.)

Had enough of these? Well, just ensure that you do not add your own personal, real life excuse to the list. What? You still do not believe that these excuses are real? Then I suggest you just read your local paper; over a period of time I bet they start showing up.

Here are the generally accepted Cardinal Rules of Handling Handguns:

1. Always assume that a handgun is loaded!
2. Never point the handgun at an object you do not intend to shoot!
3. Never put your finger on the trigger of a handgun until you are ready to shoot at the object at which you are pointing!

4. If you are preparing to shoot, be aware of what is in line with your target, both in front of and beyond.
5. Ensure that the handgun is unloaded unless you are preparing to fire it!
6. How to ensure that the handgun you are not contemplating firing is unloaded. Eject the magazine, "rack" the slide, and eject the chambered round. Visually inspect the firing chamber for a round, and then insert your finger into the firing chamber just to double check. If you are using a revolver, open the cylinder and push the ejector rod and eject all of the rounds. Then visually inspect each cartridge chamber for a round. Put on the safety, if there is one, and read Rules #2 and #3.
7. Repeat Rule #5.

Chapter 5

Ammunition

Please do not be offended because I refer to ammunition by various terms such as bullet, cartridge, shell, round, ammo or some other slightly irregular term. For the purposes of this *Companion*, please accept them all as referring to the same object. The object that you load into a revolver's cylinder or into a semiautomatic's magazine which, when struck by the firing pin, ignites the primer which in turn ignites the powder whose gases propel the projectile down the barrel.

The object that holds both the powder and the projectile is the casing. The casing is the object that, after the bullet is fired, is left in the revolver's cylinder or ejected by the semi's extractor. The object that is propelled out the end of the barrel by the powder I will variously call either a projectile or a bullet and hope that the context is clear.

Just as handguns are different in operational mechanics, caliber, material, and size; ammo also comes with a variety of nomenclature that describes its size, shape, operational mechanics, power, and caliber. Yes, we are going to review all of these areas. You will not become an expert with sufficient knowledge to work for the Winchester Arms or the Remington companies. However, you will become sufficiently knowledgeable to ensure that you do not purchase the wrong or inappropriate ammunition for your handgun. For example, should you ask for a box of 9mm jacketed hollow point ammo and the clerk hands you a box with the symbol FMJ, you will know that he has made a mistake.

Primer Location: Center-fire and Rim-fire

There are several ways to categorize handgun ammunition. One is the location at which the firing pin strikes the rear end of the bullet; either in the center, which is called *center-fire* or on the edge, which is called *rim-fire*. For handguns, the rim-fire type of cartridge is primarily used for .22-caliber ammunition, from "Short" through "Magnum" sizes, plus the .17-caliber round. There are some other rim-fire calibers lurking in the closet, but they are sufficiently rare so that you most likely can just ignore them. Let us start with the rim-fire cartridges.

Rim-fire

An article by Rick Jamison at *Shootingtimes.com* mentions many other calibers of rim-fire ammunition in addition to the .22-caliber: the 5mm Remington, a .25 Stevens rim-fire, and a .32 rim-fire. He further provides some history and insight into the rim-fire type of round:

> *At one time rim-fire cartridges were available in many bullet diameters up through the .56-56 Spencer, which appeared in the hands of Union forces at the battle of Antietam in September 1862. But the heyday of those rim-fire rounds had pretty much come and gone by the 1930s.*

One reason those rim-fire rounds faded from existence is because the case has a thin folded head that limits the pressures the case will contain. Thicker cases with solid heads are necessary for the pressures generated by modern center-fire rounds. Even so, he stated *"by far more rim-fire cartridges are sold in this country than any other sort of ammunition."*

Center-fire

Practically all other calibers of modern handguns use a center-fire cartridge system. With a center-fire weapon and cartridge, the hammer, or striker, hits the rear end of the cartridge in the center. Close inspection of an unfired round will reveal a small circular insert; that is the primer which, when struck by the hammer or striker, ignites the powder. This is not something you need to worry about. I mention it so that when you read something that uses one of the two terms you will know what is being discussed. For what it is worth, however, over my short history of handgun shooting, I have experienced and heard of a much larger number of misfires with the rim-fire type bullets than with the center-fire.

Projectile (Bullet) Composition:

There are three types of projectile (bullet) construction materials commonly used in handgun ammunition.

First, there are those projectiles **made entirely of lead**. The bullet's projectile is made of solid lead held in a casing, usually made of brass. These bullets are cast, offer specific ballistic characteristics, usually are lowest in cost, and the projectile may be lubricated with grease. "Wadcutters" are an example of this type of construction.

Second, there are **jacketed** projectiles. These bullets usually have a lead core, but also feature an outer jacket (usually **copper**) covering the lead. The copper jacket engages with the rifling in the barrel of the handgun. These bullets cost more, can have greater accuracy, and eliminate barrel "leading," but do foul the barrel to some extent. "Full Metal Jacketed" projectiles (FMJ) with copper over lead are an example of this type of construction.

There are other types of bullets, including non-copper plated bullets (thin metal coating), solid copper bullets, polymer coated bullets, solid exotic materials, partially coated projectiles, and so forth. All of these more exotic coatings and core materials result in more costly ammunition. Some states have statutes outlawing lead bullets. If you reside in one of those states, you are limited to purchasing bullets made of some other metal. That means more dollars per box of ammo. If the bullet material is not primarily lead, then the substitute material must approximate the same weight to provide the same ballistic capabilities. That is probably why the alternate materials are heavy metal, like steel, copper, or some exotic type of stuff. The box of handgun ammo lists the bullet weight in grains. The smaller the projectile's grain weight, the lighter the bullet. The lighter the bullet, the less impact it has on target plus a difference in ballistic characteristics. Point: if you change the weight of ammo that you are using, what was formerly a bull's-eye shot for you may no longer strike the target in the spot at which you are accustomed to aim.

Regardless of the projectile material, most will be housed in a **brass casing**. There are steel, tin, and other metal casings, but brass is the time honored favorite. Brass, being softer than steel, it is less likely to wear on your semi parts.

Let us discuss "grain" a little further. Handgun ammo comes with all kinds of cryptic nomenclature and initials on the box. FMJ, JHP, PPU, PHP, SCT, LF, NTX just to list a few. In addition to that will be a number of "grains." Handgun ammo lists the weight of the projectile in grains on the box. Long guns often list the powder weight in grains, just to make it confusing. Both the powder and the projectile weights are measured in grains. But with handgun ammo, the "grains" listed on the box almost always is the weight of the projectile, not the powder. This is somewhat important since the weight of the projectile impacts the projectile's flight ballistics. The higher the grain weight, the slower the bullet's speed and potentially the shorter travel distance. The 9mm Luger or Parabellum round is offered in the following grain weights: 90, 100, 115, 124, 125, 147, and 158. There may be others, but you see the point. The 158 grain weighs over 66 percent more than the 90 grain bullet. The larger the bullet the more impact on target; you remember physics: mass times speed equals energy, or something like that. This bullet grain weight is achieved by either using heavier materials or more material.

Bullet Projectile Design or Shapes

There are many different designs of bullet projectiles and each has a unique set of characteristics, and an intended use for each as well. Below are listed some of the more common types of bullet designs based on their fundamental shape and properties.

Flat Point (FP)
Flat point bullets have a flat point on the nose end, and a straight taper from the casing to the tip. These bullets punch a small hole in targets. The .45-caliber Long Colt is a close example.

Round Nose (RN)
Round nose bullets have a cylindrical body with a round tip. These bullets offer the best feeding characteristics for semiautomatic pistols and good ballistic characteristics as well. Their reputation is that they may not punch clean holes in targets, and are not optimum for hunting and defense. Looking straight down on the top view of your thumb will give you an idea of the end shape of a "RN" bullet. This round is sometimes referred to as "ball" ammunition.

Round Nose Flat Point (RNFP)
This bullet is a cross between the Flat Point (FP) and the Round Nose (RN) bullet with characteristics similar to the Flat Point (FP)

bullet. Think of your thumb's end being flat and you have a fair idea of this shape. The round nose aids in chambering and the flat point provides the advantages of the FP shape.

Beveled Base and Plain Base Bullets

Another characteristic of a bullet's shape is the base profile. Jacketed and plated bullets typically have a flat base. Lead bullets can employ a flat base (for increased accuracy) or a beveled base (the rear end edge of the projectile is cut at a slight inward angle before the base flattens out) to minimize lead shaving while seating, and to enhance bullet placement.

The Most Common Descriptions of the Ammo that You Will Purchase

When you enter a gun store to purchase ammo, you will need to select ammo based on your handgun's caliber, your intended purpose for the type of round, and the most economical ammo for your budget. Some types of ammo are more expensive to manufacture, but because they are produced in very large quantities may actually be less expensive to purchase. An example is the hollow point. On some occasions I have purchased hollow point for less than the same caliber's full metal jacket. Three possibilities for this: gun shop special, ammo manufacturer special, or the larger quantities of hollow point manufactured results in an economy of scale that permits the lower price. Point: although you may think that one type is the least expensive and you ask for that, do not be locked into only buying full metal jacket because it should be the least expensive. For target practice, always ask for the least expensive ammo for your gun's caliber. It may be a sale day. That said, I avoid less expensive steel casing rounds for my semiautomatics. The following are the most common descriptors of ammo types sold.

Full Metal Jacket (FMJ)

The standard, and usually among the least expensive bullet, is the **full metal jacket** (FMJ). As the bullet's term implies, the projectile appears to be a solid piece of metal, but actually has a solid metal core, usually lead, encased in a metal of different type. Usually the bullet's outside material is copper over lead held in a casing of brass that contains the powder and primer.

The FMJ design has the greatest penetrating power, all else being equal. Thus it has the potential to pass through your target and strike other, "non-intended" objects behind your intended target.

To further emphasize this penetrating power, think of shooting at a home-invasion perp and missing. The bullet can pass through the wall's sheet rock and enter another room(s) striking someone or thing there. Think of the "drive-by-shootings," which you may have read about or heard about, where some miscreant in a car shoots at a "target," misses, and a bullet penetrates the wall of a house and seriously injures or kills an innocent person inside the house. Also, since the bullet can pass through a human body with some degree of ease if no bones are struck, there is less force and trauma impact on the body, thus the person may still have a fairly good ability to do you harm.

Jacketed Hollow Point (JHP)

This bullet is, in all particulars but one, identical to the FMJ. That one difference is that the front end of the projectile has a hole or hollowed out space. The theory is that upon impact the hole will be pushed wider by the force of the projectile's impact on the target. As the projectile's head or point "mushrooms," it imparts more kinetic energy and thus trauma on the target. By expanding and transferring additional force on target impact, the bullet is far less likely to exit a target and hit non-intended objects. Because of these two characteristics, the JHP is often the type of round most favored for personal defense, as well as by law enforcement.

Semi-Jacketed Hollow Point (SJHP)

This bullet is similar to a JHP, but its jacket does not completely cover the lead core. A small section of core at the tip of the bullet, where the hollow hole is located, is left exposed. This older bullet design is still common in the .38 Special, .357 Magnum, and .44 Magnum calibers. I guess that the theory behind this design is that by leaving the lead uncovered at the tip of the bullet the exposed soft lead will be even more susceptible to "mushrooming."

Lead Hollow Point (LHP)

A Lead Hollow Point bullet is similar to a JHP, but is constructed completely of lead and has no jacket. Let us discuss the hollow point design for a moment. When a hollow point bullet strikes a soft target, the pressure created in the hollow pit forces the material (usually lead) around the inside edge of the hollow area to expand outwards, increasing the diameter of the projectile as it passes through. This process is commonly referred to as "mushrooming," because the resulting shape, a widened, rounded nose on top of a cylindrical base, typically resembles a mushroom.

The greater the frontal surface area of the expanded bullet, the more its depth of penetration into the target is limited. This also causes more extensive tissue damage along the wound path. Generally, a hollow point bullet should expand to be one and one-half the diameter of the bullet's original diameter. That is the design, but actual experience reveals some challenges. If the intended target is a miscreant, and that miscreant is wearing several layers of thick or tough fiber clothing, the hollow area has been known to become packed with cloth and not expand as designed. This has led to some design alternatives. Some HP rounds have tips that are of plastic or of some other fragile material designed to break apart or disintegrate upon impact. The hope is that delayed cratering and a larger hollow area will minimize the hole becoming clogged up before target penetration. Another variation is called a **Protected Hollow Point** (PHP). This HP actually has a cap of frangible material covering the hollow. Upon impact it is to disintegrate inward and force the hollow area apart.

Controlled Expansion Bullets may be designed to have special, but opposite penetration characteristics. The jacket and other internal design characteristics help to prevent the bullet from breaking apart (a fragmented bullet will not penetrate as far); or to ensure just the opposite—that the bullet does break apart to inflict more tissue damage.

More recent HP designs have the projectile with flattened sides or an elongate hollow farther down into the projectile. Each has certain design goals that the specific innovation hopes to achieve. All hollow points, regardless of design, caps or lack thereof, frangible tips or not; are designed to expand to about one and one half of their original diameter, inflict more tissue damage and trauma, and minimize pass through.

Lead Wadcutter (WC)

The wadcutter is perhaps the most basic bullet profile with a flat-nose. Typically made from lead, these bullets are basically a cylinder of lead. These bullets produce clean "punches" in paper targets. Because the flat nosed bullet is not well suited for feeding out of a magazine, wadcutters are normally best used only in revolvers or in specially-designed semiautomatic pistols.

Since wadcutters are typically made from lead, deposition of lead into the rifling grooves of barrels and into the forcing cones of revolvers limits the maximum usable velocity of wadcutters to less than about 900 fps. Shots fired at higher velocities may cause severe leading of the rifling and of the forcing cone. This introduces a potentially dangerous condition from overpressure when FMJ (Full Metal Jacket) bullets are subsequently fired without first removing the lead buildup. Either a mechanical lead removing tool and/or chemical removal techniques may be used to remove the lead build-up from shooting wadcutters at too high a velocity. Wadcutters are primarily intended for target practice.

Semi-Wadcutter (SWC)

The semi-wadcutter is a variation on the wadcutter. This bullet has a cylindrical body with a shoulder, and a flat point on the tip. These rounds which offer better ballistic performance (less drag) than wadcutters, still punch nice holes in paper targets and can be fed by automatic pistols in most cases.

Other nomenclatures are often manufacturer specific. Just for edification, here is a quick list:

PHP: protected hollow point
SCT: split core technology
LF: lead free
DPX: deep penetrating
NTX: nontoxic (presumably lead free)
PPU: Prvi Partizan of Serbia

With these unique identifiers, plus many more, you can easily see how you might pick up a box of ammo that would dazzle you with the following initials: LF NTX PHP JHP. Thankfully, most of the time, only FMJ or JHP will be listed on the box.

All Other Ammo variations plus Personal Defense Bullets (PDX)

For the sake of simplicity and brevity, I will lump all other types of ammo into two broad categories: Special Materials and Personal

Defense Designs. Most personal defense bullets are hollow point and
have some variation on the material on the front end of the projectile.
One HP design will stuff the hollow point with a frangible (don't you
just love that word) material that will prevent the hollow area from
closing, in addition, by being pushed back into the projectile, it also
helps to encourage mushrooming. Since it is frangible, it will also break
apart easily, contributing to wound trauma. This frangible material can
be as simple as a plastic plug or made of some type of exotic material.
Some hollow point designs have flattened sides with special inside design
that helps to ensure mushrooming. Since clogging the hollow area
seems to be of some concern, many of the more expensive hollow point
rounds use some type of core cover, insert, or material to help assist
mushrooming while preventing clogging. The other type, PDX ammo,
relies on multiple slugs to deliver the hit. The .410-caliber PDX round
is the perfect example of that. But do not overlook using the plain old
.410 "00" or "000" buckshot shells. Each can have four to five slugs,
depending on the brand and the shell length. They will penetrate thick
clothing yet offer little chance of pass through.

The other "lump" of ammo would encompass those rounds that are
made of special materials. The time honored standard is the lead core
and the copper jacket, but for many reasons, there are variations to this.
Some states ban lead bullets; therefore, there are bullets with other cores.
That substitute core might be steel, copper, or a more exotic material.
Other variations occur with the coating. Rather than a copper jacket,
there are rounds with what the manufacturer calls "gilding," but my guess
is that it is not gold plated. There are a few rounds that have the entire
projectile composed of an exotic material that is designed to disintegrate
rapidly upon striking the target. The theory is that as more pieces of
material expand inside the body, more trauma and force is imparted
from the projectile to the target. The larger the wound and the greater
the force imparted, the more trauma on the target and the more likely
that the target is rendered incapable of doing you harm. Even the casings
vary from brass; some are now steel, some are nickel plated. Semis have
more sensitivity to the ammo materials than do revolvers. For example, a
steel casing can cause excessive wear on the extractor parts, whereas with
a revolver, it is your finger that does the loading and a manual push bar
that does the extracting.

This is not a complete discussion of ammo materials, shapes, designs, and types, but for the average handgun owner, it is a starting point.

Ammunition Size Comparison

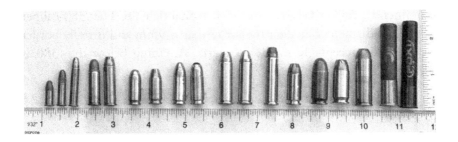

> **Picture 5.1:** Left to Right: **Group 1**: .22-Short lead RN, .22-Long Rifle lead RN, .22-Magnum FMJ; **Group 2**: .32 S&W-Long lead RN, .32 Magnum JHP; **Group 3**: .380 RNFMJ, .380 JHP; **Group 4**: 9mm FMJRN, 9mm JHP; **Group 5**: .38 Special FNFMJ, .38 Special JHP steel case, & .357 Magnum PJH steel case; **Group 6**: .40 cal. FNJHP.; **Group 7**: .45 ACP FMJ, .45 ACP JHP Steel case; .45 Long Colt lead FN; .410 2 1/2 inch PDX 3 slugs w/12 BBs; .410 2 1/2inch 4 slug buckshot.

Shot Shells

Many ammunition calibers also have what are called "shot shells." These are bullets that substitute tiny to almost regular sized BB pellets for the solid projectile. Think of a shotgun type of load encased in the handgun's bullet projectile. There are two quick "give-a-ways" that a bullet is a "shot shell." One is that the end of the bullet casing is crimped rather than having a metal projectile. The other is that the projectile has a plastic cap through which you can often view the tiny shot inside. All of the small, round, pellets (tiny BBs) are inside the shell casing, plus a few inside the plastic cap.

These types of rounds were designed primarily for varmint or snake shooting and for the most part are inappropriate for self-defense. That said, a shot shell of tiny pellets to the face would probably discourage even the most serious miscreant from further mischief.

Calibers of Ammunition

Handguns range in caliber from .22-caliber all the way up to .50-caliber and slightly beyond. That number refers to the diameter size of the bullet in either inches or millimeters. Most experts do not recommend a caliber below 9mm for personal defense. The .380-caliber is the same diameter but slightly shorter than a 9mm and is really border line of being acceptable to these experts. Anything below the .380 is definitely "Forbidden!"

Smaller Caliber Ammunition

So, if you have a .22, a .22 magnum, a .25, or a .32-caliber handgun, you should feel a little under armed for self-defense according to the experts. However, each of these smaller calibers can kill a person. They just demand better aim and selection of more precise, deadly aim points on the target. In addition, by using one of the ammo types that are designed for self-defense, you can help augment the lower firepower of the smaller caliber handgun. A review of the comparative sizes of the .32-magnum and .32-long to the .380-caliber and 9mm shows that the .32 can pack a real wallop, at least in my opinion. That said, you may well hear "urban rumors" of smaller caliber bullets literally ricocheting off of skulls. Point: smaller caliber handguns and ammunition are not the optimum for self-defense.

All that said, here is a quick bit from the USCCA Aug/Sept, 2012, magazine, page 7:

> *The .22 in your hand when you need it is better than the .45 left in your drawer at home. A Cumberland County man proved both when he used his .22 pistol he routinely carried in his pocket to fight off two men who invaded his home and were strangling him in an apparent robbery attempt. Of the three rounds the victim managed to get off, one struck an assailant, who died a short time later of the small-caliber wound to the chest.*

Placement wins!

The benefits of these smaller caliber handguns are: 1) they are smaller; 2) they are more easily concealed; 3) they weigh less; 4) they have less recoil; and 5) they are more easily controlled and kept on target. Unfortunately, except for the .22-caliber, the ammo cost is relatively higher.

The .380-caliber, called by the Germans a "9mm kurtz" (9mm short), has all the benefits of the above smaller calibers, but slightly more power. Although it is considered "borderline" for self-defense, remember:

> ***"It is better to have a handgun of small caliber on you when you need it, than to have a handgun of large caliber at home where you can't get to it in a moment of crisis."***

A visual review of the various caliber sizes in the picture 5.1 can help you to make your own assessment as to whether a smaller caliber handgun would be satisfactory for you. Remember, the "personal defense" type rounds can make up for some of the smaller powder charge and impact velocity of a FMJ round. However, there must be some validity to the concern about smaller caliber handguns for self-defense. After all, both the U.S. Army and many law enforcement departments including the FBI have upgraded their original sized handguns. The Army's first change was to move from the .38 Special to the .45 ACP, although now their standard is a 9mm semiautomatic handgun. (This 9mm decision was not based on firepower but more for political or commonality of ammo types with our NATO allies, my opinion.) Most recently, many law enforcement organizations have migrated from the 9mm to the .40-caliber semiautomatic to obtain greater knock-down power.

Bigger is better when it comes to caliber; however, your personal daily environment is also a major consideration in choosing the caliber of weapon that you can carry concealed. The good news is that even .45 ACP handguns are being made in smaller sizes, approaching sub-compact size. So your daily concealed carry environment constraints may still allow you to select a large caliber handgun. Caliber is almost the deciding characteristic determining the largest sized pistol that you can fire with comfort, enjoyment, and accuracy. Caliber equals power. Once you decide on a caliber of pistol, your firepower has now become a constant in any future gunfight situation in which you might become embroiled. You then must work on your accuracy and speed of presentation and firing. The decision is all yours: carry a smaller caliber for ease of carry and control or larger caliber for more stopping power. Whichever your choice, practice is the next most critical element in determining your ability to protect yourself and your family.

Size Comparison of Smaller Caliber Ammunition

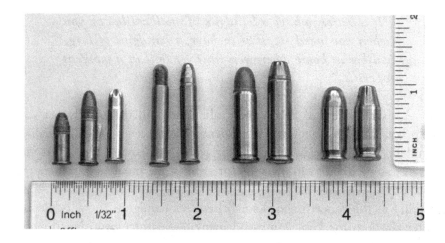

Picture 5.2: Left to Right: **Group 1**: .22 Short RN Lead, .22 Long-Rifle RN Lead, .22 Long-Rifle crimped nose Shot-shell; **Group 2**: .22-Magnum plastic tip shot-shell, .22-Magnum FMJ; **Group 3**: .32 Long RN Lead, .32-magnum JHP; **Group 4**: .380 FMJ RN, .380 JHP.

Larger Caliber Ammunition

The .50-caliber (or larger) handgun is way too strong for all but the very brave. I have read of shooters allegedly receiving hand burns from the hot gases exiting around the cylinder of a .50-caliber revolver. It is probably designed to kill lions, tigers, and bears; it packs a powerful punch. The .454-caliber Casull is designed for large game hunting and I have heard tales of first time shooters of this caliber to have the recoil plant the barrel's front sight on their forehead. Point: the very largest calibers may not be the best selection for the average armed citizen.

This leaves us with the most frequently cited calibers for personal defense: 9mm, .38 Special, .357 Magnum, .40-caliber, .44/.44 magnum, and the tried and true .45-caliber, either ACP or Long Colt. Most of these ammo calibers come in FMJ and some variety of personal-defense round. All are quite capable of dealing a miscreant a serious wound or a mortal blow. As a standard rule; the larger the caliber, the greater the recoil, the greater the projectile's penetrating power, the greater the ability to induce trauma, the greater the possibility of pass-through, and the greater your difficulty in controlling the pistol for follow-up shots.

Many law enforcement agencies migrated from .38 Special revolvers to 9mm semiautomatics. Interestingly, the .38 Special may actually be a more powerful round than the 9mm bullet. However, this change increased the number of bullets available to the policeman prior to his need to reload. A semi with 17+1 rounds gives the policeman three times the firepower without reloading over a .38 Special revolver of five or six rounds. (Reloading is a very dangerous time if engaged in a firefight.) The reason behind this change to a smaller bullet was due to the revolver's limited six-round capacity versus the semi's larger magazine capacity. Now many law enforcement agencies have migrated from the 9mm to the .40-caliber to gain more bullet penetrating and damage producing power. The story is that this change was necessitated to have sufficient fire-power to overcome "hopped up" druggies who were able to take several 9mm hits and keep on coming.

The .40-caliber S&W surfaced around 1990 and was viewed as a "compromise" round between the 9mm and the .45 ACP. The .40 S&W has more stopping power than the 9mm. It could be produced in gun frames similar to the 9mm in size and had less recoil than the .45 ACP.

For the casual shooter, the more powerful calibers may not be very much fun to shoot; thus the 9mm seems to be a good compromise. Even the most timid shooter can fire the 9mm with ease and some degree of enjoyment. Of course, this also depends on the specific gun manufacturer's make, model, and design. Additionally, the standard sized handgun normally has less recoil than the compact or small size, all else being equal. 9mm ammo is currently about the least expensive, outside of the .22 Long-Rifle, which is another factor in its favor.

A couple of rare instances allow you to fire different size or caliber ammunition in the **same revolver**. The typical .22-caliber **revolver** can usually fire three sizes of .22 bullets: short, long, and long-rifle. A

.22-caliber **semiautomatic** is more limited in shooting different sized rounds and **most likely cannot**, but if in doubt, read the owner's manual that came with the pistol. The .22 magnum round **cannot** be fired in a revolver designed for the other size .22-caliber bullets. The .22 magnum is too powerful for the typical handgun designed for the .22 long-rifle round. The .22 magnum round, even if it fits in the chamber, would potentially result in some type of incident. (Read that to mean the handgun blowing up.) The .22-magnum requires its own special .22 Magnum revolver. Repeat, there is no using the .22 magnum ammo in a handgun designed for the other three sizes of .22-caliber bullets. You might, on a rare day, discover a .22 magnum revolver that will fire the other size .22-caliber ammo; just do not try it in the reverse. (Always verify by reading the Owner's manual or calling the manufacturer.)

A .357 **revolver** can usually fire a .38 Special round, but a .38 Special revolver **cannot** fire a .357 magnum round. Why, you ask? Because the manufacturer tells us not to do it, is why. The .357 is real "cannon;" the rounds are larger and more powerful. However since the .38 Special rounds usually cost less than the .357 magnum ammo, you might consider using the cheaper .38 Special round for target practice in your .357 revolver. Again, verify that this ammo switch is recommended for your .357 revolver. However, you should load the .357 magnum with magnum rounds for self-defense.

Because of magazine function and the complexity of the loading and ejecting mechanisms, **most semiautomatics are very limited in allowing different sized ammo to be used in the same handgun.** Revolvers offer more flexibility in accommodating different caliber ammo in the same revolver. Be advised, firing a more powerful round than the handgun was designed to shoot might actually damage the handgun, and you. Be careful and very knowledgeable before you try a substitution. This brings up a special consideration. Some ammo and handguns will carry the notation "+P," or "++P," or "+P+." This notation, on a box of .38 Special for example, indicates that the powder load is greater than normal. Your individual .38 Special may not be designed to fire the "+P" or "+P+" ammo. Your owner's manual should address that as well as the handgun should have that "+P" notation stamped on it if your pistol is designed to fire that "hotter" load. The "+P" round is a minimum of ten percent more powerful than the normal round. That may not sound like a lot, but firing several rounds of a "hotter" load ammo in a non-"+P+" handgun just might damage the handgun. Since you are holding the handgun in your hand, guess what? Yep, your hand just might end up in the emergency room, hopefully, with you still somewhat attached to it. For emphasis, **when discussing using a similar but different sized round in your handgun, we are discussing revolvers only, not semis**, OK?

Two of the more popular sizes of .45-caliber ammo are the .45 ACP and the .45 Long Colt (LC), or "Cowboy Round." Both have very high "knock down" power. A story that I have long heard (you do not put really good stories to the truth test, you might discover them to be untrue), has to do with the U.S. Army switching from the .38 Special revolver to the .45-caliber handgun. The story goes that during the Philippine Insurrection, the Army discovered that the Moro rebels would get all "hopped up" on drugs prior to an attack. The .38 round was not reliable in stopping them in that hallucinogenic state. Therefore, the quick switch to the .45 caliber which can stop a buffalo; well, at least it could stop a "happy Moro." The most famous and still used design is the 1911 handgun, a semiautomatic. The .45-caliber has several different rounds and most are not interchangeable, even in revolvers. The .45-caliber ACP semi cannot fire the .45-Caliber Long Colt. Some revolver manuals will state that you can fire both calibers; some manuals are silent about that capability. Recommendation: when an owner's manual is silent about different sized ammo being OK, do not try to fire the different sized ammo. The result may not qualify you for the official "Annual Darwin Award," but you will personally believe that you should win it. The .454-Casull round should only be used in a handgun designed specifically for it. In all cases, contact the manufacturer with your model number to determine any substitution capabilities.

By this point, you should have learned a couple of key things about handgun ammunition. First, semiautomatics demand the specific caliber size round for which they were designed and do not accept substitute sizes. Second, revolvers have a little more flexibility in accepting different caliber rounds in the same pistol. The .357 magnum revolver being capable of firing .38 Special rounds is an example. Third, even within the correct caliber ammunition, there are "hotter" loads that should carry the "+P" or the "++P" nomenclature. You should not use these unless your owner's manual authorizes that "hotter" load. Fourth, even within the same size caliber nomenclature, not all handguns can use them interchangeably. The .45-caliber ACP versus the .45-caliber Long Colt and the .454-Casull is an example.

"A rose by any other name, may not be a rose and may not be sweet to fire."

OK, so I messed up a romantic poem to get your attention. Read this paragraph carefully. Not all 9mm rounds are 9mm rounds. Well, what I really mean to say is that you may see boxes of ammo that proudly list the rounds as 9mm. The problem is that they will not fire safely in the most popular 9mm handguns. The most popular 9mm handguns fire a 9mm Luger or a 9mm Parabellum round, if sanctioned by SAAMI. That certification should be on every box of ammo you purchase. (SAAMI is an association of the nation's leading manufacturers of sporting firearms, ammunition, and components. Currently SAAMI publishes more than 700 voluntary standards.) The most popular 9mm handguns will also fire the 9mm NATO round, but with this caveat; that NATO round may blow up your pistol. It is that +P+ issue. The 9mm NATO round is a military round and is "hotter" and not all handguns are designed to fire it safely, especially over a long period of time. Unless your owner's manual states that you **can use** NATO or +P+ rounds, do not use NATO ammo. For the most popular 9mm semis, here are the 9mm ammo rules:

Rule 1: **only use** SAAMI sanctioned (on box) 9mm Luger or 9mm Parabellum ammo.

Rule 2: **do not use** 9mm NATO, +P, or +P+ unless you have documentation that your handgun is manufactured to handle that type of "hot" round, and SAAMI is on the box.

Rule 3: **do not use** 9mm ammo with the following names unless sanctioned by SAAMI: 9mm Makarov, 9mm Browning, 9mm IMI, 9mm Steyr, 9mm Largo, 9mm Mauser, 9mm Dillion, 9mm Winchester magnum and not until you have verified that your unique brand and model pistol is manufactured to a design to handle these brands of 9mm ammo.

"Why not," you ask? "Because I am informed that these brands may not be sanctioned by SAAMI to fire without risk in the standard 9mm semi," is my response. "What risk" you ask. I am told that these manufacturers' 9mm ammo might be "too hot," or primers too hard, or have "dirty" powder, or increase misfires, etc. Most important, damage to your firearm from firing non-SAAMI sanctioned ammo will invalidate your handgun warranty. But don't believe me; ask your friendly gun shop expert. If I am ill-informed about one or all of the above, you at least were careful and now better informed. In addition, most gun shops will not take back ammo once you walk out the door with it. It is your responsibility to buy the caliber and spec that your handgun requires. (No, I do not have more detail about each of the above 9mm rounds as to why they might cause concern. I will admit that I might be wrong on some or all of them; after all, things change with time. I've just been told that the above is fact—one for you to check out and verify before you purchase the wrong ammo.) You should be especially careful of good bargains over the internet, newspapers, shows, etc. Ammo manufactured overseas may not meet SAAMI standards and the seller may not be providing all of the info you need to make a safe decision. Look, the point of this long discussion:

1. Be knowledgeable of the specific ammunition authorized by the gun manufacturer for your specific handgun model, as well as those types of ammo **not authorized**. EG, +P or +P+, etc.

2. Only buy ammunition that matches the specs of that ammo recommended by your handgun's manufacturer.

3. Be very careful in purchasing ammunition with differing terminology or nomenclature from that specified by your handgun's manufacturer.

4. Be very, very careful in purchasing ammo offered outside of a reputable gun store or dealer. After all, your health and the well-being of your gun just might hang in the balance of such a decision.

Size Comparison of Larger Caliber Ammunition

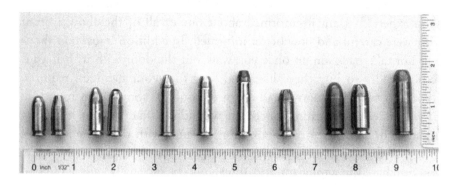

Picture 5.3: Left to Right: **Group 1**: .380FMJ; .380JHP. **Group 2**: 9mmFMJRN; 9mmJHP. **Group 3**: .38-SpecialJHP steel casing; .38-SpecialFNFMJ; .357-MagnumPJHP steel casing; .40-caliberJHP; **Group 4**: .45-caliberACPRNFMJ; .45-caliberACPJHP steel casing. **Group 5**: .45-caliber Long Colt LFN.

And You Thought That Shotguns were "Long Guns"

Just when you were beginning to think that you had a secure grasp on handgun ammunition calibers and idiosyncrasies, we get to discuss shot gun shells. "What do shotgun shells have to do with pistols?" you ask. "Good question," I respond. But do not blame me. I place that blame on the Taurus Arms Company who produced a popular handgun which incorporates the ability to shoot both a handgun bullet and a shotgun shell. The Taurus *Judge* is a five shot revolver that can chamber either the .45 Long Colt or the .410 shotgun shell. They can be mixed and matched in the cylinder so you can shoot a .410 shell followed by a .45 L.C. followed by a 410 shell, etc. Some recent competitors have added the capability to include the .45-caliber ACP round to this arsenal of ammunition types for one handgun.

Winchester has since come out with a special .410 shell especially for self-defense in the *Judge*-style of revolver. The 2 ½-inch long .410 shell has three copper disks followed by twelve BBs; the three inch long shell has four copper disks followed by sixteen BBs. These .410 rounds provide a great deal of shock power per shell, reduce "penetration through target" concerns, and reduce the need to have perfect aim, to some degree.

These "hybrid" types of handguns can fire all .410 shotgun shell loads; however, since the .410 cartridge comes in 2 ½-inch and 3-inch shell lengths, you should purchase the correct length .410 shells for your model of handgun. This is determined by the cylinder length of your handgun. A 3-inch cylinder can accommodate all sizes and loads of .410 shells; the 2 1/2-inch cylinder cannot accommodate the three-inch length shells.

In addition to the length of the .410 shell, there are over 25 options (loads) of the size of pellets or tiny BBs inside the shell. Handgun ammunition nomenclature goes higher as the size of the projectile increases. For example, the .22-caliber projectile is very small, the .38-caliber's is larger, and the .50-caliber's is very large. Shotgun shell nomenclature is just the opposite; the larger the number, the smaller the projectile size but more pellets. For example, the .410 size #7 shell has 224 lead pellets about the size of a pinhead (.095-inch diameter) in a three-quarters ounce load. Comparatively a .410 #2 shell contains 65 lead pellets (.15-inch diameter) in a three-quarters ounce load. The Winchester Arms Company lists 21 different .410 shell pellet sizes in their catalog. The size shot, or pellets, range from #9 through #1, plus "B," "BB," "BBB," and "T" in increasing size of the pellet. (The air-rifle BB is almost the size of the .410 shell #"BB" pellet.) Do you have all this? Good, next we discuss the .410 buckshot sizes.

The buckshot sizes are #4, #3, #1, #0, #00 (double ought), and #000 (triple ought). The #000 is the largest sized pellet at .36-inches in diameter; about the size of the diameter of the eraser on a lead pencil. #000 is also larger in diameter than a .32-caliber round and almost the size of the .38-caliber round. The #000 pellet is not as heavy or lengthy, but it does tear open a wound almost the size of the .38-caliber round, and the number of these pellets ranges from three to five per .410 shell. (The quantity depends on the shell length and the manufacturer.)

Now for a quick test—did you see what they did to us? They threw three curve balls at us. First, the projectile size increases as the nomenclature size declines. Second, since they failed to start at a sufficiently high number, they had to resort to using letters. Third, they reused #4, #3, and #1 size numbers with buckshot. "So what?" you ask. "Good question," I respond.

Pretend that you are planning a family outing to "Lake Snake-A-Bounda" and you think it would be a good idea to take your

Judge-style hybrid handgun along and that you think you read here that the #4 shot is the best for snake killing. You enter your local gun shop and purchase #4 size buckshot and head for snake country. You have just decreased the number of pellets from 101 available in the #4 bird-shot shell to 27 larger pellets in the #4 buckshot shell. "Is a seventy-five percent decrease in the number of pellets important?" you ask. "Maybe not," I respond. It just depends on how calm, cool, and collected you are when you hear that tell-tale sound of rattles in the tall grass just to the right of the trail where you are walking. If you draw and fire and your aim places just one of the #4 buckshot pellets on the snake's head, game over. "How tall was the grass? Did you take time to aim or just flinch and fire? Did you ever see the snake, or did you just fire at the sound in the tall grass?" The advantage of the #4 bird-shot load in this situation is that the larger quantity of pellets disperses and covers a wider area. Your chance of blistering "Mr. Rattles" is increased by 300 percent! On the other hand, if you are visiting "Lake Rabbit-Warren" hoping to kill something for dinner, the #4 bird-shot may not stop your rabbit. He just might be able to run off and either dies uneaten, or lives to run another day. Hit "Mr. Bunnytale" with the #4 buckshot and he's as good as dinner and you are one great shot.

The point of all of this is not to frighten you away from one of the hybrid-type revolvers. It is to educate you that you have to know the specific type of ammo you want and the correct nomenclature by which to request it. For small birds and very small game, .410 bird-shot sizes from 9 through 1 might be best. For slightly larger game, rabbits, squirrels, etc. probably use bird-shot #2 down through "#T." If you are considering the .410 shell for personal defense, consider only the #00 or preferably the #000. You have between three to five .36-inch sized pellets per shell, depending on length of shell. In a five-shot revolver with #000 (triple ought) .410 shells, that is fifteen to twenty-five .36 sized pellets going down range before requiring a reload. Within twenty feet, the dispersal pattern is still relatively tight and the resulting damage on target is traumatic. You see why a 12-gauge shotgun with #000 (triple ought) buckshot shells is so devastating; it contains ten .36-caliber sized pellets per shell. The .410 Buckshot shell seems to be more desirable for personal defense than the special PDX round with three or four discs and twelve to sixteen BBs because of the quicker dispersal of the BBs and thus more likely unwanted collateral damage.

There is a special shell called a "Shabot." It is a single lead projectile (slug) with a jacket designed to come off in flight. This shell type is conceptually similar to a regular handgun round and for our purposes is probably not worthy of further discussion. It is designed for shooting wild boar from a larger gauge shotgun. For personal defense, it makes more sense to use a .45-caliber round or a #000 buckshot shell, my opinion.

Just for your edification, the .410 shotgun is the only shotgun which is measured like a handgun. The size of the bore of the .410 shotgun is .410 inches in diameter. All other shotguns are measured in "gauges." A shotgun's gauge is determined by the weight of a round lead ball that is sized to fit into its barrel divided into one pound. For example, the barrel of a 12-gauge shotgun is equal to the diameter of a lead ball that weighs 1/12th of a pound. A 20-gauge shotgun's bore can fit a 1/20th pound lead ball. Using this method a .410 bore would be equivalent to a hypothetical 68-gauge, but it is not measured that way. The .410 bore is measured like the handgun; the size of the bore is measured in inches, or in millimeters in Europe. "Is this last part important?" you ask. "Nope, I am just showing off my trivial knowledge. (After all, if I cannot share it with you, with whom can I share it?) Besides, you can use it to impress your duck-hunting friends. They are probably totally ignorant of this difference."

Bird's Eye View of 3 Hollow Point Rounds

Picture 5.4: Left to Right: **Group 1**: three .22-caliber rounds; **Group 2**: .380FMJ and JHP; **Group 3**: 9mmFMJ and JHP; **Group 4**: .38 Special FNFMJ and JHP; **Group 5**: .45-caliberLLC; **Group 6**: .410 #4 bird shot, upper .410 "000" Buck shot (4 slugs), lower .410 PDX (3 disks plus 12 BBs), all are 2 1/2inch size.

"You can never have too much ammo, unless you're swimming."

Old 'Shootist' Proverb

Grouping of Hollow Point and/PDX Ammo including 2 plug inserts and 1 semi jacketed rounds

Picture 5.5: Left to right: **Back row**: .410-"000" Buckshot (2-1/2' 4 slugs); .410-PDX—3 discs+12 BBs. **Middle row**: 9mmJHP-black insert; .38-SpecialJHP-red insert; .357-magnumPJHP; .40-cal S&WJHP. **Front row**: .45-cal. ACPJHP; .32-cal.magnumJHP; .380-cal.JHP.

A Somewhat Complete Listing
of Handgun Ammunition Calibers

Many "Shootists" (by now you realize this term is borrowed from a John Wayne movie) load their own ammunition with non-standard powder and bullet grain weight, unique projectile, etc. In addition to these variations, there are special loads available from ammunition suppliers. We are not going to review any of that. "Re-loaders" swear by "doing it themselves,"—loading their own ammunition. All it requires is: spending several hundred dollars for special equipment, purchasing your casings, projectile of choice, and powder of choice in bulk, and finding a location in the house that the spouse does not mind being turned into an ammunition factory. All that accomplished, after several thousands of rounds fired, the "Re-loader" is able to claim, with great gusto and pride, that his ammo is now less expensive than the store bought, pre-assembled "stuff."

We will ignore all of the "Re-loader's" stuff and deal with what most of us casual gun owners and sometimes shooters can actually purchase. The following list will concentrate on the primary calibers popular today and not on all of the almost endless variations available. So if your friend's favorite ammo is missing from the list, tell him to just "gut up and relax."

Rim-fire Handgun Cartridges
.17 HMR
.22 Short
.22 Long
.22 Long Rifle
.22 Magnum
Specialty Loads: (shot shells)
Center Fire Handgun Cartridges
.25 Auto
.32 Short Colt
.32 S&W
.32 S&W Long
.32 H&R Magnum
.32 Auto
.357 Magnum

.357 Magnum Cowboy Loads
.357 SIG
.380 Auto (9mm short)
9mm Luger (9x19mm, 9mm NATO, 9mm Parabellum)
.38 Short Colt
.38 Smith Wesson
.38 Special
.38 Special Cowboy Loads
.40 S&W
10mm Auto
.41 Magnum
.44 Colt Cowboy Loads
.44 S&W Special
.44 Magnum
.44 Magnum Cowboy Loads
.45 ACP
.45 Long Colt (Revolver)
.45 GAP
.45 Casull
.45 Magnum
.50 Smith Wesson

It is fairly accurate to assume that any ammo round termed "Cowboy something or other" will only work in a revolver. One important reason you need to know this is to make you aware that you must ask for the specific cartridge type for your handgun. For example, if you purchase a box of .45 Long Colt (Cowboy) for your .45 ACP semiautomatic handgun, they will not fit, even though both are .45-calibers. Magazines are funny that way; they expect the bullets to all be the same size in diameter and length. Can you guess why the .45 Long Colt is called "Long"? Correct, because it is longer than the standard .45 ACP cartridge and that is why it will not fit in the semi's magazine.

Remember the original design of the semi was for round nosed ball ammunition. Despite modern improvements, semis are still very particular about the correct sized ammo being used in them. Quick quiz question: if a bullet is called "Short Colt," what does that mean? Right, that it is shorter than the standard sized ammo for that caliber.

This wraps up the quick tour of ammunition. Hopefully, now you can read or listen to experts and be capable of following most of their discussion of ammo. But before we go, here is one last thought.

This is my personal opinion and not legal advice nor is it verified by case history. It is pure speculation on my part. So here goes. Suppose that you experienced a shooting scenario and you are now being interrogated or worse yet, on trial. The D.A. needs to place your character in the worst possible light. It helps the D.A.'s case if you can be made to look like a gun crazy, trigger happy "Rambo" looking for an excuse to kill. For example, you loaded your firearm with "hollow-point" ammunition that is designed to spread on impact and do maximum damage to your target. This might negatively impress the jury about you.

An interesting fact for your consideration is that the Little Rock Police Department issues ammunition to their Law Enforcement Officers (LEOs). Guess what they issue? Jacketed Hollow Point .40-caliber rounds are the standard. The officer who shared this with me opined that they went to the .40-caliber JHP to minimize "pass through," and that is why they use hollow points. I suspect there were other considerations too, but that was what he volunteered.

So, it just might be a valid consideration for you to carry the same type of ammo that is the standard load for your local LEOs. If it is good enough for them to carry, it should also be appropriate for you too. Think of a D.A. grilling you as to why you shot the perp with a "hollow point?" The D.A. is trying to imply that you are some type of homicidal gun nut looking to really harm someone. You could retort, with all civility of course, that you just use the same type ammo that the local government issues to their LEOs.

Anyway, *"**You makes your choices and you takes your chances.**"*

Chapter 6

Holsters

It was a lot easier for gun owners back in the days when Cowboys rode the range and Wyatt Earp ruled Tombstone. You could carry a gun hidden or in the open, and the civil authorities did not have a bunch of laws governing gun usage unless you actually shot someone. Plus, if you used a holster, chances were that it was open and hanging from its own belt around your waist and the revolver hung halfway down your thigh. Now we have to hide the weapon, unless we are police or some other type of government law enforcement officer, or live in the few states that still permit "open carry." Therein is the problem we face today—how to conceal our handgun? What type of holster do we use, and where do we wear it?

I am not an expert on holsters, but I have learned a tiny bit. First of all, there are about eight or ten styles based on just where you plan to carry or wear the holster. Besides the cowboy style holster with its own belt, there are holsters worn on the pants belt, inside or outside the pants. There are pocket holsters, shoulder holsters, ankle holsters, and maybe even "thigh" holsters for dance hall girls like in the old west saloons. There are bra holsters that probably appeal mostly to females. There are even holsters that hang down the inside of the crotch of your pants; yes, on the inside. Some enterprising and talented individuals even use shirts or blouses with special pockets for carrying their pistol. A few really talented aficionados even sew the blouse or bra holster themselves to ensure a perfect match to their exact physical dimensions and carry preferences. No, I have not tried all of them, thank you very much. I am just listing them for your edification.

Holsters can be constructed of leather or some type of plastic or a combination. Some completely cover the handgun's barrel and may even enclose the end of the holster. Others look very skimpy and basically just hold onto the center of the weapon. Some have thumb straps so you can snap down a piece of leather across the grip of the pistol so it will not accidentally fall out of the holster. Many are molded to your weapon's exact brand, model, and size; some even accommodate laser attachments.

These molded holsters have very good retention on the weapon, the manufacturers assert.

It is not necessary to purchase an expensive holster made with exotic materials. After all, the purpose is concealment, so who else will see your exotic leather, tooled and decorated piece of gun holding paraphernalia?

SUGGESTION: whichever holster type and model you select, ensure that it covers the trigger guard. Remember "Plaxico Burress!"

"Stupidity Should Be Painful!"

Holster Overview

Cowboy Style
We have all seen a sufficient number of cowboy movies to understand what a "Cowboy holster" looks like. It is self-contained. The holster hangs from its own belt. The belt is wide and made of heavy leather. Around the back of the waistband are little "loops" to hold extra bullets. The holster itself hangs down from the belt and along side the thigh. Some have a single holster; some have two, one on each leg. They are not designed for concealed carry. They are deigned for a fast draw and a quick shot. If this is your choice of holster, please ensure that you have very good medical coverage.

A word to the wise:

"Don't do things you don't want to explain to the Paramedics!"

Waist Band Holsters
The closest concealed carry holster to the old cowboy western style is the "**Outside the Waistband**" (**OWB**) holster that is worn on your pant's belt and all of the holster and weapon are exterior to your clothes. Since we are talking "Concealed Carry," that means you must wear some type of coat, sweater, ill-fitting shirt, blouse, or something else to cover it up. If you do not have it covered by clothing, you had better be in a state that permits "Open Carry," or you will soon need your lawyer.

Of all the holster types, the OWB holster is probably the most comfortable to wear after you become accustomed to two or three pounds tugging at your belt and trying to pull your pants down. By the way, you will probably need to purchase a very, very strong, thick belt to carry the holster. Otherwise, the belt will probably torque on you, causing the holster to twist outward, and push the pistol out further from your body making it more likely to "print" or be seen. It will also bang into three hundred and two different things each day since it is sticking out and "aiming" for whatever you walk by. (Just another reason to ensure that your handgun has the internal hammer lock that will prevent a sharp blow on the hammer from striking the firing pin and discharging the bullet.)

Waistband holsters come "straight up" or "canted" or with slots that allow for you to select either based on which holster belt loops you thread through. "Straight up" implies the grip is in a ninety-degree angle to your belt. "Canted" implies that the grip is tilted from the vertical, usually forward and at a 15 degree angle termed the "FBI cant." (I guess because the FBI first used or popularized a 15-degree tilt forward from the vertical.) I surmise that the "cant" is to make a quick draw faster or easier, or both.

The **OWB** holster may necessitate a change in your clothing style. If you do not normally wear a coat or long sweater, you will either have to start wearing such clothing, or you will have to wear an extra-long shirt or blouse that hangs outside of your pants to cover your weapon. If your current upper wear is just right or a little tight, the outline of your weapon may press against the shirt. Remember that you are licensed for concealed carry. If every person you pass can see the outline of your pistol, then several things may happen. First, they will probably guess that you have a gun. Depending on their attitude, they may grin, ignore, scream in fright, or silently dial 911 and report that some nut is in the store with a pistol, and they are afraid you might start shooting or hold up the place. Before you know it, you are face-down on the floor with policemen pointing huge, menacing semis in your direction. So, adjust your wardrobe or dress style or both, to cover the OWB holster and pistol.

Per a *Las Vegas Times* article, the following is a real example of what can happen when a concealed weapon is seen.

> *On July 10, 2010, as Erik Scott left the Summerlin, Nevada Costco store he was killed by Las Vegas police. Mr. Scott was carrying a firearm inside the store, but had a legal permit*

allowing him to carry a gun concealed. Costco has a policy that firearms are not allowed inside their stores. Unfortunately, Costco did not have this policy posted on their entrance doors, or anywhere else that a customer might observe prior to entering. **(Arkansas has this same provision: a store or location can forbid guns, but must post the notice.)** *Police were summoned to the store after store employees called police claiming he* [Scott] *had a gun and was acting erratically.* [Per accounts, the employee(s) had observed the handgun in his holster; Scott had not drawn it or purposely exposed it.] *Other witnesses say Scott was placing water bottles in a backpack to see if they fit. Employees eventually evacuated the store. Scott was confronted by police as he left the building. Police say he pointed the weapon at officers when confronted, but several witness reports deny that. Several witnesses interviewed by the Review-Journal have said they did not see a gun and did not see Scott reach for a gun when police confronted him outside the store.*

The point of this tragic story is that you should ensure that your dress will maintain coverage of your weapon under almost every conceivable situation; otherwise the unintended consequences of flashing—allowing your weapon to be observed—can be embarrassing at best, tragic at worst. (You might also avoid Costco and other stores that discriminate against concealed carry.)

The other type of waistband holster is termed the "**Inside the Waistband**" (**IWB**) holster. As the name implies, this holster is located inside your pants waist and rests against your body or underwear, if you are so civilized as to wear such. The holster attaches to your belt with a metal or plastic device that loops over the pants waist and hooks under your very strong belt. Some of the **IWB** holsters have what is called a "Tuckable" feature. The holster is attached with a device that permits you to tuck your shirt or blouse down inside your pants between the holster and your pant's waistband for several inches. This is a great feature for "conceal-ability," but if you are a fast draw fanatic, it might slow down your draw a bit.

If you opt for the "Tuckable" featured IWB holster, you have set your destiny to a two handed draw. One hand (the off-hand) to pull your tucked shirt up and the strong side hand to actually draw. Otherwise, you will grab a bunch of shirt fabric with your hand when you reach for the pistol. (Oh come on now; you have tucked your shirt down several inches over your holster. Unless you pull your shirt up to clear your grip, it will still be covering your pistol and thus you will grab silk, so to speak. Understand?) If you do not opt for a "Tuckable" IWB holster, then you have determined that your daily wardrobe will be some type that allows for a shirt to hang loose over the pistol or you plan to wear some other garment to drape the weapon so as to conceal it. This is the same issue faced in covering an OWB holster, but with a smaller exposed pistol/holster area to conceal.

Should you opt for this type of IWB concealed carry holster, be aware that if there is no leather or some other protection on the holster's backside between the pistol grip, protruding safety, slide release, and your body, you might meet "Mr. Chafe" as the grip rides up and down and back and forth against your skin. Some holsters have this protection, some do not; but the tough gun enthusiast will tell you that carrying a concealed weapon:

"Isn't supposed to be comfortable; it's supposed to make you feel comfortable."

You know, "feel comfortable" as in feel safer since you have some means to protect yourself against a malicious miscreant intent on mischief. However, "Mr. Chafe" can still be uncomfortable until your hide develops calluses.

I have discovered as the years pass by that the waists in all of my pants have shrunk; every single one. It has been true whether the material is cotton, wool, or synthetic. Currently it takes some "gut sucking" and belt-pant waist tugging to get the top button buttoned. Why do you care about my personal pants problem, you ask? Well, if you try to stuff a holster and pistol inside your waistband and all of your pants' waists are already fairly snug, you will need to invest in a new wardrobe with pants' waist sizes from 1 to 2 inches larger than your current pants. This might be a major consideration on your type of concealed carry holster. Of course, if you do invest in a new wardrobe of pants that are actually 1 to 2 inches too large for normal wear just to allow for your IWB holster, then, when you go without your holster, your pants may fall down. (I bet that you are glad that you read about that here first, before you bought twelve new pairs of pants.)

Bra Holster

I want you to understand upfront that this is one holster with which I have zero experience or knowledge. It is designed for women who are pregnant or have other physical or personal reasons to eschew a waistband or other type holster. Some women may just not be able or willing to carry a one to two pound "boom thingee" around the waist.

The Bra holster is designed for small caliber, small size, and lighter weight pistols. The holster attaches to the bra by a strap over the front center, lowest section of the bra. It either snaps or uses Velcro or secures in a magical way and somehow holds the pistol. I have no idea how the lady so carrying actually reaches inside her blouse or dress and draws. Consider for a moment though; it is an ingenious system. A perp pushes a pistol into the woman's face and demands all her money. She blushes, acts coy, and explains that she carries her money in her bra. Blushing as she reaches for it she tells the perp, "Don't you dare look! Your Momma won't forgive you if you do." As the confused perp momentarily averts his eyes, she draws out a two-shot derringer and hits him with two .410 PDX rounds.

The one rule to remember is:

"It is better to have your gun and not need it,
than to need it and not have it."

So, if the only way you are able to carry is in a bra holster, I say, "Go for it!" But you might need some expert assistance on how the whole thing works. (Please send pictures on how this whole getup sets-up and flows.)

Ankle Holster

This is a good compromise for concealed carry. It does not require you to purchase a new wardrobe, dress more formally with a coat or jacket 24/7, or to adopt a sloppier dress code with shirttails always outside your pants. The holster wraps around the leg above the ankle and is secured by stretching a Velcro strap until it is sufficiently tight to hold the holster in place. Some even come with a garter-type belt to strap above your calf and attach to the holster with a second strap to hold the holster upright and secure. This may take a little getting used to if you have not worn a sock garter in a while.

If the holster is tight, then it should not press down too much on the ankle. If you feel excessive pain on the top of the ankle area, it is probably an indication that the holster strap is not sufficiently tight and that you need to raise the holster higher up your leg. As I said above, just like all of the other types of holsters, these may require a little getting used to.

The one drawback for an ankle holster is when you need quick access to your pistol. You are faced with one of two techniques. Either you squat down and raise your pants leg and draw your pistol out of the holster; or you lift up your leg (standing precariously on one foot rather like a Stork in water), raise the pants leg, and draw your pistol. Either technique leaves you just a little exposed or off balance for a moment. However, it is a good option if you have a job that requires you to sit most of the time as it may be easier to reach than fussing to draw from a pocket or waist holster, and it also would be much more comfortable.

A wardrobe consideration with the ankle holster is that you do need pants with a wide leg around the bottom cuff, not a slim-line, toreador pants cut. Also, the smaller, lighter pistol is probably better for this carry style. There is some debate as to whether the holster should be on the strong-side leg (the side of your shooting hand) or the off-side leg. I prefer the inside of the off-side leg, but then again I am not an experienced "shootist."

Shoulder Holster

You have seen many of these in the 1930s and 1940s movies with Humphrey Bogart playing "Phillip Marlow" or some other detective. In those movies, all the PIs, as well as the crooks, have shoulder holsters; the cops all have OWB holsters. Shoulder holsters wrap around behind both shoulders and the holster rests under one armpit. It can be vertical or have a cant of up to 90 degrees. Some actually offer a holster under both arms or extra magazine holders under the off-side arm. Either helps to offset the weight of the pistol.

The shoulder holster is a great carry technique as the pistol is readily available whether you are sitting, standing, driving, walking, running, or whatever. You wear the holster under your weak-side arm so that you can "cross-draw" with your strong-side or shooting hand. Of course, after watching all those movies, you know that this is the first area that the bad guy frisks looking for a weapon. Just do not let him get that close.

The major wardrobe issue with a shoulder holster is that you need to wear a coat or sweater all the time. If your job or daily activity does not demand this type of formal dress, you might look funny waiting tables in your Sunday suit. People, being curious like they are, will "wart" or tease you until you "fess up" and tell them what is going on. But if you do that, now half of them are freaked out, half will want you to stop bringing it to work, half will think you are a flaming paranoid lunatic, and the other half will want to see it. (I may have too many halves here.)

I think the shoulder holster is a really cool get up. However, I never wear a suit coat or sweater indoors anymore except to attend Church and you cannot carry a firearm into a house of worship in Arkansas unless the governing body of that church has authorized concealed carry on its premises. (Refer to Chapter 15, paragraph 16.) As a result, I personally had dismissed this type of holster till one Thursday when I was having lunch at local cafeteria with a bunch of old high school buddies. One old classmate, Gus, was explaining that his body repair shop, being on the "rougher" side of town, often had "strangers" wandering in looking for handouts. On one such occasion, the stranger asked for some money, and Gus told him that his only "money" was a debit card. The stranger seemed perturbed over this and picking up a tool from the bench, started toward Gus. Then Gus pulled back his open work shirt and revealed his shoulder holster. No, I do not mean he did that at his garage (although he did), I mean he did it right there at the cafeteria for the entire world to see. I guess that he was fortunate that none of the waitresses saw his Czech 9mm semi. In any case, there were no screams or shouts, just looks of surprise from those of us at the table. Three of the four of us at the table were, coincidentally, CHCL holders and quite amused at this "flashing." There was Gus, dressed in blue jeans, a polo shirt underneath an unbuttoned work shirt, and wearing a shoulder holster. Now I am thinking that is a pretty good "get-up" to allow a more comfy carry than most others. As soon as I convince my Significant Other to let me go around with my shirt unbuttoned, I am seriously thinking of going with this holster.

Pocket Holster

Most pocket holsters are little more than pouches into which the pistol slips. The pocket holster may have a "lip" or "hook-like" protrusion on one side to catch the seam edge of the inside of the pocket. This will prevent the holster from coming out of the pocket still holding onto the gun when you draw. Other pocket holsters are constructed of materials which "stick" to the inside of the pocket so that the holster is held in the pocket as the pistol is drawn.

These holsters generally cover the entire pistol, except for the grip. For a smaller, lighter pistol this is an excellent choice for concealed carry. The holster itself, covering most of the pistol, disguises any "printing." What outline or printing shows could be any object, but it does not resemble a handgun. It allows quick "presentation" and does not require any awkward body movements, unless you are sitting down. In my opinion, it is critical that the trigger guard is covered; remember "The Plaxico Burress."

There is one major disadvantage to a pocket holster. If you are sitting down, drawing it may require some real squirming and dangerous tugging of the pistol out of the pocket, especially if the pistol is in the front pants pocket. If most of your day is spent in a chair, think again about using this type of holster, or decide if you can take it out and put it your coat pocket or drawer. An alternative might be to wear cargo pants with those large pockets on the side of the thigh. This might offset some of the issues of trying to draw while sitting down.

Crotch Holster

Think of the last movie you watched with a Scotsman dressed up in his kilt. He had this little bag hanging down in front of his crotch area. I do not know what Scotsmen actually carry in those bags, but just suppose that it was a small pistol and that the bag was on the inside of his kilt, not the outside. Now, dress him in regular pants with the bag still there inside his pants, that bag is the crotch holster.

The one review that I have seen on this was from *USCCA* and the person reviewing a crotch holster was very impressed with the comfort which this style of holster provided. Just how one quickly draws and presents from this holster must require a little practice. Either you pull your pants waistband out and reach down inside your pants or you unzip your "fly." (Wearing with a button "fly" is probably not recommended.)

Either movement would probably cause consternation for your perp and perhaps gain you a few precious seconds. After all, not a lot of folks have seen a pistol drawn out of the crotch area. (Any stories of actual experiences would be appreciated.) By the way, the Scotsman's bag, worn in front of his kilt, is called a "sporran." I bet you are glad to know this and are anxious to use this new knowledge at your next competitive shoot or family gathering. (See the value you are receiving from this book?)

Thigh Holster

I have not seen this type of holster except in movies. You know, like when the dancehall girl lifts up her skirt to reveal a pearl handled derringer inside the colorful garter stretched around her shapely thigh. However, I am fairly confident that you could find one should you search long enough. They are probably along the same design as the ankle holster. Perhaps they employ a Velcro belt around the thigh with a holster, or an elastic strap with a holster. It is probably a good idea to have a strap from this "garter belt" type holster going up inside the dress to a belt around the waist to keep the whole thing from slipping down your leg. Obviously, I am not experienced in just how this might work, but in all the western movies it seemed just fine, and the dance hall lady seemed satisfied.

I would think it would take some getting used to. It must be really, really interesting to watch someone draw by either dropping the dress or pants down or lifting the dress or pants way up. (If you find and purchase one of these holsters, please send video—for instructional purposes only, of course).

Special Clothing Adapted for Concealed Carry

There are a couple of options available in ready-made clothing for concealed carry. The first is a shirt with a special compartment for concealed carry. The pistol's pocket is inside the shirt and normally around chest pocket height. It is obviously designed more for a lighter weight handgun as a three-pounder will pull the shirt down toward your knees. I have seen these shirts offered in retail establishments that cater to law enforcement personnel. I have been tempted to purchase one just for the novelty of trying it out. Turns out that they are not cheap. As I was standing at the rack selecting my size and color preference, it dawned on me that just one shirt would not be sufficient. My Significant Other would frown upon my wearing the same shirt all week, much less all of the time. Therefore, to use this type of carry would require an investment in several shirts of different colors and styles. It was daunting so I chickened out; still, I plan to return one day and invest in one. I will update you on my experience in the next version of this book.

A second option is the old fashioned seamstress approach. I have read articles of clever and industrious women actually sewing a concealed carry compartment to their bra or inside their dress. These were not "ready-wear" options that one could purchase. They were homemade, one of a kind. Exactly how satisfactory they are and how well they work is not known to me. Since the wearer is also the designer and seamstress, making modifications and experimentation would seem to be readily at hand and easy to accomplish. I am not aware of any special clothing for men other than the shirts. If you have been creative, send pictures and I will include you in the next edition.

Purse, Briefcase, and Fanny Pack Carry

In addition to the standard concept of using a holster for concealed carry, there are several other methods that you can employ to tote your pistol. There are **purses** available that are specifically designed for concealed carry and have excellent draw and presentation ability. The purses look like a real purse and they are. However they are designed with a special compartment designed to carry a weapon relatively safely. The major drawback for this type of carry in my mind, as I have never used one, is that a purse can be forgotten and left in some embarrassing location, like the grocery store checkout counter or the bank's teller window. Also some "grab and snatch artist" can run by and rip the thing right off your shoulder. A good genuine carry purse should have a reinforced shoulder carry strap. In either event, you have not only lost your purse and its contents, but your pistol.

There are **briefcases** designed to accommodate a pistol as well as papers, etc. Of course, you could just put the pistol inside a regular briefcase as well as into a regular purse, but "Remember the Plaxico Burress." You want to carry in a type of apparatus that is designed to conceal, protect, and house your weapon in some degree of safety **for you.**

The same can be said for a **Fanny Pack**. You can toss a pistol into any old fanny pack, but that is not an approach that would make me very comfortable. If a fanny pack is your choice, investigate purchasing one that is designed to carry a weapon along with your other stuff. This type of carry would be great for a jogger, hiker, biker, etc. But again I would not be comfortable just plopping the pistol into a regular fanny pack and then adding whatever else you want to throw into the mix.

Triggers are strange little creatures. They will fire whether it is your finger pulling them or by a "caught" lipstick holder, pencil, car key, etc. being forced against the little rascal. Use a fanny pack, or for that matter a purse or briefcase, that is designed for pistol carry to minimize this type of mishap by having its own secret little place for your pistol. Of course you can always use a separate holster inside the bag.

One last thought on concealed carry in a fanny pack, purse, briefcase, or carry-on bag. Most folks arrested by airport security for a concealed weapon violation had their concealed weapon in one of the above four types of carriers. Almost no one using an "on-body" holster forgets that he is carrying since he must dress and put on the holster before he heads for the airport. If you do opt to carry "off-body," please do not be so absentminded or forgetful that you show up at the airport with your weapon in a carry-on type of bag. It can be very expensive and it will absolutely ruin your plans for the day.

Just to reinforce how easy it is to be forgetful about an "off-body" type of carry, review the following article from the *Arkansas Democrat Gazette* dated January 18, 2012.

> *Jacksonville student stole gun from teacher, police say!* screams the paragraph heading. *A Jacksonville High School English teacher was arrested and suspended with pay after police say one of her students stole a handgun from her purse.*
> *. . . said officers had previously responded to the school . . . for a fight when they were told by students in . . . classroom had witnessed another student take a handgun from . . . purse and hide it in his waistband.*
> [The teacher] *told police she has a concealed carry permit but 'forgot to take the gun out of her purse' before coming to school, an arrest warrant said.*

[The teacher] *was arrested about 10 a.m. and charged with possession of a handgun on school property.*

. . . a spokesman for the Pulaski County Special School District said [the teacher] *was suspended with pay pending an investigation.*

If the teacher had been forced to put her pistol in a bra holster or waistband carry every day, she would not have forgotten, at least in my humble opinion. Actually, I would bet you a dollar to a doughnut that she had pulled this same "forgetful stunt" on several prior occasions. Unfortunately, she will most likely lose her CHCL and pay a hefty fine; even her employment may be at risk. So choose your carry method with some care. The wrong choice has consequences.

Remember: ***"Don't do things you don't want to explain to the police!"***

(Summer 2012: by way of update, the local D.A. has filed **felony** charges against the teacher.)

Summary

Many holsters have a **top opening that is reinforced** so that the holster does not collapse when the pistol is drawn. This facilitates re-holstering the pistol with a single hand. Without this reinforcement, some holsters may require that you actually take them off in order to safely reinsert the pistol after firing or presentation.

Once you try several holster types and decide which carry style you wish to invoke, please **buy a good quality holster.** Yes, I know that you may change your mind and go to another style of carry and that will necessitate purchasing another holster. However, a cheap one may not do what you need it to do. One mistake and you might have a very expensive accident, mishap, or explanation to make to the Judge.

Also, I strongly recommend that you consider having a holster with a **"Thumb Release" strap that crosses over the pistol's grip and snaps to the opposite side of the holster.** This thumb release strap helps secure the pistol, and prevents some idiot or perp from coming up to you and jerking your pistol out of the holster. It also helps to prevent the pistol from accidentally falling out. Nothing is perfect, but it helps. Yes, I know that it is one additional impediment to a fast draw and presentation. As my LEO reviewer said, *"Just keep in mind that this added retention device must be 'defeated' in order to deploy the gun. That equals more time, when time is that of which you have the least."*

However, for every day that you will need that extra fraction of a second to draw to save your life, you will have a thousand days when you will need to ensure that your handgun is safely secured in its holster. For my peace of mind, I want the extra safety of the strap to hold the pistol in the holster. There is a chance of a "bad happening" with either approach, but the safety strap improves the odds for you to avoid some misfortune day after day after day.

"You makes your choices, and you takes your chances."

I am not certain that there is a single best carry method or style since your daily work-dress and environment dictate what you can actually adopt as a conceal carry holster. I personally would favor the **OWB** holster, all other things being equal, as it handles all size pistols and allows for quick draw and presentation. Plus, it should not require the purchasing of a vast new wardrobe; just a new very strong belt. Additionally, it is also probably the least intrusive on your body. Unfortunately, it just might be the most difficult for the average person to keep concealed. After Gus's story, I would probably consider the shoulder holster if I could dress casually—shirt unbuttoned and un-tucked—or if I had a reason to always wear some outer wrap: coat, sweater, vest, etc.

Like I said earlier, each style has its pluses and minuses. There is not a best carry method. You have to review your daily dress code, work location, and make the best compromise for you. You may even use two or three different holster styles based on a specific day's destination and wardrobe requirements. Just be advised that purchasing a holster without some forethought can result in your collecting a number of holsters that really do not meet your needs. (When you fill a drawer of unwanted holsters, give me a call as I am always on the look-out for a bargain on a good holster.)

Conversation Concerning Concealed Carry Considerations

You have reviewed handguns, holsters, and ammunition, so, what can you conclude from those three chapters concerning the best concealed carry solutions? The following were distilled from the best minds in the industry. Well, actually they are mostly made up by me, but I compiled them with all the best intentions. Let us draw some serious general guidelines for your concealed carry decision process.

The Recommended Rules for Concealed Carry Selection:

1. **Select a handgun that you will carry all the time.** Do not select a handgun because another person insists it is the perfect one for you. Select a handgun that you like so well that you will carry it all the time, not just when you can wear a certain outfit or when you decide that you have the energy to tote the thing around.

2. **Select a caliber handgun that you can fire comfortably and that you will become proficient firing.** A large caliber is not what will save you in a gunfire exchange. Shot placement—accuracy—is what will save you. That, and a mind-set that you are willing to take a life to save a life. (*The Choice of Two Evils.*)

> *"A small caliber pistol on you is better than a large caliber pistol left at home."*

3. Practice until you do not miss. Reread Rule #2.

4. **Fit your concealed carry holster to your lifestyle, not your lifestyle to a concealed carry holster type.** *Change is Hell.* If you attempt to change your dress, lifestyle, etc. to fit a holster selection, chances are that you will become frustrated, encounter restrictions or obstacles, and just give up.

5. **There is no perfect answer in handgun or holster selections.** There are two annual seasons: cold and hot. Sure, there is a transition time into and out of each season, but think two seasons. Now think two concealed carry styles. OWB or shoulder holster in the winter when you wear sweaters, jackets, extra shirts, and so forth. Think ankle holster or IWB or another style in the summer when you wear fewer clothes for concealment. Think a larger handgun caliber in winter and a smaller caliber in summer. Think a large sized handgun in winter and a smaller sized handgun, same caliber, in summer. Even the .45-caliber ACP is available in compact if not smaller

size. A larger caliber does not require you to carry a large pistol.

6. **Consider the possibility that you might have two carry pistols and two holsters, to fit your lifestyle.** You can purchase two very good quality pistols and two holsters for less than $1,500.00. Sure, that is a lot of money. But if you give up one pack of cigarettes or one "latte" a week, you have paid for your protection insurance in six years. Should you have ever needed that protection during those six years, the price was worth every penny. After all, what is your life or the lives of your loved ones worth? Forgo eating out one meal per month if you require further economic justification for your "protection insurance," and that will cut your "payback" period to three years or less.

7. **Do not give the Bad Guy the Edge.** A .22-caliber pistol on you is superior to a .45-caliber revolver sitting in a safe at your house. That said; try not to compromise by taking a butter knife to a street-knife fight. Sure, shot placement is the key in a gun fight, but why give an advantage to the bad guy? Try to keep your handgun selection to the larger calibers: .40-caliber, .45-caliber ACP, a 9mm, a .38-Special, or a .357-Magnum. Unless you are going to hunt Cape Buffalos, lions, tigers, or bears, leave the very powerful calibers for the brave. Unless you just cannot handle the 9mm or larger caliber pistol, forgo selecting any caliber handgun smaller than a .380-caliber for personal protection.

8. **There is a perfect handgun selection.** It is the handgun that you love to shoot and that you will practice shooting until you never miss. (Just fall in love with a larger sized caliber pistol.) Have I mentioned that you need to practice frequently?

9. There is a perfect concealed carry holster. Care to guess which one it is? That's right. **It is the concealed carry holster that you like so well that you will wear it every day, everywhere you go;** except to forbidden zones: school grounds, government buildings, airports, posted places, houses of worship, etc. (Refer to Chapter 15, paragraph 16 on concealed carry in houses of worship.)

10. The world is not perfect; it is round. If cost is a big load resting upon your back, think practice shooting cheaply to build your skill. A fifty round box of .22-caliber ammo can be purchased for $2.00 to $3.00. A fifty round box of 9mm will cost $10.00 to $12.00. The cost of a fifty round box of any other caliber will start around $16.00. You can learn to be very accurate with a .22-caliber pistol. Just consider that in a perfect world you should practice shooting with the handgun you will carry. After all, when the time comes that a malevolent miscreant attacks you, it might be optimum if you were a really good shot with the pistol in your pocket, or where ever it is, not the one at home.

11. Cops are smart about gunfights, but **do you need the same capacity?** The story is that LEOs went from a .38-Special revolver to a 9mm semi to increase their downrange firepower from six to eighteen rounds without requiring a reload. That eighteen round capacity requires the larger sized (standard) handgun. Street smarts reports that average citizen gunfights have less than six rounds fired in total, i.e., by both sides. So, if you do not have a significant probability of engaging a street gang, some drug dusters, a meth lab, or other heavily armed group, you may not need to carry an eighteen round capacity pistol. If carrying ten rounds leaves you feeling "naked," you have two choices: carry the standard sized pistol or carry additional magazines for the ten round pistol. With practice you can reload a semi in under three seconds. Since you would have already sent around ten rounds downrange toward the miscreant, a couple of seconds to reload might not be too critical.

OK, I know that a few of the above rules might appear to be just slightly contradictory. I submit to you that it was not an oversight of pure stupidity; it was done for emphasis. Point of this review: there is probably never going to be a perfect answer to your concealed carry situation. You will need to make some compromises and trade-offs. Just make them intelligently and do not trade-off the most important thing—being armed.

Chapter 7

Gun Safes

Gun safes are a little bit like trees; they come in all sizes, from small to the very large. You can purchase a gun safe as small as a briefcase or as big as a large wardrobe or small sized closet. They come with or without fireproof ratings from minutes to hours. They offer different locks from the old spin-dial combination lock to electronic keypad to biometric fingerprint recognition. They have interiors custom designed for long guns and storage shelves. They can cost from less than a $100.00 to several thousand. Whatever your needs, there is one to fit your budget for safeguarding your handgun.

Two Basic Security Goals

There are two basic security goals for you to consider. One is protection from unauthorized use or opportunity theft of your handgun. Think of small children or sticky fingered house guests and the occasional visitor who roams looking for loose, left out items of interest. Almost any gun safe will protect your handgun from this type of opportunistic theft or unauthorized use; provided, of course, that you have locked your weapon inside the safe. However, a small gun safe that protects from unauthorized use can be picked up and carried off. To help overcome this, you can purchase these smaller safes with the capability of being bolted to a wall, shelf, or even the floor. It takes a real effort to rip one out of its bolts if they are secured to a permanent structure.

The other security option will not only prevent your weapons and valuables from being misused or stolen by the opportunistic thief, it will also afford some protection from fire and from your firearms being stolen by the professional thief who has broken into your home when you are away and has many uninterrupted hours to search, locate, and attempt to open and carry off large items. The best option to defeat this type of theft is a large gun safe that is too heavy for one person to easily move or to break into. These are expensive and require some amount of effort and friends or professionals to move them into your house. They weigh from two hundred fifty pounds to more than a thousand pounds.

Misuse and Opportunistic Theft Protection

Children are very inquisitive, undisciplined, and curiously prone to do that which you have told them not to do. A small gun safe will provide very good protection from children and teenagers. Visitors come in all sizes, sexes, and character traits. Some may wander around your house admiring the things you have. Some few are prone to pick up "targets of opportunity" and make your possession, theirs. (Of course, I know that none of your friends or your kid's friends would do this.) There might be cash sitting out, jewelry, or a handgun. They are not really bad people; they are just dishonest when presented with an opportunity they are unable to resist. A small gun safe should adequately protect your weapon from this type of opportunistic thief, unless you can envision them toting a foot-sized cube-shaped safe out the door stuffed inside their coat or underneath their dress.

Obviously, a small sized gun safe is subject to easily being taken unless you have one that you can bolt to a wall, shelf, or floor. Most that are larger than a briefcase come with holes in their back and bottom for just such a purpose. That would prevent all but the most determined thief from ripping it out of the wall; but your casual, opportunistic thief would most likely be discouraged from trying to rip the thing out while you or some family member are around. Some come with steel cables so you can wrap them around some type of post or pole to discourage the opportunistic thief.

Think protection from all but thieves who visit when you are away. When you are not at home, the thieves will be leaving with all sorts of large objects and probably have time to locate a few tools to rip safes from the wall or floor. Securing in a secret hiding place might help in this case, but the best bet is a "Big Bertha" type safe.

Large Weapon Collections and Thief Deterrence

To ensure that your weapon(s) and other valuable objects are safe from the casual as well as the determined thief, you will need to invest in one of the gun safes that are about five feet tall and from two to five feet wide. They weigh from several hundred to over a thousand pounds. Some provide thirty minutes to more than an hour of fire protection for the safe's contents. Most can be bolted to the floor.

Between their size, weight, and being bolted to the floor, only a team of thieves with lots of time and equipment can remove the safe from your premise. It is almost impossible to break into one of the better ones onsite, and if your burglar alarm is ringing its annoying outburst of claxon calls, the thieves will be very anxious and not want to spend hours or days trying to open the safe in your house. Moreover, they would need an industrial strength dolly and several strong backs to pry it out of the bolts and move it onto a truck.

This is great option as it can house your guns, ammunition, coin collection, silver flatware, Aunt Harriet's tiara, and the medals awarded to your ancestors for valor or 100% attendance at Sunday School. It is not a cheap option, but perhaps you can justify the financial outlay compared to the cost of renting a bank's lock box over a decade or three. Of course, the primary benefit is peace of mind and protection for you, yours, and some valuables.

There are several safe manufacturers and each probably has a web site for your edification. To list just a few: Liberty, Cannon, Browning, Winchester, and Sentry. There are probably many others and all probably are adequate to some degree or another. I endorse none.

Features to consider

Some features may be more important to you than others. For instance, a lifetime guarantee of some type or other may turn you on. Local locksmith service for a specific brand might also be comforting. Other beneficial features include: steel doors that are thicker than a single piece of sheet steel; the more door bolts the better (top, bottom, and sides); hinges that are internal and not exposed; slip clutch handle; easy external access to change battery on electronic models or an external key bypass; no external seams that are vulnerable to pry-bars; fireproof rating; etc.

Go look at a bunch and then make your choice. I have purchased some of the steel nine-inch by nine-inch by twelve-inch gun safes on sale for less than $75.00. The better "wardrobe" sized ones are going to start north of $500.00 unless you catch a good sale, plus you will need several friendly gorillas to help tote the thing home in a borrowed truck. The other option is to pay several hundred bucks to a mover to pick up and deliver. Be certain that their delivery includes installing it where you want it to be placed. I have heard of some safes just being dropped off at the end of the driveway. Moving three hundred pounds or more into your second story bedroom might be a real chore for just you and the better half.

Now that you are "safe" aware and security conscious, we should discuss home protection in a "safe" environment. Should you ever have the horrible experience of being awakened in the middle of the night by the sound of a window being broken or a door kicked in, the last thing you want is to attempt to retrieve your handgun from a safe whose combination seems to have been erased by the terror filling your mind and your fingers seem to have all turned to thumbs.

Here are some thoughts. They are random and not sequential as to preference. Unfortunately, the list will not be all-inclusive, and I can almost guarantee that none will be satisfactory for your situation. I am not endorsing any approach, but practicality rules.

1. Buy a small biometric gun safe. At night, place your handgun inside it and place the safe by your bedside. It will open from your fingerprints; no lock to manipulate and also safe from little fingers. Some models will allow for multiple prints to open the lock so that your spouse can also use it.

2. If you are really confident in your ability to react calmly in an adrenaline filled body when someone is roaming, uninvited, around your house in the middle of the night, consider #1 with a combination lock. This type is much less expensive.

3. I am aware of one former LEO who placed a loaded pistol under his side of the mattress at night. In that location the pistol was not easily available for little fingers to access, yet quickly retrievable by him when needed in an emergency. Do remember to retrieve it and secure it in a safer location when you get out of bed.

4. There are commercially available holsters with Velcro for attachment to the backside of the bed headboard. Again, a little awkward for small fingers to access without waking you,

but readily available in an emergency. Again, relocate come morning.

5.   Depending on the height of your tallest child, some might place the loaded handgun on top of the tallest piece of furniture in the bedroom. A five foot tall chest of drawers is too high for little tykes to reach, but readily available to you in an emergency. Again, relocate come morning.

6.   There are books as well as clocks that are sold for the specific purpose of secreting a pistol. A book might work unless you cannot read the titles in the dark and are unable to pull out the correct volume. Also, if your child is a voracious reader, well, he just might stumble upon it. Whether clock or book, it should be placed above the highest reach of your tallest child.

7.   If there are no others in your house other than your spouse, then just leave it out on the bedside table and move it to a safer location come morning.

I told you that you would not like any of the suggestions.

Chapter 8

Maintenance

This chapter is dedicated to Sam.

"Wait! What's going on? We're umpteen chapters into this and now you dedicate a chapter to someone! What's up?" Good question, so I'll explain.

I was at a party and happened to review the content of this *Companion* with Sam, an old high school buddy. He asked, "Do you have a chapter on *Maintenance?*"

I responded, "No, I wasn't planning on one."

He said, "You really need a chapter on maintenance." Sam spent a jillion years in the military, thus his obsession with maintenance.

I explained to Sam that I was adamant in my conviction. I was not having a chapter on maintenance and that was unanimous! I told him that it was not necessary; everyone knew about maintenance; clean it and oil it is all that you need to know! Rather huffily, he continued to insist that I needed one. I told him this was my *Companion* and my decision was final, no chapter on maintenance! Well, as it turned out, here is a brief, simple, easy to understand chapter on maintenance, thanks to Sam. (You see, Sam is married to Gwen who was a high school friend of My Better Half—MBH. Sam whined to Gwen, who spoke to MBH, who told me to include a chapter on maintenance. No, you don't need to know all of this, and it might be slightly exaggerated anyway.) So, my revenge is, if you have any comments to make about this chapter, please address them directly to Sam; do not send them through normal channels. OK?

Some have the belief that if you maintain things, they will work better, look nicer, and last longer. This novel concept is not just held in the gun world, but can be found scattered across users and owners of all manner of mechanical contraptions, tools, implements, and artifacts. So, just in case you fall into this belief category, let us discuss the very basics of handgun maintenance.

There are two types of maintenance: the cleaning and oiling of your weapon after firing and the repair of your weapon when it no longer functions as it should. Strangely enough, failure to perform the first can sometimes lead to the second.

Just as you need to come inside and bathe your body with soothing unguents and emollients after working outside digging in the garden or mowing or raking the lawn; you should also clean and then oil your pistol after live firing. However, **unlike** just jumping into the shower and lathering up with your favorite soap and then toweling off, cleaning your pistol is a little bit more complicated.

First, you may ask, "Why do we even need to clean and oil a pistol? The next time we fire the pistol, won't the bullet just blow all of the previous 'gunk' out the end of the barrel?" Well, not so fast, my meticulously untidy one. Pistols can rust (oxidize) and corrode. If left untouched, the powder residue may corrode the interior and exterior over time. The metal parts, especially the steel components, may rust or oxidize. Left uncared for, nature will, over time, exact its unfriendly toll on your firearm. You know—the one you agonized so long about purchasing because it cost so much money. Properly cared for your handgun will last a lifetime. At least it should unless you have little else to do than to fire tens of thousands of rounds through the thing. In fact, it should last to become a family heirloom to be passed onto your children and grandchildren or, if you lack a gun safe, then to the next thief who robs your home.

Handguns come in a variety of materials today, unlike the cowboy era when all revolvers were made of steel with wooden handles and were given little care other than an occasional rubbing with bear grease, whale oil, or something. The cowboy's revolver just wore out or rusted out and was discarded and another one was purchased or stolen. Today, you can purchase steel pistols with "bluing" (a special rust treatment) to protect the metal. You can opt for stainless steel that resists corrosion and rusting. There are pistols made from aluminum, titanium, and composites. The grip or butt can be covered in wood, rubber, composite, metal, mother-of-pearl, or some other material. The point being, not all gun parts need, nor ought to be cleaned with the same type chemicals and materials.

So what do you do? Well, a great idea is to read the manufacturer's *Owner's Manual* that comes with every new handgun purchase. In that reference manual will be recommendations on the specific care and maintenance of your uniquely manufactured firearm. What? Oh, yours is a family heirloom and the *Owner's Manual* is long gone? There are several things that you can do. The first is to call or email the manufacturer and ask them to send you one. They may charge for that, but it is a cost that is well worth it. Another option is to go the manufacturer's website and determine if they offer "Owner's Manuals" via a direct download. There may or may not be a cost associated.

A third option is a website named *www.stevespages.com*. It was a little cumbersome for me to reach the place where one can download owner's manuals, but if you need one, it is worth the hunt. He lists hundreds, maybe over a thousand owner's manuals. The listing is alphabetical by manufacturer. Then the guns are listed alphabetically by individual gun name, model name or nomenclature. For example, when I finally found the *Owner's Manual* link, I located the section "S", found Sig Sauer, located the Sig P238, and in less than 2 minutes *Steve's* had displayed in "pdf" format the 50 page Owner's Manual. On practically every screen he solicits donations; his service is worth it. Should you be required to use his good work, leave a donation of $5.00 to $10.00 or so. (Yes, I know I'm cheap.) For additional information about "stevespages," refer to *Appendix F, Sources and Resources.*

Once you have determined the cleaning system recommended by your pistol's manufacturer, it is time to go to the gun store.

There are two types of chemicals for maintenance: a solvent to clean away the residues and an oil to lubricate and protect. Purchase one each of the brands recommended for your gun. (I happen to use *Hoppe's No. 9*, but only because that is what my older brothers used when I was in grammar school. It seems to work and is still readily available.) Your friendly neighborhood gun store can also recommend to you some good cleaning solvent and oil.

Next, you will need a tool to push a cleaning rag into and through the barrel to first apply solvent and when clean, to then apply the oil. There are two basic types of cleaning tools. One is called a "snake." It is a rope with a brass brush as well as a cleaning brush wound into it. You feed the rope (snake) into one end of the barrel and pull through, first with solvent and later with oil. These "snakes" look slick and easy to use, but my friend Gaylon told me that the old ramrod tool cleaning method is superior. I have never tried the "snake," but it sure looks easy.

The ramrod tool is a longish rod with a handle on one end and a place on the other end to screw in the appropriate caliber-sized brass brush, cloth brush, or eyelet for patches, depending on which cleaning step you are on. You purchase cleaning patches at the gun store. They come in various sizes dependent on the caliber of weapon to be cleaned, but think checkerboard square size and you will have a pretty close idea.

Some semis will instruct you to push/pull the cleaning tool one certain direction only. (This is rather awkward as requires you to unscrew and remove the rod's working end to withdraw the rod, but it is what the manufacturer says to do.) With a revolver, you can only push into the barrel's end, as the cylinder opening will not accommodate the metal bar. A "snake" could be fed from the revolver's firing chamber end. I have never seen instructions that require pushing in just one direction with a revolver, but it is probably a good idea. Let's think about this "one-way" thing. The barrel bore is steel, most likely. The cleaning brush is probably made of brass. Remember from your history class the terms "Bronze Age" and "Iron Age"? Well, the "Iron (really steel since the charcoal smelting added carbon to the iron making it steel) Age" defeated the "Bronze Age" because an iron sword would swoosh right through a bronze one. Well, if it worked that way back then, why worry that much about what a brass brush will do pushed through a steel bore? So, I just ignore that warning and push-pull both directions, but gently when using the brass brush. But as they say,

"You makes your choices and you take your chances."

First, soak the cleaning patch with the solvent and push the rod or pull the "snake" completely through the barrel. Do not push the rod back and forth. When cleaning the barrel, think "one way street"—the rod only goes one way. Or, if you use my approach, just be gentle when you pull it back and don't use a forceful "scrubbing" action both ways. Repeat with clean patches and solvent until the patch shows no residue or dirt. Then run a dry patch through and double check your progress. Next soak a patch with the oil and run it through the barrel. Do this a couple of times. Inspect the oily patch to ensure it is clean. Repeat this process until the patch shows no sign of dirt or residue. That is the end of this phase unless the barrel is so heavily coated with oil that it is dripping or running oil out the barrel.

You clean the firing chamber, firing pin surface, and other areas first with solvent and then wipe dry, and only then lubricate these parts with oil. (Yes, Miss Finicky, you use your fingers to hold the patches, no tool for this.) But now comes the tricky part. The interior of the barrel is steel; thus, the above described cleaning process is how you clean the steel components. The firing chamber and firing pin are also probably steel and wiping first with solvent and then with oil is OK, but how you clean the rest of the pistol is dependent on the material. I would not clean a mother-of-pearl or wooden grip with solvent or oil. If the exterior is engraved and inlaid with gold or silver, I would not apply either chemical. (Yes, handguns do come decorated that way. Should you own one of them, you are probably sufficiently wealthy to hire a knowledgeable "shootist" to clean the weapon for you.)

You will want to lubricate the moving parts. On a revolver, these are few and fairly self-evident. Put a drop of oil on the part and let it go home. On a semi, there are different and secret places to be lubricated. Since the slide goes back and forth, it needs lubrication and the owner's manual should explain specifically where to drop a bit of oil. The trigger mechanism may also need lubrication. A little oil in unnecessary places is preferred over no oil in required places. Plus, the little oil containers are fairly inexpensive.

I know this all sounds so, well, so unentertaining. It lacks the excitement of live firing and playing hero in your own mind. But just consider that the bullet being pushed down that barrel at 1,000 feet per second may be cutting into the barrel's grooving. Since the bullet is either lead or copper, the steel barrel's sharp groves will shave off tiny particles and the inside of the barrel is very hot. Over time the barrel may become "leaded" and that is a bad thing. It may impact accuracy and safety. Left un-cleaned and uncared for, it might cause you to have to take the next maintenance step—going to a gunsmith.

Gunsmiths are artists. My friend Gaylon, in a former life, engaged in competitive Trap and Skeet shooting. He bragged that in one tournament he broke 198 out of 200. He alleges one of the two misses he actually hit, but the clay did not break. Based on my own shooting expertise, I did not expend much sympathy for him over only two misses. Once, he told me he had investigated purchasing an expensive foreign shotgun. It cost more than I pay for a car. (I know, you're thinking that it must have been a really expensive shotgun, or I buy cheap cars.) He said some competitors spend thousands of dollars on a single shotgun and then take it to a gunsmith before they even shoot the thing. The gunsmith does magical things to the weapon, and when it is returned, it shoots better. I queried Gaylon, "What does the gunsmith do to it? If the modifications are so good, why don't the gun manufacturers just make them that way to begin with?" Gaylon looked at me like I was the slow child in class and said he did not think I had the proper technical knowledge to comprehend the details of the work, or some such lame explanation. In any case, gunsmiths are like doctors. When your weapon is sick, take it to a local gunsmith or call the manufacturer. "When is a gun sick?" you ask. Luckily, it is fairly easy to determine. For example, if your pistol is misfeeding regularly, it is sick. If it only misfeeds occasionally, it is probably an ammo problem, or with a semi, perhaps a magazine issue. If it fails to load or revolve, it is sick. Occasional problems do occur, especially with semis. It is when they have a habit of bad performance that a gunsmith is needed. (In the case of a semi misfeeding, remember to check the magazine as the first source of trouble. This might save you a "doctor's fee.") Unlike your suffering through the flu without medical assistance, an unattended to faulty weapon could result in your injury, or in extreme cases, death. If a semi is not functioning properly 99% of the time, try changing ammo brand and/or a new magazine. If these two actions do not resolve the problem, think "gun medical assistance required."

Some manufacturers offer a lifetime warranty on their weapons. I am not positive that all do. Some provide, via E-mail, postage paid shipping labels within their warranty service. You have already been thrilled to learn of my sending a weapon back to the manufacturer for repair. In that case, it was a Sig Sauer, and the Customer Service Rep emailed me a pre-paid mailing label, plus Sig paid the cost of returning the weapon. Now, I do not know where you live, but here in central Arkansas, only UPS ships weapons. You must drive out to their depot at the airport and drop it off with a lady who then locks it up tighter than a drum until some special dude comes and sends it off in some type of special container to its proper destination. That costs in excess of $50.00 one-way. So the Sig adventure saved me over a $100.00 because they have one of these good type warranties.

There is a gun shop in the central Arkansas area that actually offers to sell you an insurance policy under which they will ship the weapon back to the manufacturer at no cost to you, should you ever have the need. Well, you do have the cost of their insurance policy, but they pay the UPS bill. You know, it is similar to the insurance offering for repair service that is offered to you when you buy a new TV or other electronic item. Anyway, this store does not offer it for some manufacturers because, like Sig, the manufacturer covers that expense. I will not mention the name of the gun shop because, for all I know, they all offer that type of insurance policy.

If you call the manufacturer and you own one of those "you pay the shipping, not them" pistols, then you just might decide to take your pistol to a local gunsmith since the postage is going to set you back between $50.00 and a $100.00 anyway. You find a good local gunsmith two ways. He is the only one in the area is the first way. Hopefully he is good since he has survived and folks apparently still use him.

The second technique to locate a good gunsmith is the same that you use to locate a good doctor; you ask your friends for recommendations. A third technique is actually just blind luck; you look in the phone book, newspaper, or on the Internet for one in your area. Once you have found one, you take the weapon to the gunsmith and explain as best you can the malfunction or problem. He will take the weapon from you and examine it cursorily with the experienced eye of a brain surgeon. You will then ask for an estimated cost to fix "Mr. Boom" and make him all better again. The gunsmith will sigh, shake his head, and tell you it is difficult to estimate the repair cost until he has taken it all apart and finds the true problem. He will share with you that in addition to his time, there will be the cost of the necessary repair parts. You both agree that neither of you knows how much it will cost. He will then chuckle and opine that it will probably be less costly than buying a new gun. (I know what you're thinking. You think that I have danced this dance before. I told Shirley that only the more astute would purchase this *Companion*, much less read it.)

Remember, I warned you that this chapter might not "tickle your gizzard." In any case, when treated with respect and care, your handgun should last a very, very, long time. When it shows signs of malfunctioning beyond an occasional hiccup, call the gunsmith or manufacturer. Firing a faulty pistol may prove hazardous to your health. Remember:

"Do not do things that you do not want to explain to the paramedics."

Chapter 9

Requirements for a Concealed Handgun Carry License

Below is a synopsis of the disqualifiers and requirements for an Arkansas Concealed Handgun Carry License (CHCL). Despite the length, if you are a law-abiding citizen with no criminal record, no substance abuse issues, or other stuff like that, it is relatively easy to meet the requirements and to get legally authorized to carry a concealed weapon. Read the quick review list below, and if you see something that raises a red flag for you, go to the Arkansas State Police website (*Appendix F*) and read it in its entirety.

Let us review two important concepts concerning a CHCL. First, per state statute *5-73-301: Concealed means to cover from observation so as to prevent public view.* You are responsible for keeping your weapon from being seen in public by anyone. (Visit *Chapter 24 Aggravated Assault.*)

Second, a CHCL **only** grants you the legal authority to **carry** a concealed weapon. **It does not authorize** you to be an unofficial policeman, a bounty hunter, a societal bodyguard, a vigilante, or a reincarnated "Rambo." It does not authorize you to show, display, draw, point it, shoot into the air or ground, or threaten others. **All a Concealed Handgun Carry License lawfully allows you to do is carry a concealed weapon**, and keep it concealed. OK?

A Synopsis of CHCL Requirements: (§5-73-309. License Requirements.)

*The Director of the Department of Arkansas State Police **shall issue** a license to carry a concealed handgun if the applicant:*

(1).   Is a citizen of the United States;

(2).   Is a resident of the state continuously for ninety (90) days;

(3).   Is twenty-one (21) years of age or older;

(4).   *Does not suffer from a mental or physical infirmity that prevents the safe handling of a handgun and has not threatened or attempted suicide;*

(5).   *Has not been convicted of a felony;*

(6).   *Is not subject to any federal, state, or local law that makes it unlawful to receive, possess, or transport any firearm;*

(7).   *A background check successfully completed through the Department of Arkansas State Police and the Federal Bureau of Investigation's National Instant Check System;*

(8).   *Does not chronically or habitually abuse a controlled substance or has been voluntarily or involuntarily committed to a treatment facility for the abuse of a controlled substance;*

(9).   *Does not chronically or habitually use an alcoholic beverage to the extent that his or her normal faculties are impaired nor has been voluntarily or involuntarily committed as an alcoholic to a treatment facility;*

(10). *Desires a legal means to carry a concealed handgun to defend himself or herself;*

(11). *Has not been adjudicated mentally incompetent;*

(12). *Has not been voluntarily or involuntarily committed to a mental institution or mental health treatment facility;*

(13). *Is not a fugitive from justice or does not have an active warrant for his or her arrest;*

(14). *Has satisfactorily completed a training course as prescribed and approved by the director; and*

(15). *Signs a statement of allegiance to the United States Constitution and the Arkansas Constitution.*

If you meet the requirements and decide to pursue obtaining your CHCL then the first step is to locate a State Licensed Instructor. If you do not know one, then key *www.asp.state.ar.us* on your web search line. The resulting screen will be the Arkansas State Police web site.

1.   On Main ASP screen, under "Online Services" select the "Licensing" Tab.

2.   On the "Licensing" options, CLICK on second option "CHCL Safety Instructors."

3. The next screen will display "Fill in the Blank" boxes for names, etc. Since the reason you are doing this is because you have no names, leave all that blank. On the "County" box CLICK on the "Drop-Down Menu Arrow."
4. Select your county and CLICK on "Search."
5. The next screen will list all the licensed instructors in your county.

There is no state mandated fee for the instructors. Each sets his or her own price. $100.00-$125.00 is a close estimate at this time. Some may include range fees if applicable. The instructor, or some helper, must fingerprint you and fill out some paper work after you have attended the class and demonstrated that you can fire a handgun with: both hands, left hand only, right hand only, and not injure yourself or anyone else. You will want to qualify with a semiautomatic. Reason being, in Arkansas if you qualify with a revolver, your license will not authorize you to carry a semiautomatic handgun. If you qualify with a semi, you can carry any type of legal handgun.

Once you have successfully completed the course and received the signed paper work and fingerprint paper from the instructor, you mail it, along with a check, to the Arkansas State Police. They have two fees: one for the license and one for the background check. Think around $150.00 for both as an estimate.

If you have something in your background that disqualifies you, per the statute's requirements, from obtaining a license, the ASP will probably find it out and now you are out this money and maybe facing some charges relating to false documents, etc. Therefore, play this honest and save us all some trouble. If you have just been released from the pokey serving a short sentence as a drug-crazed, suicidal maniac, who has a long list of felony convictions, six outstanding warrants from Timbuktu, you never obtained your citizenship papers and you are under 21 years old, please do not apply. It takes the ASP up to three months to do a normal request and you will just delay others from obtaining their license.

And besides, if you do submit a false application:

Any person who knowingly submits a false answer to any question on an application for a license issued pursuant to this

121

subchapter, or who knowingly submits a false document when applying for a license issued pursuant to this subchapter upon conviction is guilty of a Class B misdemeanor.

If you are with Law Enforcement or the military, then go to the ASP website and read the complete section on CHCL as there are some accommodations for you all.

To view all the Arkansas statutes on firearms and CHCL regulations: Put *www.asp.state.ar.us* on your web search line and press ENTER.

The screen will be the Arkansas State Police Website. Across the "tabs" at top, CLICK *Services and Programs*. On the next screen titled: *Services and Programs*, scroll down to section titled: *Regulatory Services*. About 9th is the line: *Concealed Handgun Licensing*; CLICK

On the next screen titled *Concealed Handgun Licensing*, scroll down to the second section titled: *CHCL Laws and Administrative Rules*. There are two options, CLICK on the title: *Concealed Handgun Carry (CHCL) Law*. You will be shown about a fourteen-page document with all kinds of legal stuff.

For further edification, after reading all of that go back to the prior screen and CLICK on the second option titled *CHCL Administrative Rules*. After reading both, you will be a flaming expert in something or other.

Chapter 10

The Gun Fight's "Rule of Threes"

My longtime friend, Ray, shared this with me. Ray said that law enforcement often dissects gunfights by their compliance with the "Rule of Threes."

The premise: gunfights, or encounters when gunfire is exchanged, typically occur within the Rule of Threes:

1. The shooting is over within **three** seconds;
2. The total number of shots fired is **three**;
3. The exchange distance is within **three** yards (9 feet).

Many experts who teach advanced gun courses quote similar types of statistics. For example, the 1993 NYCPD Firearms Discharge Assault Report by Deputy Inspector John C. Cerar reported:

In 1993, 48% of all gunfights of a known distance occurred [within] *7yards-21 feet-or less.* [The FBI also reports on such statistics. Their annual *Law Enforcement Officers Killed and Assaulted,* provides the following figures]: *that pertain to 1,246 LEO's feloniously killed by firearms nationwide between 1978-1994: inside 5ft-54%,* ***inside 10ft-73%,*** *inside 20ft-88%, and inside 50ft-95%.*

There is sufficient similarity in all of these statistics to give some credence to the *Rule of Threes* on distance, so let us run with all three as gospel.

Rule of Three Seconds

Whether the time duration is two seconds, three seconds, or five seconds, the key point is that the typical gunfire exchange is over very, very quickly. Too quickly for you to open your briefcase, carry-on bag, backpack, or purse and then draw and engage. If you are thinking of concealed carry as a new lifestyle, these statistics should have a major influence on your selection of carrying method. OWB, IWB, Shoulder, and maybe pocket holsters would seem to be about the universe of a three second window. Ankle, bra, crotch, upper thigh holsters, or some other concealed carry holster would seem to require more than the three seconds just to locate, grasp, and start to draw; no time to switch off the safety, aim, fire.

Rule of Three Rounds

These same experts, who teach gun-skill classes to ordinary citizens, as well as to law enforcement and to the military, also address the "three rounds." Their common mantra is, *"It's not the first one to shoot, it's the first one to hit, that wins!"* Shot placement is their constant harping, verbal blast. Of course our cowboy heroes were both the first to shoot and the first to hit. They always won. The bad guy, even if he drew first, he never shot first and he always missed anyway. The lesson for me, and for you, be very fast, but be accurate.

"You can't miss fast enough to catch up in a gun fight."

Shot placement is the product of several factors. The most important is practice. Practice dry fire and live fire over and over again until you are perfect, or until you do not miss that silver dollar sized bulls-eye at ten feet (the three yards).

The second major factor is your comfort with the caliber of handgun that you are using. You may have read about or know of someone who carries a .357-magnum because he was told, based on gelatin tests, the .357-magnum is the best "one shot stopper." Wanting to have the best protection, he buys one of the best calibers for a "one shot stopper." But when he fires the .357-magnum, the recoil is so severe, he flinches, jerks, closes his eyes, and adopts other poor shooting techniques to compensate for the excessive recoil he fears will result when the trigger finally releases the hammer. We all do that, boys, men, women, even new military recruits. It takes practice to eliminate a natural instinct and to finally realize you will not suffer from the recoil. That said, if you shoot the .357-magnum and your hits on target at 20 feet appear similar to a world map, you may be in real trouble in a gunfight. A .380-caliber JHP into the torso is superior to a .357-magnum round hitting in Rhode Island. In fact, a single .380 JHP into the torso is superior to all six .357-magnum rounds hitting in Rhode Island.

"Where are we going with this?" you ask. You must select a caliber size that you will be comfortable firing so you will practice with it until you are very, very accurate. It is true, most gelatin tests confirm the .357-magnum, .45-caliber ACP, and the .40-caliber rounds are among the best "stoppers." But they are only "stoppers" when they are hits on center of mass; read that as the thoracic cavity of the miscreant. If those calibers are so fear-inspiring to you that you cannot hit the bulls-eye, try a step down. The 9mm with a JHP on the target is better than a .45-ACP hitting the moon. Heck, a .22-magnum HP on target is better than a .45-ACP hitting the moon.

You must choose a caliber with which you will become very, very accurate. Then you have the chance to win those rare situations when a gunfight erupts upon you. Three shots: you want yours to be number one and number two and number three; all in the center of the thoracic cavity. You do not want to be dreading to pull the trigger and hesitating, or moving your front sight toward the North Pole, when the first boom sounds.

You will encounter very experienced "Shootists" who will inspire you to only pack a standard sized semi with 17+1 plus two extra, fully-loaded magazines. That is not bad advice. Once a generation, you might even need that kind of firepower; police often do. But under the "Rule of Threes," a small pistol of six rounds would meet most gunfight scenarios. It is easier on your body, physical comfort, and wardrobe to carry a smaller handgun. This is a major decision and not one to make lightly.

The Rule of Three Yards-nine feet

Three yards is only nine feet and your extended arm is about two to three feet. You can see the color of their eyes and hear their labored breathing at nine feet. It is up close and personal; very, very personal. A reasonably healthy person can cover a distance of twenty feet in less than three seconds. At ten feet, if the perp is coming toward you, you have about one second till he has you.

You have no time, and may have no chance, for a second shot. The first shot needs to be on mass. You have no time to reach into your purse or pack and rummage around for your pistol, hopefully in a holster; pull it out of the holster; turn; flip off the safety; aim, and . . . how many seconds have expired? Unfortunately, under the "Rule of Threes," you will never know how many seconds passed.

Speaking of Rules, let us make our own Rule of Fives:

1.   Select a handgun caliber which you can shoot comfortably.
2.   Practice with that handgun until you are very, very good at twenty feet.
3.   Select a concealed carry technique which will permit you to be a survivor under the Rule of Threes.
4.   Practice drawing and presenting until you are under two seconds with the front sight on target.
5.   Practice drawing, presenting, and firing at a target until you are a "bulls-eye" shot at twenty feet in less than three seconds.
6.   Have fun; go to some gun shoots; take an advanced class; train a significant other.

Yes, I can count and that is six, but what the heck, they are our rules. Besides I wanted to check and see if you were really paying attention.

Chapter 11

Protecting Your Assets and Limiting Your Liabilities

Engage a Good Criminal Defense Attorney—Now

We all know a lawyer: either from probating Dad's will, or creating our own will, or trust, or living will, or divorce, or cousin Jane's sister-in-law's 3rd cousin is one, or there is one in our neighborhood. In any case, we all know one. He or she may be very qualified to do wills, divorces, trusts, and family law; but he or she may not be an **expert in and experienced with criminal law**.

When and if you ever have a non-social incident involving you and your firearm, you want the best, the absolute best criminal defense attorney in your town, county, or state. Also, you want to actually talk to him **before you ever need his professional services**. You either call, or meet face to face, and explain that you desire to have him or her represent you should you ever have a handgun episode. If he agrees, whether he asks for a retainer or not, get his cell phone number, his home phone number, his office number, and the number of his Mama. You will want to contact him immediately after such an episode, and most likely it will not be during normal working hours. He should give you some upfront advice, like tell the police nothing or some variation of that. He may even opine that you will be your own worst enemy if you provide a statement at the "shooting" scene without him present.

A Scenario

Let us assume that a fifteen-year-old "plebe" of the "Black Beard Pirates" gang is trying to earn his entrance fee and credentials. He selects your house, and late one evening you hear a "bump in the night" and get up to investigate. You meet face to face. He thrusts the largest semiautomatic that you have ever seen into your face. He actually hits your nose with the barrel tip as he shouts, "Give me your cash and jewels or I'll kill you!" As you reach for your wallet in your bathrobe pocket using your weak side hand, his eyes follow that hand. With your strong side hand you pull out your "home defender" and fire two .410 PDX rounds into his torso.

The police arrive and you are giving the cop a statement. "He pointed his pistol in my face and said that he would kill me if I didn't give him my money and jewelry. But he was in my house! I have the right under Arkansas law to use lethal force if he's in my house threatening me! I was starting to just give up my stuff, but then I saw my chance and I shot him!" Guess what may happen next?

Unfortunately, many newspapers, TV and radio stations have a bias against guns, gun owners, and citizens taking the law into their own hands, even when justified and legal. The local reporter, may have grown up in New York, graduated from Vassar, and may be striving to make a name for herself in this "one-horse-hick-town" so that a real newspaper in a cultural metropolis will hire her. She picks up this story of a grown man deciding to shoot a fifteen-year-old child. Just to make this your "perfect storm," the D.A. is up for re-election in a tough campaign. The TV and papers are filled with your night-time episode, but they report it as "*man shoots child*" with all your talkative details. The local minority rights advocates march and get interviewed. "What's the D.A. doing about this?" they shout. The ACLU, Brady Gun Control Advocacy Group, and "Gun Control America" all get involved and make you the "Poster Child" for abolishing gun ownership.

From reading various newspaper accounts of arrests, I have formed an opinion of how the typical D.A. operates—they pile on every conceivable charge possible. For example, a miscreant was arrested recently and charged with: "kidnapping, rape, aggravated robbery, theft of property, aggravated residential burglary, second degree battery, possession of marijuana, and criminal attempt to commit capital murder." The D.A. must hope that surely a jury of twelve will find one of these charges to like. The D.A. takes your case to the Grand Jury. The Grand Jury only hears what the D.A. presents; the D.A. does not present your side, you know. The D.A. convinces them that it is up to a trial jury to really determine if you are guilty. All the G.J. needs to decide is if there is sufficient evidence for a "true bill." After all, you told the cop on-scene: "I saw my chance and shot him." Guess who learns how much a Bail Bondsman charges for a $50,000.00 bond? But then we all have

$5,000.00 sitting around for just such an occasion. By the way, to my knowledge, it is non-refundable.

You hire the only lawyer you know, the guy who prepared your will. In comes the typical family law attorney and pleads the long list of charges down to just one felony charge, and then explains to you how fortunate you are to have hired him. All those other charges—gone. You do not even have to plead "guilty." You can plead "Nolo Contendere."

Guess who gets to spend six years in jail? Guess who gets to pay a fine of $15,000.00? Guess who loses his right to vote? Guess who loses his right to own a firearm? Oh, by the way, guess who just might become the "piggy bank" of the miscreant's family as they sue for wrongful death? So, after paying for the lawyer to plead down to a lesser charge, guess who gets to hire a new lawyer to defend against the miscreant's family's suit? Guess who is now being housed and fed at taxpayer expense? I guess that you are happy that you read all this here before any of this happened to you. (I'm being a little self-serving, aren't I?)

Is there a lesson to be learned from this? Yes, make contact and conversation with a good **criminal defense attorney** before you ever need one. Also, understand that you are not "Mirandized" until the cops decide to take you into custody or arrest you. Any and everything you tell 911 is recorded and everything that you tell the sympathetic cop at the scene is fair game for the D.A. (See *Chapter 32, History to the Victor, Facts to the First Caller,* for more discussion of this area.)

Line up a good criminal defense attorney now! Ask him what to say and how to handle the cop's interrogation prior to your lawyer's arrival. A few hundred bucks for advice now might save your entire fortune later, not to mention time in the jailhouse. If you do not handle yourself intelligently during those first few minutes, or hours, after a handgun incident; well, I can hear the words to that old song now:

"He's in the jailhouse now;
He's in the jailhouse now.
I warned him once or twice,
Not to blab his mouth, just play it nice.
He's in the jailhouse now,
He's in the jailhouse now.
He blabbed once or twice,

But the lady cop, she sure was nice.

He's in the jailhouse now."

(Yes, I know; I did change the words a little, but you get my point.)

So how do you find a good criminal defense attorney? Here are a few suggestions for your consideration:

1. Ask friends and neighbors whom they might know or recommend. Of course they will want to know what you have done that you now need a criminal defense attorney. Tell them some guy at work needs one and since he owes you a bunch of money, you want to find a good one for him.

2. Ask the lawyer who did your last bit of legal work whom he would recommend. Better yet, ask what lawyer would he hire as a criminal defense attorney if he shot his wife or mistress.

3. Call the D.A. and offer a free lunch or campaign contribution. Then ask the D.A. to name the top three lawyers he would seek out if his child needed one.

4. There is always the *Yellow Pages*.

5. Maybe the local bar association would supply you a listing of such attorneys and with their won-loss record. (Yes, sure, in your dreams.)

However you drag up the name, go meet, or at least call, and talk to your very own criminal defense attorney today!

Consider Special Insurance for Criminal Defense Expenses

Even if you have the absolute best criminal defense attorney since *Matlock* and *Perry Mason*, he will cost you some money; lots and lots of money. These types of gun related criminal defense expenses are not covered under your homeowner or renter's insurance policies. They are probably not covered under some fancy "umbrella" policy either. Nope, coverage is exclusively limited to just you and your bank account, IRA, 401K, and home equity. Does your wife work? That would help, since you may well be housed at public expense and unable to bring in any income.

So what is a "suspenders and belt" type of person to do? Well, there are a couple of options that might provide you some insurance protection and peace of mind. Understand that I know very little of the details of these policies and exactly what is or is not a good or a less-good option. You get to dig that out for yourself. First, The National Rifle Association, NRA, (1-817-232-5556 reaches their corporate office) has some type of insurance offering. Call or contact them and seek details of what it covers and how much it costs. The Concealed Carry Association (USCCA reachable at 1-877-677-1919) also offers "insurance type" coverage for a handgun defense incident. Currently, they offer three coverage levels at three cost levels. Their coverage is not exactly "insurance," but is a trust or some other type of set up.

There may be some other associations offering some type of insurance for gun related episodic defense expenses. I am just unaware of them. Ask your local gun dealers and shooting enthusiasts for information. Actually, when you contact either of the above, ask them how their offering compares to their competitor's. Perhaps you will get some additional names that way.

Two or three hundred bucks a year is a lot of money for this type of insurance coverage. Heck, two or three hundred bucks is a lot of money, period. But I suspect that you have car insurance, homeowner or renter's insurance, health insurance, and life insurance. I also suspect that you hate to write out the checks to pay any of them. I also bet that you hope that you never have to actually put in a claim against any of them either. But you continue to buy them and pay their premiums each year. Why? Why do you do that? "Just in case," is the answer. "Just in case" disaster strikes and it costs you a whole lot more than you could afford. You pay for the insurance every year, hoping you never use it, hating the cost, but glad to have the protection. That is why you should look into gun episode insurance, for peace of mind and protection of assets.

Call those two associations today and educate yourself. Then make an intelligent decision as to what, if anything, you will, should, or can do. And remember:

"Stupidity should be painful."

Chapter 12

Practice Shooting on the Cheap

The shooting gallery that is most convenient for me is a pretty good deal. The current fee is about $12.00 for as long as you want to shoot and each target is only $1.00. You can bring your own ammo. It is indoors, so weather is no concern. The men who run the place are knowledgeable and helpful. They also rent guns so you can try before you buy. Also, there is a complete gun store with very knowledgeable men to help.

Even with all that said, to practice live fire shooting once a week for fifty-two weeks can add up. Now my friend Gaylon shoots skeet or trap or whatever once a week and handguns whenever the urge grabs him, but he owns his own business so he can do all kinds of stuff whenever he wants to. The rest of us are a little less blessed; well, actually he works a whole lot harder. Anyway, I must have whined to him about the cost of shooting or something equally petty.

One day, he calls me up and tells me to go to my computer and look up something online. Turns out it is a laser target and pistol set up. You can "dry fire" your own handgun at a target with a laser light inside your gun and it will register on the target up to about fifty feet. The video looked really neat and the audio must be very informative but my old computer's audio has died so I do not know what the guy on the video actually said. He probably covered all the exceptions, caveats, and things it will not do, but I did not hear any of that.

Turns out if you buy the target and the special shell for your very own handgun the cost is approaching $350.00 or so. That sounded pretty expensive until I put a pencil to it. The batteries last for three thousand laser shots. So if you planned to go shooting and shoot about a hundred rounds per trip, then three thousand laser shots equal about thirty trips to the range. This would cost, in range fees, targets, and ammo, over $1,100.00, and that is just for you. If you take your spouse, the cost would double. I think that the laser's batteries are probably cheap and to replace all three would probably equal the cost of a hundred rounds of ammo or even less.

You, your spouse, and your kids could all practice at home. You could teach gun safety, remove fear of firearms, and make crack marksmen of the entire clan. A family "live-fire" outing in your own living room!

No, I have never seen one of these systems. No, I have never talked to anyone who owned one. No, I have never talked to anyone who has tried one. No, I do not have a clue as to what I am talking about, but I am going to encourage Gaylon to buy one. Then I'll try it out. If it is as slick as it looks, I just might bite. Of course, when Gaylon tires of his new toy, I could probably just borrow it. Better yet, I will offer to let him store the thing at my house! Go look for yourself at *www.laserlyte. com.* There are probably several other such systems, but Gaylon did not give me their website addresses.

All that said, dry firing is only part of becoming an accurate shooter. You can practice proper grip, squeeze, target-sight alignment, etc. You can eliminate a lot of bad form and instill some good techniques. That said, it does not provide the real live fire recoil. Dry fire every day and hone your skill, but you still must live fire to validate your skill and learn that "Mr. Recoil" is not as fierce as you might fear. Combine the two and you may some day equal my shooting skill. (OK, Little Orphan Annie already surpasses my skill.) If you do both dry fire and live fire, you will be the kind of person who no criminal would ever intentionally want to confront, accost, or attack. Therefore, do both: dry fire daily; live fire at least once or twice monthly until you get very, very good. You know, be capable of emptying the full magazine or cylinder into a circle under six-inches at twenty feet. At least that is my suggestion.

"But you makes your choices and you takes your chances."

(Please let me know if you get one of these gizmos, how you like it, and if it is worth the money. I might make you an offer if you tire of it.)

A couple of points about dry firing, or live firing for that matter, have someone show you how to grip your pistol properly. This is the foundation, the bedrock, of all your future accuracy. You should learn how to grip it properly and then grip the pistol that same proper way every time you pull the trigger. Soon, your muscle memory will have control, and you can concentrate on aiming.

Aiming is a three-point process. First, you align the front sight in the center of and level with the rear sight slot, if there is a slot. Second, you "place" the front sight on your target's center. Third, you focus on your front sight as you point the pistol's barrel at your target's center.

To fire, you squeeze the trigger rearwards with a slow and steady pressure. No quick trigger press, jerk, or snap backward; that will probably cause your hand to pull the pistol off target. Squeeze the trigger slowly and steadily rearward until the trigger releases the hammer. When dry firing, there is no recoil, so you can maintain the sight picture and have a look downrange to ensure that you still have the proper sight picture. If you desire you can balance a penny or dime on the end of the barrel; it will fall off if you are flinching or jerking. When live firing, there is immediate recoil, and that will force the pistol backwards and upwards and off target. You will have to inspect the hole in your target to determine if your sight picture was accurate.

You can see the advantage of dry firing or using some type of simulator as discussed above. With no recoil, you will concentrate on proper gripping, proper sight alignment, proper trigger squeeze, and maintaining a steady sight picture while pressing the trigger slowly to the trigger release point. Since there is no recoil you will not jerk or flinch in anticipation. If you practice this for a sufficient time, when you do live fire, your mind and muscles will not be trained to flinch. You have trained them otherwise. Therefore, you should be a much better shot.

The key to marksmanship is the "front sight." Believe it or not, the bullet will leave the end of the barrel and go in the direction that the front sight is pointing. Therefore, focus on the front sight; align it properly with the rear sight grove and the target's center, but **focus on the front sight**.

Dry firing or simulator firing can be used to develop proper habits, aiming, etc. However, at the end of the day, you will need to "live fire" your weapon. We have discussed this before, but a quick a review. The least expensive ammunition to shoot is the .22-caliber; after that is the 9mm Luger round. The .22-caliber pistol offers a fun shooting experience for all sexes and ages with minimum recoil and the least noise. The 9mm is a relatively easy to handle caliber pistol, and with the low cost of its ammunition and the pistol's ability to be your primary defense weapon, it is a solid choice for all purposes.

If you have tried everything to hit the target, and you still are at my level of shooting expertise, you might consider: *shoot first and call whatever you hit "the target."* (Did I say it was a last resort?) Just kidding, if your skill just does not improve, you require some instruction. So, if after several months of dry firing, simulator firing, and live firing your aim is still poor—get professional instruction.

Chapter 13

Review of Some Basic Legal Statutes

After many an afternoon hour spent at the Bowen School of Law Library, I have formed two conclusions. First, there is just no organization to our laws that helps you find something unless you already know where it is located. Second, should one be so fortunate as to finally locate the statute that seems to be the one for which you are searching, it may not be written for the normal person's comprehension.

Despite all my whining, perhaps it would still be a good idea to look at some of the basic Arkansas statutes that relate to violence, guns, and real examples of running afoul of the law. After all, we all have an enhanced opportunity to run afoul of the law as handgun owners and concealed carry license holders. Therefore, the more we know the laws, the less likely we are to do something really dumb. I have used Arkansas statutes, but they are probably very similar to those in most states. It should be easier to dig out your own state's statues using these as a guide

Although I did my best to locate these statutes in the library legal archives, there are umpteen jillion books and you need skill, knowledge, and a law degree to find stuff. So please assume at the best that the following is incomplete and that all my opinions are wacky. Of great assistance to me in some of the reference research was *LexisNexis*. They graciously granted me the ability to use their database for inclusion. That saved many additional hours of keyboarding.

Generally, the actual statute will be in *italics*. My (Editor) emphasis within the statute itself will be in **bold type.** Editor (My) comments are interspersed and will appear as normal type font; neither italics nor bold.

You should assume several things:

1. First, the *LexisNexis* library stated that it was accurate only through 2011.
2. There are many other statutes and laws that are probably just as important and critical, but you need to have some skill and legal training to really dig them out. I lack both.

3. Any comments made by me are just that, comments. I am not a lawyer and none of the comments made should be construed as, or considered to be, legal advice. You need to go to your own attorney for legal advice.
4. Any comments made by me are just observations of a layman trying to understand legal jargon, and my liabilities and requirements to obey them. You may totally disagree with any and all comments, and are encouraged to do so as many of my own prejudices probably show up.

That said, the statutes that follow are the most obvious areas for our review and discussion, or at least it seems that way to me. This section begins with the general laws about transporting guns and some of those issues. Then it moves to lethal force followed by the various levels of lethal force that are actually listed in the statutes. At the end are some miscellaneous things.

Again, I am not a lawyer. None of the following should be construed as legal advice. Hire your own lawyer to get that. Consider the following to be just a "conversation" between a couple of folks with similar interests and concerns discussing these statutes as if we were sitting together in your den. (I drink tea or coffee should you invite me over.) Let us start with the big picture.

Crimes of Violence

Just for your edification, the following are the general crime categories that in Arkansas are considered "Crimes of Violence" as defined in Arkansas Statute 5-73-202:

(1) *"Crime of violence" means any of the following crimes or an attempt to commit any of them:*
(A) Murder;
(B) Manslaughter;
(C) Kidnapping;
(D) Rape;
(E) Mayhem;
(F) Assault to do great bodily harm;
(G) Robbery;

136

(H)   Burglary;
(I)   Housebreaking;
(J)   Breaking and entering; and
(K)   Larceny.

Why list these? Well as we passed into 2012 and beyond, only criminals who perpetrate a "violent" crime will be sent to prison in Arkansas. Miscreants who commit "non-violent" crimes will be returned to your highways and byways, dear citizen. This is just another reason to get armed, get legal, get prepared and stay alert.

An outstanding resource from a lawyer's perspective on similar issues is a book by Ken Hanson, an attorney as well as a gun owner. His book, *The Ohio Guide to Firearm Laws,* is about 50 percent actual Ohio law concerning firearms. It is the other half that is most instructive for your reading. He covers such areas as to what to do after a shooting incident, "Castle" interpretation, and "Stand your Ground" considerations from an Ohio law perspective. There is some difference in Arkansas and Ohio law in respect to these areas, but his discussion really helps with perspective. His book, since I am unaware of one for Arkansas laws, is worth the $19.95 list price.

Depending on the specific legal area you may have fallen afoul of, there are levels or degrees of severity and punishment. The table below lists an overview of penalties for several Felonies and Misdemeanors which relate to firearm statutes.

Sentence Guidelines

Crime	Prison/Jail Sentence	Fine	Statute of Limitations
Felony:	**Statute 5-4-401**	**Statute 5-4-201**	**Statute 5-1-109**
Class Y	Min.10 yrs.-Max.40 yrs., or life. Cap. Murder = life w/o parole or death		Within 6 yrs.*
Class A	Min. 6 yrs.-Max. 30 yrs.	$15,000.00 max.	Within 6 yrs.*
Class B	Min. 5 yrs.-Max. 20 yrs.	$15,000.00 max.	Within 3 yrs.
Class C	Min. 3 yrs.-Max. 10 yrs.	$10,000.00 max.	Within 3 yrs.
Class D	Not to exceed 6 yrs.	$10,000.00 max.	Within 3 yrs.
Misdemeanor:	**Statute 5-1-107**	**Statute 5-4 201**	**Statute 5-1-109**
Class A	Not to exceed 1 year	$1,000.00 max.	Within 1 yr.

Class B	Not to exceed 90 days	$500.00 max.	Within 1 yr.
Class C	Not to exceed 30 days	$100.00 max.	Within 1 yr.
			* Some exceptions, such as murder, rape, etc.

Chapter 14

Carrying and Transporting Firearms

A private citizen carrying a weapon is not exactly looked upon with a friendly smile in Arkansas, at least not by law enforcement. In fact, you might easily run afoul of the law if you purchase a handgun or go shooting in one area of town and then travel back to your residence in another section of town with the handgun sitting safely on the seat next to you. I know that may be just a little alarmist, but then you read the law and decide for yourself.

Arkansas Statute: 5-73-120. Carrying a weapon. (Statute in *italics*; Editor's emphasis in **bold**, not the statute's; Editor's comments not italicized or bold.)

(a)   *A person commits the offense of carrying a weapon if he or she possesses a handgun, knife, or club on or about his or her person, in a vehicle occupied by him or her, or otherwise readily available for use with a purpose to attempt to unlawfully employ the handgun, knife, or club as a weapon against a person.*

So, if you purchased your pistol for self-defense and have it with you in your car, have you run afoul of the law? What if you are stopped by the police on the way to or from the shooting range? After all, the purpose for which you purchased the firearm is to "employ as a weapon against a person" when attacked or threatened with violent physical harm. Yes, I see where it said "to attempt to unlawfully employ . . . as a weapon." But be advised, it is not you that gets to decide on what your "intent" is. It is the cop, the D.A., the Grand Jury, and the judge that get to determine that.

(b)   *As used in this section:*

(1) *'Club'* *means any instrument that is specially designed, made, or adapted for the purpose of inflicting serious physical injury or death by striking, including a blackjack, billie, and sap;*

(2) ***'Handgun'*** *means any firearm with a barrel length of less than twelve inches (12") that is designed, made, or adapted to be fired with one (1) hand; and*

(3) *(A) 'Knife' means any bladed hand instrument that is capable of inflicting serious physical injury or death by cutting or stabbing.*

(B) 'Knife' includes a dirk, sword or spear in a cane, razor, ice pick, throwing star, switchblade, and butterfly knife.

(c) *It is **permissible to carry a handgun** under this section if at the time of the act of carrying a weapon:*

(1) *The person is in his or her own dwelling, place of business, or on property in which he or she has a possessory or proprietary interest;*

This probably means that if you sneak it home from the gun store, you are OK once you are running around on your own property or your driveway.

(2) *The person is a law enforcement officer, correctional officer, or member of the armed forces acting in the course and scope of his or her official duties;*

There is no help here as this does not apply to most of us.

(3) ***The person is assisting a law enforcement officer,*** *correctional officer, or member of the armed forces acting in the course and scope of his or her official **duties pursuant to the direction or request of the law enforcement officer,** correctional officer, or member of the armed forces;*

This is an interesting item. It does not appear to cover your carrying a weapon up until the point that you are asked by the LEO to help. Have you broken the law if you now reveal that you had a firearm before you were impressed into service by the LEO? In any case, no help here either as most of this does not apply to the majority of us. You would be well advised, I would think, to give this situation some pre-incident thought. You are asked by a policeman to help him in a very dangerous situation. This policeman risks his life every day for us. Yet, despite the appeal to your hidden "Ramboette" persona, you have no police training, no experience, no body armor, no badge, no pension if injured or killed for acting as a policeman, and probably limited training on a live gunfight plus probably limited ammunition with you. Still, it is an opportunity to make the newspaper: headlines and/or obituary.

(4)   *The person is **carrying a weapon when upon a journey**, unless the journey is through a commercial airport when presenting at the security checkpoint in the airport or is in the person's checked baggage and is not a lawfully declared weapon;*

This is a lawyer's delight. You are OK if carrying the pistol on a "**journey**." Definition of a "journey" formerly was up to the cop arresting you, and then the D.A., and then the Judge. My friend Gaylon tells that his lawyer friend swears that a local judge considers a "journey" to be more than twenty-five miles. That is probably too many miles to cover the short distance to get you back home from the gun store or most shooting ranges. Having a map of Oklahoma spread out on the seat next to you might work, but do not count on it. The cop would probably ask "Where in Oklahoma are you going? What is the address and what is the name of the people you are 'journeying' to visit?" (You do understand that it is probably against the law to lie to a LEO?) I wonder if the twenty-five mile is a standard and if it includes total mileage—you know, round trip mileage? Well, thanks to the April 4, 2013 signing of Arkansas Act 746 by the Governor, you no longer have to worry about all of this. They now define journey as: beyond the county in which the person lives. Now, a state map is all you need, or two residencies in different counties.

(5) The person is a licensed security guard acting in the course and scope of his or her duties;

No help here, as this does not apply to most of us.

*(6) The person is hunting game with a **handgun** that may be hunted with a **handgun** under rules and regulations of the Arkansas State Game and Fish Commission or is en route to or from a hunting area for the purpose of hunting game with a **handgun**;*

The above statute might be confusing. What it says to me is: if you are hunting with a legal handgun and hunting game that can be hunted with a handgun under state rules when that game can be hunted, then you can transport your weapon. So if you are wearing your fatigues; if it is the right time of year; and if you are carrying your hunting license, you just might get away with this excuse, but for most of us, no help here. (If you have a .45-ACP with JHP and claim to be after quail, you might just be suspect.)

(7) The person is a certified law enforcement officer; or

No help here, as this does not apply to most of us.

*(8) **The person is in possession of a concealed handgun and has a valid license to carry a concealed handgun under SS5-73-301** et seq., **or recognized under SS5-73-321 and is not in a prohibited place as defined by SS5-73-306.***

The emphasis here is all the Editors. This is an outstanding reason to go obtain your Arkansas CHCL. Go get a CHCL and avoid all of the above hassle.

(d)   **(1)** *Any person who carries a weapon into an establishment that sells alcoholic beverages is guilty of a misdemeanor and subject to a fine of not more than two thousand five hundred dollars ($2,500) or imprisonment for not more than one (1) year, or both.*

This one is very tricky. There is an exception under another statute, but you have to meet about three hurdles to escape this crime. Your best course of action would seem to be as follows: if liquor, wine or beer is served, do not carry a weapon inside the establishment. Better yet, go to eateries where they **do not serve** alcohol. It is not only cheaper, but since you are armed, it is safer. See *Chapter 15* for the exception for restaurants. This section of SS5-73-120 (d) (1) appears to have been repealed by Act 746 of 2013, but since it is referenced in other statutes, it is left here for your consideration. Remember, you lose your license if caught consuming alcohol with a firearm.

(2) Otherwise, carrying a weapon is a Class A misdemeanor. (That could be up to a $1,000.00 fine and up to one year in jail.)

So, what have we learned here? Good common sense plus fear of untimely police roadblocks, speeding tickets, or just bad luck would tell me to go and obtain an Arkansas CHCL. For about a $150.00 State Police Fee and a $100.00 or so class fee, you can avoid a lot of potential lost time, court trouble, and much greater expense via fines, etc. But,

"You makes your choices and you takes your chances."

CAVEAT: I am not a lawyer. I have zero legal training. Do not construe any of the bold font wording or my comments as legal opinion or advice. They are not. They are my opinion only. Consult your own attorney for legal advice or interpretation of laws and statutes.

Chapter 15

Prohibited Places to Carry
Even With a CHCL

There are places where concealed handguns are prohibited even if
you have a CHCL.

Even if you go through the appropriate class, pass the State Police
background check, pay for, and receive your CHCL, there are many
locations forbidden to your entry with a concealed weapon. Below is the
quick list. (State statutes are in *italics*; **bold** is Editor's emphasis; Editor's
comments are not italicized or bold.)

Arkansas Statute: **ACA §5-73-306**

*No license to carry a concealed handgun issued pursuant to this
subchapter authorizes any person to carry a concealed handgun into:*

*(1)   Any police station, sheriff's station, or Department of Arkansas
State Police station;*

*(2)   Any Arkansas Highway Police Division of the Arkansas State
Highway and Transportation Department facility;*

*(3)   (A) Any building of the Arkansas State Highway and
Transportation Department* ***or onto grounds adjacent*** *to any
building of the Arkansas State Highway and Transportation
Department.*

*(B) However, subdivision (3)(A) of this section does not apply to
a rest area or weigh station of the Arkansas State Highway and
Transportation Department;*

(4)   Any detention facility, prison, or jail;

(5)   Any courthouse;

(6)   (A) Any courtroom.

*(B) However, nothing in this subchapter precludes a judge from
carrying a concealed weapon or determining who will carry a
concealed weapon into his or her courtroom;*

(7)   Any polling place;

(8)   Any meeting place of the governing body of any governmental entity;

(9)   Any meeting of the General Assembly or a committee of the General Assembly;

(10) Any state office;

*(11) **Any athletic event** not related to firearms;*

*(12) **Any portion of an establishment, except a restaurant as defined in § 3-9-402, licensed to dispense alcoholic beverages for consumption on the premises**;*

*("Restaurant" means: any public or private place which is kept, used, maintained, advertised, and held out to the public or to a private or restricted membership as a place where complete meals are actually and regularly served, such place being provided with **adequate and sanitary kitchen** and dining equipment and a seating capacity of **at least fifty (50) people** and having employed a sufficient number and kind of employees to prepare, cook, and serve suitable food for its guests or members. **At least one (1) meal per day** shall be served, and the place shall be **open a minimum of five (5) days per week**, with the exception of holidays, vacations, and periods of redecorating. (This definition is in another section of the Statutes. **Do not under any circumstances drink intoxicants while you are carrying.**)*

(13) Any portion of an establishment, except a restaurant as defined in § 3-9-402, where beer or light wine is consumed on the premises;

(See definition of "restaurants" under (12) above.)

*(14) Any school, college, community college, or university campus **building or event**, unless for the purpose of participating in an authorized firearms-related activity;*

Effective March 1, 2013, by ACT 226 (SS 5-73-322) this was modified **to permit: licensed staff and faculty to carry a concealed handgun on a university, college, or**

community college campus *under certain circumstances. That the governing board of the* (institution) *does not adopt a policy expressly disallowing the carrying of a concealed handgun by staff members in the buildings and grounds of the* (institutions) *and posts notices as described in SS 5-73-306(19). A policy disallowing the carrying of a concealed handgun by staff members into the* (institutions) *expires one (1) year after the date of adoption and must be readopted each year by the governing board of the* (institutions).

(15) *Inside the passenger terminal of any airport, except that no person is prohibited from carrying any legal firearm into the passenger terminal if the firearm is encased for shipment for purposes of checking the firearm as baggage to be lawfully transported on any aircraft;*

(16) *Any church or other place of worship.*

Effective February 11, 2013 by ACT 67 SS 5-73-306(16) this was modified to state: *(B) However this subchapter does not preclude a church or other place of worship from determining who may carry a concealed handgun into the church or other place of worship . . . that the Second Amendment of the Constitution of the United States ensures a person's right to bear arms; and that this act is immediately necessary because a person should be allowed to carry a firearm in a church that permits the carrying of a firearm for personal security . . .* (Senate Bill 896, if enacted, would permit a church that authorizes concealed carry to also authorize concealed carry in its own church schools.)

(17) *Any place where the carrying of a firearm is prohibited by federal law;*

(18) *Any place where a parade or demonstration requiring a permit is being held, and the licensee is a participant in the parade or demonstration; or*

(19) *(A) Any place at the discretion of the person or entity exercising control over the physical location of the place by placing at each entrance to the place a written notice clearly readable at a* *distance of not less than ten (10) feet that 'carrying a handgun is prohibited.'* (Remember the Costco Store incident? Read the signs on the doors of the establishments you frequent and avoid those that don't allow citizens legally armed.)

(B) **(i)** *If the place does not have a roadway entrance, there shall be a written notice placed anywhere upon the premises of the place.*

(ii) *In addition to the requirement of subdivision (19)(B) (i) of this section, there shall be at least one (1) written notice posted within every three (3) acres of a place with no roadway entrance.*

(C) *A written notice as described in subdivision (19)(A) of this section is not required for a private home.*

(D) *Any licensee entering a private home shall notify the occupant that the licensee is carrying a concealed handgun.*

So what is the general lesson from this section? Generally, if it is a public, tax payer supported property, just do not carry there. That is easier to remember than to memorize three hundred and seven exceptions. If it is an athletic event or other school activity, do not carry there. Do not carry into houses of worship unless it has been authorized. (Refer to Chapter 15, paragraph 16.) Do not carry where it is posted as prohibited. Watch out for restaurants, plus a few others.

And speaking of bars, saloons, gentlemen's clubs, late-night entertainment spots, etc., they are very dangerous places. They are especially dangerous after midnight based on continued newspaper reports of shootings at such watering holes. If you feel compelled to go there, do not go armed, do not get intoxicated, do not get into an argument, and do leave early. **And do not drink and carry!**

But, "*You makes your choices and you takes your chances.*"

CAVEAT: I am not a lawyer. I have zero legal training. Do not construe any of the bold font wording or my comments as legal opinion or advice. They are not. They are my opinion only. Consult your own attorney for legal advice or interpretation of laws and statutes.

Chapter 16

Reciprocity for Concealed Carry with Other States

There is some degree of mutual recognition between most states that issue concealed carry licenses. In Arkansas, this is empowered in a statute to grant reciprocity recognition to other states' CHCL holders if that state recognizes Arkansas CHCL as valid in their state. This facilitates Arkansas CHCL holders going to the other such states with a handgun. The Arkansas State Police are responsible to coordinate, facilitate, and report this to Arkansas citizens.

Arkansas Statute: 5-73-321; Recognition of other states' licenses.

(a) *A person in possession of a valid license to carry a concealed **handgun** issued to the person by another state is entitled to the privileges and subject to the restrictions prescribed by this subchapter if the state that issued the license to carry a concealed **handgun** recognizes a license to carry a concealed **handgun** issued under this subchapter.*

(b) *The Director of the Department of Arkansas State Police shall:*

    (1) *Make a determination as to which states' licenses to carry concealed **handguns** will be recognized in Arkansas and provide that list to every law enforcement agency within the state; and*

    (2) *Revise the list from time to time and provide the revised list to every law enforcement agency in this state.*

To find out which states currently have reciprocity with Arkansas:

1. Go to the State Police Web site: *http://www.asp.state.ar.us/*
2. On the "Tabs" across the top, SELECT "Services and Programs."
3. On the resulting page titled "Services and Programs," Scroll down to the section titled: "Regulatory Services."

4. About 3/4s of the way down the "Regulatory Services" section, CLICK on "Concealed Handgun Licensing."
5. On the resulting screen titled: "Concealed Handgun Licensing" SCROLL to the very bottom of the page under the section titled: "Applicable Laws".

At this time (2013), there were about 39 states listed as having reciprocity with Arkansas for CHCL recognition. This list currently includes our surrounding states of Missouri, Oklahoma, Texas, Louisiana (state only), Mississippi, and Tennessee.

The Arkansas State Police site has the interesting words *"state only"* by Louisiana. On a call to the Louisiana State Police (225-925-4867), the person said that their law was statewide and thus reciprocity was statewide and she had no clue why Arkansas had that notation by Louisiana. A call to the Arkansas State Police number resulted in umpteen message options but no return call. A call to a CHCL instructor produced this information, *"Louisiana lacks a state law restricting the Parishes and municipalities from having their own gun control laws. So any municipality might have a concealed carry ban. For example, New Orleans prohibits concealed carry."* Therefore, be careful in Louisiana, or at least call their state and the Parishes through which you will be traveling. If you are stopped, their police have the legal right to "pat you down" and to temporarily disarm you after you inform them that you are an armed CHCL holder.

Be very, very careful of travel in the North East. For example, no reciprocity is listed for the states of: Maryland, Massachusetts, New Jersey, New York, Vermont, Connecticut, and Rhode Island. There are a few other states that lack reciprocity, but these in the N. E. are clustered. On December 30, 2011, it was reported in the local paper:

> *Meredith Graves, a 39-year-old tourist who has a legal permit to carry a weapon in Tennessee, was arrested on a gun-possession charge in New York, where gun laws are stricter, when she asked New York City police where she could check her loaded pistol while visiting the Sept. 11 memorial at the World Trade Center site, the New York Post reported.*

Vermont may be an interesting wrinkle, so to speak. My LEO reviewer opines, *"While no 'true' reciprocity exists with Vermont, I believe that is because Vermont does not issue CHCLs to its citizens. Vermont allows its citizens to carry based on the Second Amendment and similar state laws. Therefore, they issue no license for Arkansas to recognize. But I believe Vermont honors the Arkansas CHCL."* An Internet search resulted in a site titled *"Concealed Carry."* That site shows that Vermont recognizes all states' CHCL but Illinois. It also shows that Arkansas recognizes Vermont. The Arkansas State Police list does not verify that. Which do you believe? If traveling to Vermont, do not travel armed through New York, but do call ahead and ask Vermont about reciprocity.

You can see from the above that any one website may not have the correct answer to your questions about traveling while armed. That said, if you wish to travel interstate with your handgun, you should access the website of the individual states through which you will travel. Verify that they list Arkansas as a state with whom they have reciprocity. (This is a belt and suspenders approach to life.) You might also review any of their statues related to their requirements concerning carrying a handgun in a vehicle. Some states may require your handgun to be carried in some combination of: unloaded, locked in a safe, in a car compartment not accessible from inside the car, ammo and gun locked separately, or some other such restriction.

In the fall of 2011, the U.S. House of Representatives passed a law that overrides the need for individual states to engage in mutually negotiated reciprocity agreements. It would establish nationwide reciprocity among states issuing CHCL. Only Illinois and DC were exempt. If this passes the Senate and the President signs it into law (doubtful), then reciprocity becomes more of a "right" across state lines and lot less of a worry. That said, **every state does have its own specific peculiarities, so one is still advised to consult the specific laws of the states to be visited.**

Let me repeat that last bit of information. Each state has its own CHCL rules and regulations. Just because they recognize the Arkansas CHCL does not remove your requirement to abide by their laws while in their state. So, if you are traveling across country and only pass through states that honor Arkansas CHCL, you may still have a bunch of different laws and regulations to salute and obey as you cross from one state into another.

Do not expect police to have a sense of humor or an understanding of your forgetfulness on carrying handguns into prohibited states or locations or a leaning toward granting "second chances." They are hired to uphold the law; good and bad ones. They enforce the law or run the risk of losing their own employment.

On the other hand, should you find yourself suddenly standing in a place that prohibits concealed weaponry and no one at the moment is aware of that fact but you, then it would seem that you have no obligation to turn yourself in to the police. Turn around and exit that location and when you are in a "gun OK" location, disarm. Then return, if you must go back.

If you see those upright metal posts with a guard standing close by herding all folks through the detector, think real quick—*am I carrying a weapon?* If so, those uprights and the guard are visible reminders that you are about to enter a "No Gun" zone. What to do? Act as if you have just received a cell phone call, step aside, pull out your phone, listen and then exclaim in horror that your Aunt Harriet has just had a close encounter of the third kind and you must leave immediately, or something. You should avoid New York.

Have I mentioned that I am not a lawyer? None of the above should be construed as legal advice.

Chapter 17

When to Show
Your CHCL to a Policeman

There may be some confusion on when one should hand over their CHCL to a policeman. Some folks say "When Asked." Others, including the police who teach the CHCL class, will tell you: *"Whenever a policeman requests your Driver's License, hand over your CHCL also."* Well, what does the law say? It states: *"display both . . . upon demand."*

Arkansas Statute: 5-73-315: Possession of license; Identification of licensee.

(a) Any licensee possessing a valid license issued pursuant to this subchapter may carry a concealed **handgun.**

(b) The licensee shall:

(1) Carry the license, together with valid identification, at any time when the licensee is carrying a concealed **handgun;** and

(2) Display **both** the license and proper identification **upon demand by a law enforcement officer.**

Does this mean if the policeman does not **demand** your CHCL when he **demands** your Driver License, that you are only required to *display* the DL? Not so fast "Mr. Sneaky Legal Beagle." Let us give this some thought. You are driving and subsequently are pulled over by a patrol car.

1. Initially, the policeman does not know that you have a CHCL. In fact, he does not even know that you have a driver's license, just that you are supposed to have a driver's license.

2. Second, he **will** know that you have a CHCL as soon as he puts your DL # into the system. (Hey Dude, remember it is the State Police who issue and track CHCLs.)

3. Policemen do not like surprises, especially when out on patrol and of the unpleasant kind. Do you remember the video of

the Ohio cop who made a routine traffic stop in 2011? The motorist did not inform the officer that he was a CHCL holder and that he was currently carrying a loaded weapon despite Ohio law requiring this. When the officer subsequently learned that the driver was armed, he went berserk. The scene turned very ugly with the cop even threatening the motorist with what he "should do to him." The motorist did not help when he actually pulled out his concealed weapon. Fortunately, no one was shot or injured. The motorist probably received a ticket for every citation that the policeman could dream up plus four unrelated ones for good measure. Because the incident was caught on tape, the policeman is in big trouble. However, if the policeman is still on the force and making traffic stops, how would you like to be stopped by him and fail to inform him of your CHCL status? (Pretty dumb move if you do not inform him, or any other LEO, is my opinion.)

4.   Remember, in a traffic stop you are hoping the policeman will only give you a warning, not a real ticket, so be very courteous, compliant, and understanding.

When a policeman asks for your ID, whether driver license (or something else that you may conjure up for sake of argument) **also give him your CHCL**, and inform him if you are "HOT" at that moment. (Just thought that I would throw in the "Shootist" term—"hot.") In other words, tell him if you have a weapon with you and if it is loaded or not.

Are we in agreement then? Tell the policeman, as you hand over both your driver's license and your CHCL, that you are a CHCL holder and that you **are not** currently armed, or that you **are** currently armed and if you are armed, whether it is loaded.

I guarantee you that the policeman will be very appreciative of your forthrightness and will not go ballistic over learning such information from you. He may ask some questions concerning your weapon and even ask that you turn it over to him. He should not get into this, but he just might since he is the one wearing a badge, and the police are always a little apprehensive when encountering armed civilians. Yes, turn your pistol over to him. Should he fail to return it, very politely and nicely ask him to return it. Failing that, ask for a receipt.

No, he should not retain it unless he is arresting you for some other legal infraction. Still, he may be having a very bad day. Do not make yours worse than his; surrender your handgun(s). Ask for a receipt; mentally note his name and badge number and record both a soon as you can discretely do so.

Unless the reason for being stopped by him turns into a felony, you will be able to regain possession of your handgun(s). It might take some time, and even a lawyer in the worst case, but it will happen. Barring that the stop was for a felony, he will probably return your handgun(s) to you after the ticketing process. Be nice! Be Courteous! Be conscious of the fact that all the laws, rules, and force are in his favor at this moment in time. And by the way, please do not leave home with the handgun and without your CHCL! In the gun world this is termed stupid! And Remember:

"Stupid Should Be Painful."

And it will be painful. Not only financially and time wise, but also from anxiety and self-recrimination.

Here is the Arkansas statute that gives me the confidence that your weapon would be returned to you.

12-12-324. Testing by State Crime Laboratory.

(a) (1) *All firearms used in the commission of a crime that come into the custody of any law enforcement agency in this state shall be delivered to the State Crime Laboratory within thirty (30) calendar days for ballistics testing.*

(2) *However, if the firearm is being used as evidence in a criminal case, then delivery shall take place within thirty (30) calendar days after the final adjudication of the criminal proceeding.*

(b) (1) (A) *The laboratory may conduct ballistics tests on all firearms received and input the resulting data into the National Integrated Ballistics Information Network of the Bureau of Alcohol, Tobacco, Firearms and Explosives.*

(B) The ballistics tests may include, but not be limited to, firing of the weapon and electronic imaging of the bullets and casings.

(2) The laboratory shall coordinate with all participating agencies when investigations require the use of the National Integrated Bullet Identification Network's computer database.

(3) The laboratory shall provide written analysis reports and experts for testimony when feasible.

*(4) **After completion of the testing, the firearms shall be returned to the law enforcement agencies.***

*(5) **When the law enforcement agency regains possession of the firearm, the law enforcement agency shall immediately notify the owner, unless the owner is prohibited by law from possessing the firearm, that the owner may regain possession of the firearm at the offices of the law enforcement agency.***

(c) A law enforcement agency in this state may request the assistance of the Department of Arkansas State Police in tracing a firearm.

(d) A firearm seized by the Arkansas State Game and Fish Commission for violation of a commission regulation is exempt from this section.

(e) The State Crime Laboratory Board may adopt rules for the implementation of this section, including, but not limited to, rules regarding testing and submission procedures.

If the state returns a weapon used in a crime back to its owner, surely it would return a weapon confiscated during a routine traffic stop back to the owner. Yes, I know that the world is not perfect and that I am not a lawyer. Therefore: **Do not construe any of the bold font wording or my comments as legal opinion or advice. They are not. They are my opinion only. Consult your own attorney for legal advice or interpretation of laws and statutes.**

Chapter 18

Lethal Force: When Should I Shoot?
Is It the ONLY Option?

There is a quote that is well worn, overused, but very germane to this section:

> *"To a man whose only tool is a hammer,*
> *every problem looks like a nail."*
> A Shootist's Proverb

You may have heard such terms as "Castle Law" or "Stand Your Ground Law" justifying the use of deadly force. In a broad sense the Castle Doctrine has two parts: the ability to defend yourself inside your home (Castle Doctrine) and the ability to defend yourself outside your home (Stand Your Ground). Arkansas does not have laws so titled, but does afford you approximately the same protection under two separate statues: 5-2-620 and 5-2-607. Under Arkansas Law, you are legally afforded the option to take another person's life **ONLY** under certain, very specific circumstances. But before we even look at that specific set of circumstances, here is an excellent piece of advice lifted from another "Shootist:"

> *"If you have to think if you should shoot,*
> *you probably should not shoot."*

"Castle Doctrine" or while in your home

Arkansas criminal statute 5-2-620 codifies for Arkansas what might be termed "The Castle Doctrine." Some assert that it offers tremendous protection and gives an unprecedented benefit-of-the-doubt to the **home owner**. (All bold print is the Editor's emphasis, not the statute's emphasis.)

*5-2-620. Use of force to defend persons and property **within** [the] **home***

(a) The right of an individual **to defend himself or herself and the life of a person or property in the individual's home against harm, injury, or loss** by a person unlawfully entering or attempting to enter or intrude into the home is **reaffirmed as a fundamental right** to be preserved and promoted as a public policy in this state.

(b) There is a legal presumption **that any force or means used to accomplish a purpose described in subsection (a) of this section was exercised in a lawful and necessary manner,** unless the presumption is overcome by clear and convincing evidence to the contrary.

(c) The public policy stated in subsection (a) of this section shall be strictly complied with by the court and an appropriate instruction of this public policy **shall be given to a jury sitting in trial of criminal charges** brought in connection with this public policy.

Editor's comment: **Please note: the above only applies when you are in your home!** If you drive up and see your lights on and you know that no one is supposed to be home, do not get out of your car and go inside to look for the perp. Call 911 and stay outside and wait for experts who have been trained on how to clear a house. Also, if you go inside and locate the perp and shoot him, you have, legally speaking, probably just become the hunter, not the homeowner fearful for his life.

"Stand Your Ground Doctrine" or when you are away from home

Before we read the law itself, the following is another's assessment of the protection under the Arkansas law. What might be termed "The Stand Your Ground" protection is primarily codified in Arkansas criminal statute 5-2-607. **You have a duty to retreat.** However, our duty to retreat has two very important caveats:

1. The **individual must know that he can retreat**, and
2. He must know he can retreat with **complete safety** . . . not some safety, or a predominate amount of safety, but **complete safety**.

Some advise that these two caveats provide exceptional legal protection for the individual using deadly force in his/her self-defense because the prosecution is required to prove beyond a reasonable doubt that the person claiming self-defense knew he could retreat and knew he could retreat with complete safety. Some opine that this is almost an insurmountable burden for the prosecution to overcome, but, my opinion, "buyer beware."

That said, read the law.

Arkansas Statue: 5-2-607. Use of deadly physical force in defense of a person.

(a)   *A person is justified in using deadly physical force upon another person if the person reasonably believes that the other person is:*

   (1)   *Committing or about to commit a **felony involving force or violence**;*

   (Review *Chapter 13* for definitions of "crimes of violence.")

   (2)   *Using or about to use **unlawful deadly physical force**; or*

   (3)   ***Imminently endangering the person's life or imminently about to victimize the person as described in 9-15-103 from the continuation of a pattern of domestic abuse.***

(b)   *A person **may not use deadly physical force** in self-defense if the person knows that he or she can avoid the necessity of using deadly physical force **with complete safety**:*

   (1)   **(A)**   ***By retreating**.*

      (B)   *However, a person is not required to retreat if the person is:*

         (i)   *In the person's dwelling or on the curtilage surrounding the person's dwelling and was not the original aggressor; or*

         (ii)   *A law enforcement officer or a person assisting at the direction of a law enforcement officer; or*

   (2)   ***By surrendering possession** of property to a person claiming a lawful right to possession of the property.*

(c)   *As used in this section:*

(1) *'Curtilage' means the land adjoining a dwelling that is convenient for residential purposes and habitually used for residential purposes, but not necessarily enclosed, and includes an outbuilding that is directly and intimately connected with the dwelling and in close proximity to the dwelling; and*

(2) *'Domestic abuse' means:*

(3) ***(A)*** *Physical harm, bodily injury, assault, or the infliction of fear of imminent physical harm, bodily injury, or assault between family or household members; or*

   (B) *Any sexual conduct between family or household members, whether minors or adults, that constitutes a crime under the laws of this state.*

It's all perfectly clear, right? You now know and understand all that you need to know, right? Well bully for you, because I get all hung up on some of the little words and thus I am just a little uncertain. You are probably well equipped to understand the mental state of the attacker: is he "about to commit." Plus, you are versed in the law and know what is a "felony" and what is "unlawful" deadly force. (In my mind, any force is "deadly force" when applied against me and is also "unlawful" when attempted against me, but then I'm a wimp). Maybe these definitions from state statute 5-2-601 can help us:

5-2-601. Definitions.

(2) ***'Deadly physical force'*** *means physical force that under the circumstances in which it is used is **readily capable of causing death** or serious physical injury;*

(6) *'Physical force' means:*
   *(A) **Any bodily impact**, restraint, or confinement; or*
   *(B) **The threat of any bodily impact**, restraint, or confinement*

(8) ***'Unlawful physical force'*** *means physical force that is employed **without the consent** of the person against whom it is directed and the employment of the physical force constitutes a criminal offense or tort or would constitute a criminal offense or tort except for a defense other than the defense of justification or privilege; and . . .'*

A very important consideration seems to be the implication that you are defending **your life** or the life of another, **not property**. For example, if you are in your car and a miscreant comes and points a pistol at you and tells you to move over, he is threatening your life. However, if you come out of the drug store and see the perp "hot-wiring" your Lexus, you are not lawfully authorized to take lethal action; your life is not at risk, just your Lexus. But those are just my thoughts. Go consult your attorney; now, back to the statute.

First, the term "curtilage" is hazy. Sure they defined it. I understand that if a perp is inside my attached garage and my life is threatened, I can (in my case) unsnap the thumb strap, draw, flick off the thumb safety, aim, and fire. But what if I am one hundred yards away from my house by the back fence and the miscreant is climbing over the fence screaming, "I'm gonna' beat your butt?" Am I in danger of this person about to "commit a felony" or use "unlawful deadly force?" Is "beating my butt" deadly force? Does he have to be armed for me to be threatened? Should I run back to my house first and then wait for the rascal? (Oh, by the way, do you think if I've been seeing his wife that it might have an influence with the D.A.? Am I now considered the "original aggressor?" If I shoot this fellow, do you think that it would probably be poor judgment on my part to marry his widow before the D.A. makes a decision about this case?)

Second scenario: A perp breaks down the door and screams that he wants all his property returned—all of his jewelry and cash. He is red-eyed, foaming at the mouth, arms flailing, mad, and seemingly upset. He screams that if you don't give him the goods, he'll kill you. You unsnap the thumb strap, draw, flick off the thumb safety, aim, and fire. All five witnesses, visiting church Deacons soliciting your annual pledge, swear to the police that the perp was screaming that he would kill you if you did not return his property. Can you guess what happens next? It's an extremely good idea to carry your lawyer's phone number (cell and home) in your wallet. The police may allow you to make the call at the jail house.

Third scenario: You are speeding along the highway minding your own business when suddenly at the next stoplight a car pulls in front, partially blocking you. The door opens and a two hundred-fifty pound gorilla lumbers out and comes toward you with a tire iron in his hand, shouting uncomplimentary terms related to your family's ancestry and accusing you of cutting him off in traffic. Your eight-year-old son in the back seat shouts for you to "Whup the guy's butt!" Your daughter screams, "Daddy, he's using foul language!" Your wife demands, "Make that man stop using vulgar words around the children!" Should you unsnap your thumb strap, draw, flick off your thumb safety, aim, and fire? (Do you have plans for the next 50 years?)

OK, here is an easy one. Walking to your car parked on a downtown street, you look across the street and see a rather disheveled person coming in your direction, a bottle grasped by its neck with his right hand. You make the casual assessment that he is drinking and, with a disapproving sniff, guess that it is some cheap, screw-top wine. In the middle of the block, he crosses the street to your side. You keep walking toward him and it becomes apparent that he also has his eyes on you. You move slightly aside to pass and suddenly he moves in front of you, raises the bottle and strikes a misaimed blow at your head and hits your left shoulder. No words, nothing said. He raises the bottle for a second try. You unsnap the thumb strap, draw, flick off the thumb safety, point, and fire. ("*Why didn't you just reverse your direction and retreat to the restaurant and wait or call the police? Why didn't you ask for someone to accompany you back to your car? Couldn't you have just run away and escaped?*" It's these types of questions that the D.A. is prone to ask if you take the stand at your trial.)

No, Shirley, these little scenarios aren't silly and a total waste of time. The experts recommend that you play out scenarios in your mind and have a plan **before** certain things might happen. Think of a specific solution to scenarios like the above, and then you can generalize that solution to many other types of similar encounters quickly when the unexpected arises. Discussion and review with your real lawyer might be a great idea. (See *Appendix B* for some discussed actions to these scenarios.)

I have been wondering about that quote that "every problem looks like a nail if all you carry is a hammer that goes boom." Do I really want to shoot a drunk or homeless person if there is a less lethal response level? For your consideration: **buy a second tool to augment your "hammer that goes boom."**

Perchance it's time for a true story. My Significant Other went through the CHCL class, passed, got licensed, found a handgun she liked and could operate and shoot with accuracy, and encouraged me (or at least acquiesced to my pressure) to purchase it for her. It sits very safely at our house wherever I happen to put it. After all of that, she refuses to carry the pistol daily. She understands that there really are some bad folks out there, but in her words, "I don't go to dangerous places and if I go out at night I'm with you. You can protect me."

Of course, my "manhood quotient" soared to incredible heights, and any logical discussion or argument was delayed several minutes or hours since I was now her super hero, and my ego was running roughshod over common sense and safety. Of course, this is not a very satisfactory situation: even IHOP and Walgreens have become dangerous places.

We went to a gun show. (Just the one; she tells me that once is enough for her.) At that show, we bought several "pepper spray" gizmos that one can attach to a car key-ring. I convinced her to start carrying one of these. However, they are only effective for about three feet, and if the wind is blowing toward the user and not the perp, both can catch an eye full.

One day at *BULLSEYE Guns and Ammo,* I spied a "pepper spray pistol" type gizmo. It is a red plastic thingy that is shaped like a pistol and has a trigger and two shots of pepper gel. It claims that it shoots out a pepper gel to a distance of about 13 feet; a far better distance to engage a perp than the "within three feet" for the normal pepper spray container. She now carries that. She's content now that I spent $19.95 on its holster so it will not accidentally mess up her purse. I am slightly pacified, but not totally convinced.

I now carry one of these red *Kimber Pepper BlasterII* thingies from *BULLSEYE.* In theory, if some rude, menacing, huge Alabama fan wants to "beat my . . ." when we crush them on the gridiron next season, one well-aimed shot from this *"Kimber Blaster"* will give me about a thirty minute head start to get away. Should you decide to purchase one, be advised that they come with a five year shelf-life from the date of manufacture. Each package lists the date for its "Blaster." Pick one with the date that gives you the entire five years, or try to negotiate a discount for each year short of five. That said, it is so **in**expensive for the protection that it offers, a "one year carried" is better than a "five year never purchased."

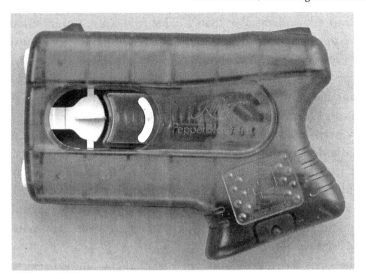

Picture 18.1: A Kimber *PepperBlaster II*: 2 shots, each travels at a speed of 90 mph; range from 2 to 13 feet; OC inflammatory agent, symptoms last 45 minutes.

In addition to the Kimber *Blaster,* there are other non-lethal options: *Tasers, Spitfire* spray with a ten-foot range, and probably many others I don't know about. Even some wasp spray cans are said to be very effective deterrents and have a range up to thirty feet, but it just might be a little cumbersome to carry a can of wasp spray everywhere, plus it may even blind someone permanently.

So what is the point to this long tale? If you're going to carry a handgun, why not carry an optional "first responder" of lesser lethality? Should you ever have the terrible misfortune to actually have to shoot someone, having tried something of a lower lethal nature first, or even having it on your person just might help the D.A. and/or jury decide that you do not view every problem as a "nail to be hammered with a big boom thingy." That said, be advised:

"Violence is seldom the answer, but when it is the answer, it is the only answer." A *Shootist's proverb.*

By the way, several experienced experts do not like this idea. Their concern is that it puts too many decisions into a time frame that is already incredibly short, frightening, and potentially deadly. Their advice is sound advice and from gentlemen who are much more experienced and far more knowledgeable than I. That said, in my opinion, another defensive device is a good option. A handgun should not be **my only tool** for every situation. You should consider whether **you** should acquire some type of less lethal deterrent and carry that even as much or more than your handgun. "Why more?" you ask. Good question, "Because you can carry Mr. Pepper into places where guns cannot legally go." **This is a very personal decision. The consequences of this decision may be potentially devastating—whichever decision you make.**

You may have noticed that none of the above scenarios involved an intruder or assailant armed with a handgun or knife, obviously bent on doing you or yours serious and/or potentially deadly harm. Such dangerous situations are probably fairly straight forward and potentially far more deadly.

If the perp has a gun, you can make several immediate (without further "hem-hawing") decisions that would probably hold up in any legal surrounding:

1. You think the gun is real;
2. You think the gun is loaded;
3. You think the perp has reasonable knowledge of how it works. You know, pull the trigger and it goes bang;
4. You think the perp is prepared to use it to obtain his desire;
5. You think that your life is of little consequence or value to him in his current state of mind.

As a matter of fact, make those decisions now so if that fearful, dreaded situation ever arises, you are already five mental decisions ahead and can concentrate on what, if anything, you can or should do at that moment.

As the Arkansas law states:

A person is justified in using deadly physical force upon another person if the person reasonably believes that the other person is:

(1) **Committing or about to commit a** *felony involving force or violence;*

(2) **Using or about to use** *unlawful deadly physical force;* **or**

(3) **Imminently endangering the person's life.**

There are many scenarios that can be built to describe an armed encounter. Read your daily paper. Chances are that you will have a scenario reported regularly. Not all of the details may be reported to allow you to understand the exact situation, but you can hypothesize and build your own scenario and then visualize several responses. Just remember, statistics indicate that most encounters are within nine feet and happen fast, very fast. The standard time for gunfire fights taught in "shooting schools" is a 2-3 second response time.

To use the "old west" term, if someone has the "drop" on you, initial compliance may be a very easy or a very tough decision. For example, FBI statistics that I have heard indicated that getting into a car with an armed perp increases your chance for harm about threefold. But if the perp is pointing a pistol at your face, well, you have a tough decision: get in the car, try to escape, or fight—somehow. However, in your favor, the perp may be feeling very much in control and not too worried about you causing a problem. On the other hand, he is probably nervous, shouting, acting very mad and commanding your immediate compliance with his demands. You must quickly determine what to do now: comply, flee, or fight. If the decision is to comply, may God help you, because you are in the hands of the perp. If you decide to flee, again may God help you, as you are again at the mercy or aim of the perp. But, if you decide to fight, then you have to instantly determine how you can seem to be in compliance with the perp's demands and at the same time put your body into a position that you can draw your handgun without the perp seeing you do so. Next, you must point and fire before the perp can visually comprehend what you are doing and send the instruction to his trigger finger to pull. Again, may God help you.

You are not a policeman. You are not a bounty hunter. You should not be worried about disarming or arresting the perp. Your only worry is about getting out alive. You probably will not survive a standoff by asking the perp to put down his pistol as you point yours at him. If you reject compliance and flight, then "Shoot" would seem the only prudent action. But can you shoot him? Boy, that is the question for all of us who are basically law-abiding citizens. Let us hope and pray that it will never come to that, but if it does, you have less than 2-3 seconds to make up your mind, so decide now. Or you comply and hope that this perp "leaves eyewitnesses alive."

Further considerations just to muddy the mind: who else might be in jeopardy if you try to draw and fire? Is your wife and are your kids standing there with you as the armed perp points the pistol and demands your money, your wife's jewelry, and your kid's *iPad*? If you start to draw and the perp reacts fast, how many of you will be harmed? Will he leave living eyewitnesses even if you do comply?

The best advice is avoidance, vigilance, and having your weapon in your hand, but concealed, when in any place where a situation is likely to occur. Some sound advice to avoid dangerous situations is to follow these rules:

1). *Don't hang out with stupid people,*
2). *Don't go to stupid places,*
3). *and Don't do stupid things.*

Follow these three rules and it should reduce the possibility that any of the above will ever become an issue. However, perps do come into "safe" neighborhoods. Let us hope that being embroiled in a dangerous encounter never occurs, but meanwhile, we should conduct ourselves with vigilance, be alert, and be prepared.

A Final Perspective

What is the basis for one human legally taking the life of another? When is the use of deadly force by a private citizen against another human considered judicious, sensible, prudent, cautious, careful, justified, well thought out, and should not result in arrest, prosecution, and conviction? How can a private citizen be authorized to kill another human using his own summary judgment? The very simple answer is that **deadly force is recognized as a last resort to be used only** when you need to save your life.

This is often referred to as the "doctrine of competing harms" and/or the "doctrine of necessity." Put very simply, you are allowed to break the law (in this instance—killing) in the rare circumstances where following the law (i.e. not killing) would cause more injury to you or other innocent humans than your breaking the law would.

This is actually addressed in the Arkansas statutes under the interesting title *Choice of Evils.*

Choice of Evils (5-2-604)

(a)   Conduct that would otherwise constitute an offense is justifiable when:

   (1)   The conduct is necessary as an emergency measure to avoid an imminent public or private injury; *and*

   (2)   According to ordinary standards of reasonableness, the desirability and urgency of avoiding the imminent public or private injury outweigh the injury sought to be prevented by the law proscribing the conduct.

(b)   Justification under this section shall not rest upon a consideration pertaining to the morality or advisability of the statute defining the offense charged.

(c)   If the actor is reckless or negligent in bringing about the situation requiring a choice of evils or in appraising the necessity for his or her conduct, the justification afforded by this section is unavailable in a prosecution for any offense for which recklessness or negligence, as the case may be, suffices to establish a culpable mental state.

This concept was put into layman-style language by Taylor Tarwater in the Aug/Sept, 2012, *Concealed Carry Magazine*, page 9: *"The second worst thing that you can ever do is take someone else's life, but the worst thing is to lose your life or the life of a loved one because you didn't act."*

One last word of warning about the use of deadly force: Remember, your decision to use deadly force will be thoroughly examined and re-examined by the judicial system. Here are the results from two cases that plead self-defense.

Lethal Force Case Notes 5-2-607:

A condition precedent to a plea of self-defense is an assault upon the defendant of such a character that it is with murderous intent, or places the defendant in fear for his life, or great bodily harm; **a mere assault is not sufficient to justify the plea of self-defense.** *(Girtman vs State 1985; Heinze vs State 1992)*

Gentle reader, the lawful use of lethal force is a rare occurrence and should be used only in the rarest of difficult circumstances. That said, remember,

"Violence is seldom the answer,
but when it is the answer it is the only answer."

Unfortunately, you may have only two to three seconds to decide and respond.

CAVEAT: I am not a lawyer. I have zero legal training. Do not construe any of the bold font wording or my comments as legal opinion or advice. They are not. They are my opinion only. Consult your own attorney for legal advice or interpretation of laws and statutes.

Chapter 19

Murder in All Degrees
Means Lots of Trouble

I am not certain if this crime category should even be included in this *Companion*. Should you be arrested and charged with murder, then things have really gone wrong. Plus, you will have an attorney, hopefully a very good one—a very good criminal defense attorney. But in the interest of trying to give a quick review of most of the areas with which one could run afoul of the law with a handgun, here it is.

Apparently there are several degrees of murder: Capital Murder, Murder in the First Degree, and Murder in the Second Degree. I have also included Manslaughter and Negligent Homicide. I was unable to find a Third Degree Murder. Perhaps that category does not exist; after all, four would seem to be sufficient, even for lawyers.

5-10-101. Capital murder
A person commits capital murder if:

(1)   *Acting alone or with one (1) or more other persons:*
   (A)   *The person commits or attempts to commit:*
   (i)   *Terrorism, as defined in § 5-54-205;*
   (ii)   *Rape, § 5-14-103;*
   (iii)   *Kidnapping, § 5-11-102;*
   (iv)   *Vehicular piracy, § 5-11-105;*
   (v)   *Robbery, § 5-12-102;*
   (vi)   *Aggravated robbery, § 5-12-103;*
   (vii)   *Residential burglary, § 5-39-201(a);*
   (viii) *Commercial burglary, § 5-39-201(b);*
   (ix)   *Aggravated residential burglary, § 5-39-204;*
   (x)   *A felony violation of the Uniform Controlled Substances Act, §§ 5-64-101-5-64-508, involving an actual delivery of a controlled substance; or*
   (xi)   *First degree escape, § 5-54-110; and*

169

(B)   In the course of and in furtherance of the felony or in immediate flight from the felony, the person or an accomplice causes the death of a person under circumstances manifesting extreme indifference to the value of human life;

(2)   Acting alone or with one (1) or more other persons:

(A)   The person commits or attempts to commit arson, § 5-38-301; and

(B)   In the course of and in furtherance of the felony or in immediate flight from the felony, the person or an accomplice causes the death of any person;

(3)   With the premeditated and deliberated purpose of causing the death of any law enforcement officer, jailer, prison official, firefighter, judge or other court official, probation officer, parole officer, any military personnel, or teacher or school employee, when such person is acting in the line of duty, the person causes the death of any person;

(4)   **With the premeditated and deliberated purpose of causing the death of another person, the person causes the death of any person;**

(5)   With the premeditated and deliberated purpose of causing the death of the holder of any public office filled by election or appointment or a candidate for public office, the person causes the death of any person;

(6)   While incarcerated in the Department of Correction or the Department of Community Correction, the person purposely causes the death of another person after premeditation and deliberation;

(7)   Pursuant to an agreement that the person cause the death of another person in return for anything of value, he or she causes the death of any person;

(8)   The person enters into an agreement in which a person is to cause the death of another person in return for anything of value, and a person hired pursuant to the agreement causes the death of any person;

(9)   (A) Under circumstances manifesting extreme indifference to the value of human life, the person knowingly causes the death of a person fourteen (14) years of age or younger at the time the

murder was committed if the defendant was eighteen (18) years of age or older at the time the murder was committed.

(B) It is an affirmative defense to any prosecution under this subdivision (a),(9) arising from the failure of the parent, guardian, or person standing in loco parentis to provide specified medical or surgical treatment, that the parent, guardian, or person standing in loco parentis relied solely on spiritual treatment through prayer in accordance with the tenets and practices of an established church or religious denomination of which he or she is a member; or

(10) *The person:*

    (A) **Purposely discharges a firearm from a vehicle at a person or at a vehicle, conveyance, or a residential or commercial occupiable structure that he or she knows or has good reason to believe to be occupied by a person; and**

    (B) *Thereby causes the death of another person under circumstances manifesting extreme indifference to the value of human life.*

It is an affirmative defense to any prosecution under subdivision (a) (1) of this section for an offense in which the defendant was not the only participant that the defendant did not commit the homicidal act or in any way solicit, command, induce, procure, counsel, or aid in the homicidal act's commission.

(1) Capital murder is punishable by death or life imprisonment without parole.

5-10-102. Murder in the first degree

(a) *A person commits murder in the first degree if:*

    (1) *Acting alone or with one (1) or more other persons:*

        (A) *The person commits or attempts to commit a felony; and*

        (B) *In the course of and in the furtherance of the felony or in immediate flight from the felony, the person or an* **accomplice causes the death of any person under**

> *circumstances manifesting extreme indifference*
> *to the value of human life;*
>
> (2)   *With a purpose of causing the death of another person,*
> *the person causes the death of another person; or*
>
> (3)   *The person knowingly causes the death of a person fourteen*
> *(14) years of age or younger at the time the murder was*
> *committed.*
>
> (b)   *It is an affirmative defense to any prosecution under subdivision*
> *(a)(1) of this section for an offense in which the defendant was*
> *not the only participant that the defendant:*
>
> (1)   *Did not commit the homicidal act or in any way solicit,*
> *command, induce, procure, counsel, or aid the homicidal*
> *act's commission;*
>
> (2)   *Was not armed with a deadly weapon;*
>
> (3)   *Reasonably believed that no other participant was armed*
> *with a deadly weapon; and*
>
> (4)   *Reasonably believed that no other participant intended*
> *to engage in conduct that could result in death or serious*
> *physical injury.*
>
> (c)   Murder in the first degree is a Class Y felony.

5-10-103. Murder in the second degree

> (a)   *A person commits murder in the second degree if:*
>
> (1)   **The person knowingly causes the death of another**
> **person under circumstances manifesting extreme**
> **indifference to the value of human life;** *or*
>
> (2)   *With the purpose of causing serious physical injury to*
> *another person, the person causes the death of any person.*
>
> (b)   Murder in the second degree is a Class A felony.

Summary of Murder

To me, all three of the above seem to contain the same description of the murderous act: "*knowingly causes the death of another person under circumstances manifesting extreme indifference to the value of human life.*" Therefore, the D.A. would appear to have some latitude in which of the three levels of murder one is charged. Regardless, if you find yourself with one of these charges hung around your neck—call your lawyer ASAP.

5-10-104. Manslaughter

(a)   A person commits manslaughter if:

(1)   (A)   **The person causes the death of another person under circumstances that would be murder, except that he or she causes the death under the influence of extreme emotional disturbance for which there is reasonable excuse.**

(B)   *The reasonableness of the excuse is determined from the viewpoint of a person in the actor's situation under the circumstances as the actor believed them to be;*

(2)   *The person purposely causes or aids another person to commit suicide;*

(3)   *The person recklessly causes the death of another person; or*

(4)   *Acting alone or with one (1) or more persons:*

(A)   *The person commits or attempts to commit a felony; and*

(B)   *In the course of and in furtherance of the felony or in immediate flight from the felony:*

(i)   *The person or an accomplice negligently causes the death of any person; or*

(ii)   *Another person who is resisting the felony or flight causes the death of any person.*

(b)   *It is an affirmative defense to any prosecution under subsection (a)(4) of this section for an offense in which the defendant was not the only participant that the defendant:*

(1)   *Did not commit the homicidal act or in any way solicit, command, induce, procure, counsel, or aid the homicidal act's commission;*

(2)   *Was not armed with a deadly weapon;*

(3)   *Reasonably believed that no other participant was armed with a deadly weapon; and*

(4)   *Reasonably believed that no other participant intended to engage in conduct which could result in death or serious physical injury.*

(c)   Manslaughter is a Class C felony.

5-10-105. Negligent homicide

(a) (1) *A person commits negligent homicide if he or she negligently causes the death of another person, not constituting murder or manslaughter, as a result of operating a vehicle, an aircraft, or a watercraft:*

(A) *While intoxicated;*

(B) (i) *If at that time there is an alcohol concentration of eight hundredths (0.08) or more in the person's breath or blood based upon the definition of breath, blood, and urine concentration in § 5-65-204, as determined by a chemical test of the person's blood, urine, breath, or other bodily substance.*

(ii) *The method of chemical analysis of the person's blood, urine, or breath shall be made in accordance with §§ 5-65-204 and 5-65-206; or*

(C) *While passing a stopped school bus in violation of § 27-51-1004.*

(2) *A person who violates subdivision (a)(1) of this section is guilty of a Class B felony.*

(b) (1) *A person commits negligent homicide if he or she negligently causes the death of another person.*

(2) *A person who violates subdivision (b)(1) of this section is guilty of a Class A misdemeanor.*

(c) *As used in this section, 'intoxicated' means influenced or affected by the ingestion of alcohol, a controlled substance, any intoxicant, or any combination of alcohol, a controlled substance, or an intoxicant to such a degree that the driver's reactions, motor skills, and judgment are substantially altered and the driver therefore constitutes a clear and substantial danger of physical injury or death to himself or herself and other motorists or pedestrians.*

The above negligent homicide statute seems to exclude a firearm related death. Therefore, it follows that if you cause the death of another person by means of a firearm, it had better be a "justifiable homicide." Since there is no "justifiable homicide" statute that I was able to locate, your only protection is under the *Choice of Evils* statute (5-2-604) and its children statutes: 5-2-607 and 5-2-620. (Refer to *Chapter 18 Lethal Force.*)

Per my admission above, I am not certain that this section has great relevance to you, but there it is. Any of these charges are big time trouble, and should you be accused of any of them, you will need a big time lawyer. A couple of the items that are obvious to all but the completely, totally unwary, not-paying-too-much-attention type of reader:

1. Do not drink and drive (Have you heard that before?).
2. Do not pass a stopped school bus (No news here either).
3. Do not draw, present, or put your finger on the trigger unless you are prepared to shoot and you are lawfully authorized to do so. (This, too, should not be the first reading of this warning for you.)

CAVEAT: I am not a lawyer. I have zero legal training. Do not construe any of the bold font wording or my comments as legal opinion or advice. They are not. They are my opinion only. Consult your own attorney for legal advice or interpretation of laws and statutes.

Chapter 20

Battery in the First Degree

The Arkansas statute is printed in *italics*. The **bold** print is the Editor's efforts to highlight those portions that appear to be most pertinent to the average citizen, but not necessarily to a law enforcement officer.

5-13-201.Battery in the first degree
(a)   *A person commits battery in the first degree if:*
   (1)   **With the purpose of causing serious physical injury to another person, the person causes serious physical injury to any person by means of a deadly weapon;**
   (2)   *With the purpose of seriously and permanently disfiguring another person or of destroying, amputating, or permanently disabling a member or organ of that other person's body, the person causes such an injury to any person;*
   (3)   *The person causes serious physical injury to another person under circumstances manifesting extreme indifference to the value of human life;*
   (4)   *Acting alone or with one (1) or more other persons:*
      (A)   *The person commits or attempts to commit a felony; and*
      (B)   *In the course of and in furtherance of the felony or in immediate flight from the felony:*
         (i)   *The person or an accomplice causes serious physical injury to any person under circumstances manifesting extreme indifference to the value of human life; or*
         (ii)   *Another person who is resisting the felony or flight causes serious physical injury to any person;*
   (5)   *With the purpose of causing serious physical injury to an unborn child or to a woman who is pregnant with an unborn child, the person causes serious physical injury to the unborn child;*

(6) *The person knowingly causes physical injury to a pregnant woman in the commission of a felony or a Class A misdemeanor, and in so doing, causes serious physical injury to the pregnant woman's unborn child, and the unborn child is subsequently born alive;*

(7) *The person knowingly, without legal justification, causes serious physical injury to a person he or she knows to be twelve (12) years of age or younger;*

(8) **With the purpose of causing physical injury to another person, the person causes physical injury to any person by means of a firearm; or**

(9) *The person knowingly causes serious physical injury to any person four (4) years of age or younger under circumstances manifesting extreme indifference to the value of human life.*

(b) *It is an affirmative defense in any prosecution under subdivision (a)(4) of this section in which the defendant was not the only participant that the defendant:*

(1) *Did not commit the battery or in any way solicit, command, induce, procure, counsel, or aid the battery's commission;*

(2) *Was not armed with a deadly weapon;*

(3) *Reasonably believed that no other participant was armed with a deadly weapon; and*

(4) Reasonably believed that no other participant intended to engage in conduct that *could result in serious physical injury.*

(c) (1) *Except as provided in subdivisions (c)(2) and (3) of this section, battery in the first degree is a Class B felony.*

(2) *Battery in the first degree is a Class Y felony under the circumstances described in subdivision (a)(9) of this section.*

(3) *Battery in the first degree is a Class Y felony if the injured person is a law enforcement officer acting in the line of duty.*

Battery in the 1st Degree seems to require "intent" or "purpose" rather than just stupid, dumb, careless "recklessness." You can commit 1st

Degree Battery without a firearm, but that is not our focus. I guess, then, if you really, honest to goodness, cross your heart and hope to die, insist that you did not intend to shoot the person, you might plead down to 2nd Degree Battery—which is still a felony with prison time. Suggestion: keep your pistol in the holster and memorize the rules of Good Gun Handling.

Here are the generally accepted Cardinal Rules of Handling Handguns:

1. **Always assume that a handgun is loaded!**
2. **Never point the handgun at an object you do not intend to shoot!**
3. Never put your finger on the trigger of a handgun until you are ready to shoot at the object at which you are pointing!
4. If you are preparing to shoot, be aware of what is in line with your target, both in front of and beyond.
5. Ensure that the handgun is unloaded unless you are preparing to fire it!
6. Ensure that the handgun you are not contemplating firing is unloaded. Eject the magazine; "rack" the slide and eject the chambered round. Visually inspect the firing chamber for a round, and then put your finger into the chamber just to double check. If a revolver, open the cylinder and push the ejector rod and eject all of the rounds, and then visually inspect each cartridge chamber for a round. Now put on the safety, if there is one, and read Rules #2 and #3.
7. *Repeat Rule #5.*

You will discover that the differences between the three degrees of Battery are subtle. I will attempt to supply some level of differentiation in *Chapter 23.*

CAVEAT: I am not a lawyer. I have zero legal training. Do not construe any of the bold font wording or my comments as legal opinion or advice. They are not. They are my opinion only. Consult your own attorney for legal advice or interpretation of laws and statutes.

Chapter 21

Battery in the Second Degree

The Arkansas statute is printed in *italics*. The **bold print** is the Editor's efforts to highlight those portions that appear to be most pertinent to the average citizen not protected by the shield of being a law enforcement officer.

5-13-202. Battery in the second degree
  (a)   A person commits battery in the second degree if:
    (1)   With the purpose of causing physical injury to another person, the person causes serious physical injury to any person;
    *(2)   With the **purpose** of causing physical injury to another person, the person causes physical injury to any **person by means of a deadly weapon other than a firearm;***
    *(3)   **The person recklessly causes serious physical injury to another person by means of a deadly weapon;** or*
    (4)   The person knowingly, without legal justification, causes physical injury to or incapacitates a person he or she knows to be:
      (A) (i)   A law enforcement officer, firefighter, code enforcement officer, or employee of a correctional facility while the law enforcement officer, firefighter, code enforcement officer, or employee of a correctional facility is acting in the line of duty.
           (ii)   As used in this subdivision (a)(4)(A):
                  (a) (1)   'Code enforcement officer' means an individual charged with the duty of enforcing a municipal code, municipal ordinance, or municipal regulation as defined by a municipal code, municipal ordinance, or municipal regulation.

(2) *'Code enforcement officer' includes a municipal animal control officer;*

(b) *'Employee of a correctional facility' includes a person working under a professional services contract with the Department of Correction, the Department of Community Correction, or the Division of Youth Services of the Department of Human Services; and*

(B) *A teacher or other school employee while acting in the course of employment;*

(C) *An individual sixty (60) years of age or older or twelve (12) years of age or younger;*

(D) *An officer or employee of the state while the officer or employee of the state is acting in the performance of his or her lawful duty;*

(E) *While performing medical treatment or emergency medical services or while in the course of other employment relating to his or her medical training:*

(i) *A physician;*

(ii) *A person licensed as emergency medical services personnel, as defined in § 20-13-202;*

(iii) *A licensed or certified health care professional; or*

(iv) *Any other health care provider; or*

(F) *An individual who is incompetent, as defined in § 5-25-101.*

(b) **Battery in the second degree is a Class D felony.**

I warned you that the differences between the degrees of Battery are subtle. (We will attempt to address the differences in *Chapter 23*.) My guess is that the subtle differences allows the D.A. to charge you with the 1ˢᵗ Degree that carries more prison time and a higher fine and then allows you to plead down to a lesser Degree. Next, we will review 3ʳᵈ Degree Battery. However, battery with a firearm will probably always start with a charge of 1ˢᵗ Degree Battery.

It appears that the primary difference between "Battery" and "Assault" is under battery you must actually do the other person some physical injury, short of death. If no physical injury results, it seems to just be an "assault." In any case, if you draw your weapon, fire and wound another person, it had better be under circumstances that the police and D.A. do not consider "reckless," whatever that is, or worse—intentional. Per the above statute, if you are "*the person* [**who**] *recklessly causes serious physical injury to another person by means of a deadly weapon,*" that means you may go to jail.

Go back and read the *Lethal Force* chapter to gain a better insight into what might **not** be considered "reckless." Note that you are also liable for injury to any other person.

CAVEAT: I am not a lawyer. I have zero legal training. Do not construe any of the bold font wording or my comments as legal opinion or advice. They are not. They are my opinion only. Consult your own attorney for legal advice or interpretation of laws and statutes.

Chapter 22

Battery in the Third Degree

The Arkansas statute is printed in *italics*. The **bold print** is the Editor's efforts to highlight those portions that appear to be most pertinent to the average citizen.

5-13-203. Battery in the third degree
(a)   A person commits battery in the third degree if:
(1)   With the purpose of causing physical injury to another person, the person causes physical injury to any person;
(2)   The person recklessly causes physical injury to another person;
(3)   **The person negligently causes physical injury to another person by means of a deadly weapon;** *or*
(4)   The person purposely causes stupor, unconsciousness, or physical or mental impairment or injury to another person by administering to the other person, without the other person's consent, any drug or other substance.
(b)   **Battery in the third degree is a Class A misdemeanor.**

It might be some comfort to learn that if you are just dumb, stupid, careless, did not intend to harm the other person, they were not seriously harmed, and some kind policeman or D.A. decides that you were just **negligent**, then you might get off with a misdemeanor. Even so, just keep your weapon holstered until you or someone close is having a life threatening exposure. Remember the 7 rules of gun safety:

1.   **Always assume that a handgun is loaded!**
2.   **Never point the handgun at an object you do not intend to shoot!**
3.   Never put your finger on the trigger of a handgun until you are ready to shoot at the object at which you are pointing!
4.   If you are preparing to shoot, be aware of what is in-line with your target, both in front of and beyond.

5. Ensure that the handgun is unloaded unless you are preparing to fire it!

6. Ensure that the handgun you are not contemplating firing is unloaded. Eject the magazine; "rack" the slide and eject the chambered round. Visually inspect the firing chamber for a round, and then put your finger into the chamber just to double check. If a revolver, open the cylinder and push the ejector rod and eject all of the rounds and then visually inspect each cartridge chamber for a round. Now put on the safety, if there is one, and read Rules #2 and #3.

7. Repeat Rule #5.

Think of shooting your pistol into the air to diffuse a dangerous—in your mind—situation. The bullet ricochets or just comes down again, as they all will, and hits someone. If that person is not killed, only injured, you might get to plead to Battery in the Third Degree. The good news, you are only guilty of a misdemeanor; the bad news—you are guilty of a misdemeanor.

CAVEAT: I am not a lawyer. I have zero legal training. Do not construe any of the bold font wording or my comments as legal opinion or advice. They are not. They are my opinion only. Consult your own attorney for legal advice or interpretation of laws and statutes.

Chapter 23

The Three Degrees of Battery Compared

The Arkansas statute is printed in *italics*. The **bold print** is the Editor's efforts to highlight those portions that appear to be the most pertinent differences between the three levels of "Battery" to the non-legally trained citizen.

*5-13-201. Battery in the **first degree***
*(a)   A person commits battery in the **first degree** if:*
    *(1)   With the **purpose** of causing **serious** physical injury to another person, the person causes **serious physical injury to any person by means of a deadly weapon;***
    *(3)   The person causes **serious** physical injury to another person **under circumstances manifesting extreme indifference to the value of human life.***
    *(8)   With the purpose of causing physical injury to another person, the person causes physical injury to any person **by means of a firearm.***

*5-13-202. Battery in the **second degree***
*(a) A person commits battery in the **second degree** if:*
    *(1.)   **With the** purpose **of causing physical injury** (omitted word serious) **to another person, the person causes** serious physical injury **to any person;** (No mention of "deadly weapon.")*
    *(2.)   With the **purpose** of causing physical injury (omitted the word serious) to another person, the person causes physical injury to any person by means of a **deadly weapon other than a firearm;** (Apparently if a firearm is used, it is First Degree.)*

(3.) *The person **recklessly** causes serious physical injury* (the word serious is included) *to another person **by means of a deadly weapon.*** ("Reckless" versus "with purpose.")

5-13-203. *Battery in the **third degree***
(a) *A person commits battery in the **third degree** if:*
   (1) *With the purpose of causing physical injury to another person, the person causes physical injury to any person;* (Omits the word "serious").
   (2) *The person recklessly causes physical injury to another person;* (Omits the words "means of a deadly weapon," and requires recklessness).
   (3) *The person negligently causes physical injury to another person by means of a deadly weapon; or . . .* ("Negligence" is added to use of a deadly weapon.)

"Firearm" is only used in 1st Degree Battery; all three use the term "deadly weapon," which actually includes firearms. My guess is that if a firearm is used, you go straight to First Degree. Some major differences would seem to be as follows:

1st Degree seems to require the **intent** to cause serious injury. Lacking the intent to cause serious physical injury would seem to drop the charge to 2nd or 3rd Degree Battery.

1st and 2nd Degrees both have serious physical injury results. So if the physical injury is determined to be "not serious physical injury," the charge may go to 3rd Degree.

2nd Degree introduces the action being "reckless" versus "with purpose."

3rd Degree introduces the action being "negligent" versus "with purpose" or "reckless."

You do not want to be charged with any of these three degrees of "Battery." Unlike "Assault," to be charged with "Battery," apparently you must "cause physical injury," not just threaten to injure someone. Therefore, to be charged under one of these three degrees of battery, it would appear that you must either shoot someone or beat the person with the weapon or some other object and that person does not die from your attack. Friends, be careful!

Battery Degree	Descriptors	Key Words	Penalties
First Degree Battery	1. With the purpose of causing serious physical injury to another person, the person causes serious physical injury to any person by means of a deadly weapon; 2. The person causes serious physical injury to another person under circumstances manifesting extreme indifference to the value of human life; 3. With the purpose of causing physical injury to another person, the person causes physical injury to any person by means of a firearm;	With the purpose; causes **serious** physical injury; by means of a **deadly weapon;** manifesting **extreme indifference** to the value of human life; With the purpose . . . by **means of a firearm;**	Class Y felony or Class B felony
Second Degree Battery	(1) With the purpose of causing physical injury to another person, the person causes serious physical injury to any person; (2) With the purpose of causing physical injury to another person, the person causes physical injury to any person by means of a deadly weapon other than a firearm; (3) The person recklessly causes serious physical injury to another person by means of a deadly weapon	With the purpose; causes **serious** physical injury. With the purpose of causing, person by means **of a deadly weapon other than a firearm;** **recklessly** causes, by means of a **deadly weapon.**	Class D felony
Third Degree Battery	(1) With the purpose of causing physical injury to another person, the person causes physical injury to any person; (2) The person recklessly causes physical injury to another person; (3) The person negligently causes physical injury to another person by means of a deadly weapon; or	With the purpose, causes physical injury. **recklessly** causes physical injury. **negligently** causes physical injury by means of a deadly weapon.	Class A mis-demeanor

CAVEAT: I am not a lawyer. I have zero legal training. Do not construe any of the bold font wording or my comments as legal opinion or advice. They are not. They are my opinion only. Consult your own attorney for legal advice or interpretation of laws and statutes.

Chapter 24

Aggravated Assault: Flashing and Brandishing Can Send You to Jail

If you have watched any television coverage of turmoil in the Middle East, you have probably seen some persons lifting rifles upward and firing the weapons into the air. Apparently, this is a type of victory celebration in that part of the world. You may wonder where the bullets fall to the ground and if there are any innocent victims from the celebratory firing; at least I sometimes wonder about that. As it turns out, so do our representatives. In fact in most cities, it is illegal to discharge a firearm, along with firecrackers.

So, OK, you swear and aver to not engage in that type of unnecessary weapons firing. Good! But having a handgun of a concealed carry variety has some additional issues for you to contemplate. You cannot draw your weapon and fire it into the air or into the ground in a misguided effort to gain the attention of others who may be engaged in some type of conduct that is either illegal, harmful to others, or disgusting to you. (Refer to *Chapter 35.*)

"Why", you ask? Well, because it is against the law and will probably result in you being the one arrested and sent to the "pokey." You have just conducted armed assault and endangered the lives of others. You see, the fact that you did not hit anyone can/might/will be construed as poor marksmanship. It will not be viewed as a low level, non-lethal attention gaining technique. Police and D.A.s are funny that way. Also, everyone in the crowd will testify that they were terrified by you and fearful for their life. Sound familiar? A second consideration why this is a bad idea—is anyone in the crowd armed? You can see where that might lead? So, if you fire a shot into the air (for whatever misguided reason you can proffer), you have now used "potentially deadly force" in their mind and thus, you are now the "perp." So much for your ill-advised attempt to be a "Good Samaritan."

I know, you do not believe me and you disagree. OK, then read the law and make up your own mind. Better yet, call your real lawyer and discuss it with the expert.

The Arkansas statute is printed in *italics*. The **bold print** is the Editor's efforts to highlight those portions that appear to be most pertinent to the non-Law Enforcement person.

Arkansas Statue 5-13-204: Aggravated assault.

(a)   *A person commits aggravated assault if, under circumstances manifesting* **extreme indifference to the value of human life, he or she purposely***:*

(1)   *Engages in conduct that creates a substantial danger of death or serious physical injury to another person;*

(2)   **Displays a firearm in such a manner that creates a substantial danger of death or serious physical injury to another person; or**

(3)   *Impedes or prevents the respiration of another person or the circulation of another person's blood by applying pressure on the throat or neck or by blocking the nose or mouth of the other person.*

(b)   Aggravated assault is a **Class D felony**.

(c)   *The provisions of this section do not apply to:*

(1)   *A law enforcement officer acting within the scope of his or her duty; or*

(2)   *A person acting in self-defense or the defense of a third party.*

5-13-205. Assault in the first degree.

(a)   *A person commits* **assault** *in the first degree if he or she:*

(1)   **Recklessly engages in conduct that creates a substantial risk of death or serious physical injury to another person; or**

(2)   *Purposely impedes or prevents the respiration of another person or the circulation of another person's blood by applying pressure on the throat or neck or by blocking the nose or mouth of the other person.*

(b)   *Assault in the first degree is a Class A misdemeanor.*

(c)   *It is a defense to prosecution under subdivision (a)(2) of this section if the other person consented to the impeding or prevention of his or her respiration or circulation of blood.*

5-13-206. Assault in the second degree.
(a)   **A person commits assault in the second degree if he or she recklessly engages in conduct that creates a substantial risk of physical injury to another person.**
(b)   *Assault in the second degree is a Class B misdemeanor.*

5-13-207. Assault in the third degree.
(a)   **A person commits assault in the third degree if he or she purposely creates apprehension of imminent physical injury in another person.**
(b)   *Assault in the third degree is a Class C misdemeanor.*

Nice try, but I would not want to bet my next six years on using 5-13-204, (c), (2) above to justify the firing of my pistol into the air or ground as self-defense. (You know what I mean. "Judge, I didn't threaten them with the pistol. Instead I fired a warning shot!" Yeah, sure the judge might agree with you, if he is your dad.) Yes, you probably could draw your weapon and face the person or persons engaged in violent physical force and tell them to desist and maybe even live to be an un-incarcerated hero. But do not dare to even put your finger on the trigger, much less fire your weapon into the ground, into the air, or into one of the miscreant's legs. At least do not put your finger on the trigger until you are ready to fire to protect your life or the life of another person, as per the above.

But read the statue carefully:

> *"He or she . . .* **Displays a firearm** *in such a manner that creates a* **substantial danger** *of death or serious physical injury to another person."* (Aggravated Assault, Class D felony.)

> *"A person commits assault in the third degree if he or she purposely creates* **apprehension of imminent physical injury** *in another person."* (I guarantee that another person

190

witnessing you firing your weapon into the air or ground, or even just waving it about, will tell the police that he/she was "*Apprehensive of imminent physical injury.*")

You are not the one who gets to decide if flashing or brandishing your weapon creates a "substantial danger" or "apprehension of imminent physical injury." The police investigate and gather all the facts and witness testimony they can and then send it to the D.A. The D.A. reads the stuff and listens to the public outcry on TV and in the daily paper about some CHCL nut brandishing a pistol and scaring the crowd half to death and just may decide that you are a threat.

So what's a poor CHCL holder supposed to do? Keep the pistol concealed unless you plan to use it, is probably the best advice. You are not a cop. You are not a bounty hunter. You are not a Societal Security Guard looking for an opportunity to become a hero. Call 911 and ask for the professionals who are trained, equipped, and paid to handle these things.

"But some poor schmuck is being beaten to death!" you scream at me. Well, you have completed the CHCL class; you have read the chapter on lethal force, and you have read the above statue. You should make up your mind right now, before the above happens, as to what you should do, after you call 911.

If you see some poor soul being beaten, a bank robbed, a store held up, a woman being abused, **what will you do after** you call 911? Decide now, and discuss with somebody who is legally wise and "situationally" smart. It might take several folks to cover all the bases, but give it some thought before it ever arises, would be my best advice.

As this book is being written, a big alleged sex abuse scandal surrounding Penn State University hit the news. Many are saying what they would have done had they been the person to walk into the shower room and see a ten-year old being sexually abused. That is all well and good, and sort of what I am suggesting. No, not walk into the shower. You know, think it through and decide what you would do before you get thrown into the live situation when all the consequences, laws, morals, and ethical responsibilities get confused in your adrenalin filled brain. Try to decide, before it ever occurs, what is the best course of action for you to take if you ever find yourself in a situation where some other citizen(s) is in trouble.

Be very, very careful of becoming involved in the aid of third party. For example, if that third party is able to defend himself and you enter into the fray on his behalf, you may have just shifted the odds so the perp is now the one facing *"substantial risk of death or serious physical injury."* Unless it is you, your spouse, your children, or your Aunt Harriet, be very careful of getting involved to assist a third party. THINK, and then act, after calling 911. Remember:

"No Good Deed Goes Unpunished."
And
"Fools Rush In Where Angels Fear To Tread."
And just to round it all out,
"All that is necessary for the triumph of evil is for good men to do nothing."

Some Suggestions for Your Consideration:
1. Do not "brandish" your handgun as a threat to others, unless you are ready to take a life.
2. Do not expose your handgun as an intimidation to others, unless you are ready to take a life.
3. Do not assume that warning shots are a good idea. They are not. (Refer to *Chapter 35*.)
4. Do understand that if you expose, draw, or "brandish" your handgun, it is probably a life-threatening act in the mind of others. Only do so if you are prepared to shoot under the legal statutes that enable you to do so.
5. You can shout at the person and inform them that you are armed. You can shout that you are prepared to defend yourself if they do not stop. But your weapon is not being waved about; it is still "concealed." However, my LEO reviewer advises, *"Verbal warnings could be given with the weapon in hand, but we tell our students to not plan on verbal warnings having any effect."*
6. Call 911 when you see a "bad" situation and keep them on the line.
7. **Remember, you are not the person that gets to decide if your conduct creates a *"risk of death or serious physical injury."***

I bet that this has been no help at all, but I have an excuse—I am a 1st Degree Wuss. My advice: consult a lawyer and stay out of harm's way.

A quick comparison of the four degrees of assault:

1. *Aggravated Assault:* **under circumstances manifesting** *extreme indifference to the value of human life,* **he or she purposely: (engages in) conduct that** *creates a substantial danger of death* **or serious physical injury to another person;(or) Displays a firearm in such a manner that creates a substantial danger of death or serious physical injury to another person;**

2. *1ˢᵗ Degree: Recklessly engages in* **conduct that creates a substantial risk of death or serious physical injury to another person;**

3. 2ⁿᵈ Degree: **or** she recklessly engages **in conduct that creates a substantial risk of physical injury to another person.** (Omits word serious before physical.)

4. 3ʳᵈ Degree: **she purposely creates apprehension of imminent physical injury in another person.**

The degrees of Assault seem to go from *"extreme indifference,"* to *"substantial risk of death,"* to *"substantial risk of physical injury,"* to *"create apprehension."* Per the state statutes, the main difference between Aggravated Assault versus Assault in the First Degree is: *"One who commits an Aggravated Assault must act Purposely, but one who commits an Assault in the First Degree need only act recklessly." (Rust vs. State 1986).*

Just to cover all the bases about drawing and pointing but not firing your pistol and the problems that you might face, read the two cases below that resulted in convictions for Aggravated Assault from the mere act of pointing a gun.

Aggravated Assault (5-13-204) Pointing a Gun.

1. *Assault committed where the defendant, after a previous argument with one victim, pointed a gun at that victim and another; although the defendant did not verbally threaten the victims, the fact that a gun is pointed at someone is enough to create a substantial danger of death or serious physical injury to another person. (Harris vs State 2000)*

2. *Evidence was sufficient to support a conviction of aggravated assault where the defendant pointed a gun at another person and a search of her vehicle, shortly thereafter, found a loaded gun with one round chambered and the safety off. (Dillehay vs State 2001)*

Unless you actually fire your weapon or beat the person with it, these are the statutes that would seem to be the most likely for us to stumble into as concealed carry license holders. You know what I mean—trying to be a hero, we draw our weapon and tell the perpetrator to "Cease and desist!" while waiving the pistol around and gesturing sufficiently to get the entire world's attention, and apprehension.

My free and un-legal advice is to keep your weapon holstered; keep it concealed! Get out of harm's way if you can! Only draw if you believe that your life or the life of another person is in imminent danger. It is OK to retreat to live and laugh another day. No one will think the worse of you, and it sure beats spending time in jail to rethink the whole episode. (I will send you written permission to retreat if you so desire. It will be suitable for framing and signed by "Chief Wuss 1st Degree.")

CAVEAT: I am not a lawyer. I have zero legal training. Do not construe any of the bold font wording or my comments as legal opinion or advice. They are not. They are my opinion only. Consult your own attorney for legal advice or interpretation of laws and statutes.

Chapter 25

Police Authorized Citizen's Arrest

Citizen's Arrest sounds like a powerful authority, but to some it also comes with even more powerful problems involved. Such power probably dates back into ancient times to the old "hue and cry" search and chase of outlaws by all the citizenry of a hamlet, village, or town. Under Arkansas law, we, as private citizens, appear to have the lawful authority to make a citizen's arrest; I just have not been successful in determining exactly how we are to go about it. You can make your own determination from reading the statute below.

The following statutes seem to empower the private citizen to make an arrest, but **under law enforcement's verbal authority.** (The Arkansas statute is printed in *italics*. The **bold** print is the Editor's efforts to highlight those portions that appear to be most pertinent to the non-Law Enforcement Officer.)

Arkansas Statute: 5-2-612. Use of physical force in resisting arrest.
Whether the arrest is lawful or unlawful, a person may not use physical force to resist an arrest by a person who is known or reasonably appears to be a:

(1)   Law enforcement officer; or
*(2)   **Private citizen directed by a law enforcement officer to assist in effecting an arrest***

16-94-214. Arrest without warrant.
*(a)   **The arrest of a person may be lawfully made** also by an officer or a private citizen without a warrant upon reasonable information that the accused stands charged in the courts of another state with a crime punishable by death or imprisonment for a term exceeding one (1) year; but when so arrested the accused must be taken before a judge or magistrate with all practicable speed and complaint must be made against him or her under oath setting forth the ground for the arrest as in*

the last section; and thereafter his or her answer shall be heard as if he or she had been arrested on a warrant.

(b)   *Notwithstanding any other law to the contrary, a law enforcement officer shall deliver a person in custody to the accredited agent or agents of a demanding state without the Governor's warrant provided that:*

(1)   *Such person is alleged to have broken the terms of his or her probation, parole, bail or any other release of the demanding state; and*

(2)   *The law enforcement agency has received from the demanding state an authenticated copy of a prior waiver of extradition signed by such person as a term of his or her probation, parole, bail or any other release of the demanding state. The copy shall contain photographs, fingerprints or other evidence properly identifying such person as the person who signed the waiver. A.C.A. § 14-52-202 (2011)*

14-52-202. Powers and duties of police chiefs.

(a)   *The chief of police in cities of the first class shall execute all process directed to him by the mayor and shall, by himself or by someone else on the police force, attend on the sitting of the police court to execute its orders and preserve order therein.*

(b)   (1)   *The chief of police shall have power to appoint one (1) or more deputies from the police force, for whose official acts he shall be responsible, and by whom he may execute all process directed to him.*

(2)   *He shall have power, by himself or by deputy, to execute all such process in any part of the county in which the police court is situated or in which the municipal court has jurisdiction.*

(3)   *For serving city warrants only, the chief of police or his deputies shall be entitled to the fees allowed to the sheriffs under § 21-6-307 for similar services in similar cases.*

(4)   *All fees collected by the police chief and his deputies for similar services shall be paid over to the city treasury.*

(c)   **It shall be the chief of police's duty to suppress all riots, disturbances, and breaches of the peace. To that end he may**

**call upon the citizens to assist him to apprehend all persons
in the act** *of committing any offense against the laws of the state
or the ordinances of the city, and he shall bring them immediately
before the proper authority for examination or trial.*

*A.C.A. § 16-81-107 (2011), Title 16 Practice, Procedure, And Courts,
Subtitle 6. Criminal Procedure Generally, Chapter 81 Arrest, Subchapter
1—General Provisions, 16-81-107. Procedures of arrest, Arkansas Code of
1987 Annotated Official Edition © 1987-2011 by the State of Arkansas All
rights reserved.*

(a) *An arrest is made by placing the person of the defendant in
restraint or by his or her submitting to the custody of the person
making the arrest.*

(b) **No unnecessary force or violence shall be used in making the
arrest.**

(c) *To make an arrest, a law enforcement officer may break open the
door of a house . . . . purpose for which admittance is desired.*

(d) **A law enforcement officer making an arrest may summon
orally as many persons as he or she deems necessary to aid
him or her in making the arrest, and all persons failing
without reasonable excuse to obey the summons shall be
guilty of Class C misdemeanors.**

(e) *The person making the arrest shall:*
(1). *Inform the person about to be arrested of the intention to
arrest him or her and the offense for which he or she is to
be arrested; and*
(2). *If acting under a warrant of arrest, give information of the
warrant and show the warrant if required.*

(f) *The law enforcement officer making an arrest in obedience to
a warrant shall proceed with the defendant as directed by the
warrant.*

Apparently, you, as a private citizen, can make a "citizen's arrest" but
under three very specific circumstances all requiring prior authorization
or impressments by law enforcement:

1.   **The Citizen is directed** by a law enforcement officer to assist in effecting an arrest.
2.   (It shall) . . . be the chief of police's duty to suppress all riots, disturbances, and breaches of the peace. To that end **he may call upon the citizens to assist** him to apprehend all persons in the act of committing any offense against the laws of the state or the ordinances of the city.
3.   A law enforcement officer making an arrest **may summon orally as many persons** as he or she deems necessary to aid him or her in making the arrest.

Unfortunately, about the only guidance given as to how you, the private citizen, engage in this activity is:

1.   No unnecessary force or violence shall be used in making the arrest.
2.   Inform the person about to be arrested of the intention to arrest him or her and the offense for which he or she is to be arrested.
3.   If acting under a warrant of arrest, give information of the warrant and show the warrant if required.
4.   An arrest is made by placing the person of the defendant in restraint or by his or her submitting to the custody of the person making the arrest.

It gives me very little comfort to know that if a "Hulk Hogan" look-a-like rearranges my body parts during the arresting activity, he has broken the law. After all, as it clearly states, the *"person may not use physical force to resist an arrest by a person who is known or reasonably appears to be a: Private citizen directed by a law enforcement officer to assist in effecting an arrest."*

So what non-legal advice can we deduce from the above? First, nowhere does it discuss, imply, or insinuate that you are an authorized concealed carry license holder. Therefore, the above must assume that you are NOT armed unless supplied by the police officer impressing you into aiding him. Therefore, since you cannot use *"unnecessary force or physical force,"* you should be very hesitant to draw your weapon. These statues do not seem to provide the authority to empower you as a part of an armed posse.

Second, the situation must be pretty dire for a policeman to ask for the assistance of some "happen-to-just-wander-by" type of citizen. Thus, you just might be placed into a very dangerous situation lacking body armor, training, insurance, plus being scared witless. Third, you have zero immunity under these statutes to any litigation resulting from your involvement. The Law Enforcement authorities have some, plus they are insured through their political entity, etc. You are all by yourself; so keep that handgun holstered unless your life or the life of the officer is endangered.

If you do not help, at least under one of the statutes, you can be charged with a Class C misdemeanor. The police put their lives on the line for you and me every day. I would do almost anything to aid and assist one in trouble. That said, is being charged with a Class C misdemeanor better or worse than being shot, beaten to death, or otherwise rendered unable to resume normal daily life? You may have an Arkansas CHCL and be armed with some big .45-caliber boom stick, but that license only authorizes you to CARRY. It does not authorize you to draw, to shoot, to become a vigilante, to assume that you are a "Rambo" incarnate, or that you are an unofficial law enforcement person who can do what is necessary to make an arrest.

You have all of the powers and responsibilities shown above without ever having received a CHCL. The fact that you have a CHCL gives you no additional powers over any other private citizen helping under the above statutes. If you are armed, it probably means that you are more likely to get into trouble than the non-armed citizen. You know what I think? I think you need to discuss this whole area with your lawyer. At least think, and then,

"You makes your choices and takes your chances."

CAVEAT: I am not a lawyer. I have zero legal training. Do not construe any of the bold font wording or my comments as legal opinion or advice. They are not. They are my opinion only. Consult your own attorney for legal advice or interpretation of laws and statutes.

Chapter 26

The Power to Make a Citizen's Arrest

Just to ensure that we do not keep this whole area simple to understand, there is another statute that appears to give you, John Doe Citizen, the authority to make a "citizen's arrest" without prior Law Enforcement Officer (LEO) authorization.

The Arkansas statute is printed in *italics*. The **bold print** is the Editor's efforts to highlight those portions that appear to be most pertinent to the non-Law Enforcement Officer.

16-81-106. Authority to arrest.

(a) ***An arrest may be made** by a certified law enforcement officer or **by a private person.***

(b) *A certified law enforcement officer may make an arrest:*

    (1) In obedience to a warrant of arrest delivered to him or her; and

    (2) (A) Without a warrant, where a public offense is committed in his or her presence or where he or she has reasonable grounds for believing that the person arrested has committed a felony.

        (B) In addition to any other warrantless arrest authority granted by law or court rule, a certified law enforcement officer may arrest a person for a misdemeanor without a warrant if the officer has probable cause to believe that the person has committed battery upon another person, the officer finds evidence of bodily harm, and the officer reasonably believes that there is danger of violence unless the person alleged to have committed the battery is arrested without delay.

(c) *(1) A certified law enforcement officer who is outside his or her jurisdiction may arrest without warrant a person who commits an offense within the officer's presence or view if the offense is a felony or a misdemeanor.*

(2) (A) *A certified law enforcement officer making an arrest under subdivision (c) (1) of this section shall notify the law enforcement agency having jurisdiction where the arrest was made as soon as practicable after making the arrest.*

  (B) *The law enforcement agency shall then take custody of the person committing the offense and take the person before a judge or magistrate.*

(3) *Statewide arrest powers for certified law enforcement officers will be in effect only when the officer is working outside his or her jurisdiction at the request of or with the permission of the municipal or county law enforcement agency having jurisdiction in the locale where the officer is assisting or working by request.*

(4) *Any law enforcement agency exercising statewide arrest powers under this section must have a written policy on file regulating the actions of its employees relevant to law enforcement activities outside its jurisdiction.*

(d) **A private person may make an arrest where he or she has reasonable grounds for believing that the person arrested has committed a felony.**

(e) **A magistrate or any judge may orally order a certified law enforcement officer or private person to arrest anyone committing a public offense in the magistrate's or judge's presence, which order shall authorize the arrest.**

(f) *For purposes of this section, the term 'certified law enforcement officer' includes a full-time wildlife officer of the Arkansas State Game and Fish Commission so long as the officer shall not exercise his or her authority to the extent that any federal funds would be jeopardized.*

(g) *The following persons employed as full-time law enforcement officers by the federal, state, county, or municipal government, who are empowered to effect an arrest with or without warrant for violations of the United States Code and who are authorized to carry firearms in the performance of their duties, shall be empowered to act as officers for the arrest of offenders against the laws of this state and shall enjoy the same immunity, if any, to the* same extent and under the same circumstances as certified state law enforcement officers:

(1)   Federal Bureau of Investigation special agents;

(2)   United States Secret Service special agents;

(3)   United States Citizenship and Immigration Services special agents, investigators, and patrol officers;

(4)   United States Marshals Service deputies;

(5)   Drug Enforcement Administration special agents;

(6)   United States Postal Inspection Service postal inspectors;

(7)   United States Customs and Border Protection special agents, inspectors, and patrol officers;

(8)   United States General Services Administration special agents;

(9)   United States Department of Agriculture special agents;

(10)   Bureau of Alcohol, Tobacco, Firearms and Explosives special agents;

(11)   Internal Revenue Service special agents and inspectors;

(12)   Certified law enforcement officers of the United States Department of the Interior, National Park Service, and the United States Fish and Wildlife Service;

(13)   Members of federal, state, county, municipal, and prosecuting attorneys' drug task forces; and

(14)   Certified law enforcement officers of the United States Department of Agriculture, Forest Service.

(h)   Pursuant to Article 2.124 of the Texas Code of Criminal Procedure, any certified law enforcement officer of the State of Arkansas or law enforcement officer specified in subsection (g) of this section shall be authorized to act as a law enforcement officer in the State of Texas with the same power, duties, and immunities of a peace officer of the State of Texas who is acting in the discharge of an official duty:

(1)   During a time in which:

(A)   (i)   The law enforcement officer from the State of Arkansas is transporting an inmate or criminal defendant from a county in Arkansas that is on the border of Texas to a hospital or other medical facility in a county in Texas that is on the border between the two (2) states.

(ii) *Transportation to such a facility shall be for purposes including, but not limited to, evidentiary testing of that inmate or defendant as is authorized pursuant to laws of the State of Arkansas or for medical treatment; or*

(B) *The law enforcement officer from the State of Arkansas is returning the inmate or defendant from the hospital or facility in Texas to an adjoining county in Arkansas; and*

(2) *To the extent necessary to:*

(A) *Maintain custody of the inmate or defendant while transporting the inmate or defendant; or*

(B) *Retain custody of the inmate or defendant if the inmate or defendant escapes while being transported.*

(i) *A certified law enforcement officer trained pursuant to a memorandum of understanding between the State of Arkansas and the United States Department of Justice or the United States Department of Homeland Security is authorized to make an arrest in order to enforce federal immigration laws.*

Yes, Shirley, an ordinary citizen can make an arrest without LEO authorization. Also an ordinary citizen can be authorized by a magistrate or any judge to make an arrest under the guidelines above. What is clearly lacking is full information and instruction on just how one does this "Citizens Arrest" thing? Again, let me repeat in case I have forgotten to mention this elsewhere, an Arkansas CHCL authorizes you to legally **carry a concealed weapon. It does not authorize you to show, to draw, or to use a weapon.** There is a great difference between legally toting a cannon around under your shirt and actually pulling the pistol out, pointing it at someone, and saying, "You are under a citizen's arrest per Arkansas Statue 16-81-106, authority to arrest." The perp just might not be all that impressed with you in your blue jeans, loose shirt and lack of uniform and badge.

It is time for a true story. A friend of mine, richer than Croesus, and his wife attended his company's annual soiree. The occasion was fitting for her to be adorned with the finest jewelry that she had accumulated over the years. She retrieved it all from the safe, went to the gala event, had a ball, returned home in the wee hours somewhat worse for wear.

The late hour and inconvenient location of their safe resulted in all her jewelry being removed and carefully placed on her bathroom counter.

The next day one of the yardmen she had previously asked to return to assist her arrived. The two of them successfully completed the planned yard activities, and she invited this worker, who had been there before and was deemed reliable, to come inside and she would get his money to pay him. While the transaction was being completed, the worker asked to use the bathroom. She supplied directions and after his return she drove him to the bus stop. Upon arriving back at her house, the thought struck her that her jewels were still on the counter in the bathroom, and with some understandable panic, she rushed in to its confines. Yep, you guessed it; the jewels were nowhere to be seen.

In a panic, she phones her husband who cannot be located. She then calls the police. They invite her to come down to the precinct. She explains that she knows the bus and the location where the suspect yardman lives as well as the bus stop where he will get off the bus. She begs the police to go with her to confront the man and to retrieve her jewelry. The police tell her that she must first come down and fill out a report. She speeds downtown to the precinct and repeats her plea for a quick response to catch the suspect at the bus stop. The police person insists that she must first complete her report. Three hours later, report finished, she finally exits the police station, without any escort to attempt to apprehend the yardman who probably has been home for a couple of hours anyway. Sad to say, the jewels were never recovered. The yardman was questioned but there was no evidence, and surprisingly, he did not confess to the heist.

Upon hearing this tale of loss and misery, my significant other opined that she would have grabbed her Sig .380 with night sights and laser and headed off for the perp's bus stop. (No, she did not actually say her Sig .380 with night sights and laser; she just said her "gun." I was just trying to impress you with gun talk.) When asked what she would then do, she said, "I'd make a citizen's arrest! I would wait for the bus. When the yardman got off I would draw and tell him to 'Get on his knees and to hand over the jewelry!' Then I'd call 911."

Now, she may or may not have made a citizen's arrest. Since she is all of five foot two and less than a heavy weight, the suspected perp could have made a "quick meal" of her citizen's arrest efforts. Overcoming that probability, she might even have retrieved the jewelry. But let us view this situation from a bystander's perspective.

A "gentleman" gets off the bus and some old woman draws down on him and shouts for him to get on his knees and hand over the jewelry! All twenty-three witnesses on the bus testify to this. The perp states that he was fearful for his life. Now just suppose that one or more of those witnesses had been prudent and had previously procured an Arkansas CHCL to protect themselves from robbery in their "tough" neighborhood. Now just suppose that they were sitting there on the bus too, armed and safe. What do you think might have been the outcome?

If you were on that bus, what would be your conclusion? Would you get involved to stop what looked from all appearances to be an armed robbery? Would you shoot if the old lady turned to face you with her gun still sticking out? Would she shoot back at you, thinking that you were in cahoots with the perp? Could we have a real shoot out at the Route 66 bus stop?

Citizen's arrest seems to be a very tricky thing to me; even if you think you know who, what, where, when, and how. All those other folks standing around lack that knowledge and may have different conclusions.

Think the above is not a good, representative conclusion? OK, we will take the scenario a step farther. Good fortune has a police patrol car show up about the time that the "gentleman" is begging the little old lady, "Please don't shoot me lady!" The lady flags down the patrol car. With some relief, but great irritation, she drops her pistol and kneels on the pavement at the officer's request. The police query both suspects. She explains that he stole her jewelry. "Where do you live?" asks the cop looking around and seeing only the convenience store, a pool hall, and several empty buildings. She explains that she lives in the Golden Acres Subdivision and had followed the bus to catch the thief here. After hearing her long, complete tale, they give the older lady the benefit of the doubt and make the gentleman suspect empty his pockets. Next they frisk him. No jewelry. Guess who is handcuffed, put into the squad car and driven downtown? Guess who hopes her husband is now reachable by phone? Guess who hopes her husband can reach a lawyer on Saturday afternoon? Guess who meets some new friends overnight? Guess who hopes the lawyer can locate a judge on Sunday? Guess who hopes that Monday is not a holiday?

"Where is the jewelry?" That is a good question. Perhaps the "gentleman" called ahead on his "Obama" phone and a "Fence" met him at an earlier stop and the gentleman gave the jewelry to him. Instead of a "Fence," perhaps he called his wife, girlfriend, brother, or someone else and they met him and took the jewelry. Maybe he did not take the jewelry at all. Perhaps another of the yard crew had overheard the conversation and knew that there would be several hours when the lady and the "gentleman" would be digging in the backyard and came and went before they had finished. My point: what you think you know to make a *citizen's arrest* may not be what others perceive or even what actually transpired.

I wish that there was a little bit, no, a lot more detail on just how one does a "citizen's arrest." Have you read *Chapter 25*?

Remember: *"Stupid will get you killed."*

CAVEAT: I am not a lawyer. I have zero legal training. Do not construe any of the bold font wording or my comments as legal opinion or advice. They are not. They are my opinion only. Consult your own attorney for legal advice or interpretation of laws and statutes.

Chapter 27

Municipal Firearm Ordinances and Codes

One might argue that in Arkansas, we are fortunate that the State Legislature has limited the power of counties, cities, towns, and municipalities to enact additional firearms laws. The state did authorize one power to the municipalities. They can pass ordinances concerning the discharge of firearms. Yep, you guessed it, about every one of them jumped on that bandwagon and passed a law making the discharge of a firearm within their limits illegal. The City of Little Rock even went further and controls the use of various bows, air rifles, and pellet guns. However, they were considerate and gave permission for the legality of such weapons at an approved range.

To determine what, if any, laws your specific municipality may have dreamed up and enacted, there are two sources. First, you might call your local city attorney or chief of police. The other source, *Municode.com,* is available via the Internet for a small number of participating cities in Arkansas and perchance for other states too. Give it a try, you might get lucky and find your city or county listed.

To access the online site *Municode.com* do the following:

1. Enter *www.municode.com* on your search bar and press "Enter."
2. A purple box should appear on the next screen titled *Access to Municipal Codes* with several options within. "Click" on the option *Search Free Municipal Code Library.*
3. Next a map of the U.S should appear. Either "Click" over the location for *AR* or click on the arrow for the "drop down list box" and select *"Arkansas"* and then click on *"GO."*
4. The next screen: *Ordinances and Minutes for the State of Arkansas Are Listed Below.* This screen lists the participating cities in alphabetic order. If your city is listed, "Click" on your city.

5. On the next screen, enter "firearms" in the *Search* box and click "GO."

6. The next screen lists all ordinances that contain the word *firearms*. Click on each listed ordinance to read the entire detail.

To provide some examples, here are the firearm controls for the City of Little Rock.

City of Little Rock: Sec. 18-102.—Discharge of firearms, air guns, etc.

The discharging or firing of any weapon, bow instrument where the pull of the bow is forty (40) pounds or more, compound bow, crossbow, recurved bow, long bow, air rifle, pellet gun, or firearm of any description within the city is prohibited with the following exceptions:

(1) When discharged or fired by a duly certified law enforcement officer when necessary in the performance of his duty.

(2) The chief of police may issue a permit to a licensed and qualified pest exterminator with the state authorizing the use of either an air rifle, air gun, or pellet gun for the purpose of eradicating pests causing injury or damage to property, or the existence of which creates a health hazard within this city. Such permit will restrict the use of such weapon to a designated area, for a limited period of time and to a specific person, and shall identify specifically the weapon to be used.

(3) The discharge of any weapon by a certified law enforcement or regulatory officer of any local, state or federal agency if the discharge is necessary to the performance of the officer's duty.

(4) The discharge of any bow instrument where the pull of the bow is forty (40) pounds or more, compound bow, crossbow, recurved bow, long bow, or firearm on any public or private archery, rifle or pistol range, or shooting gallery, approved for use in writing by the chief of police.

(5) The discharge of any bow instrument where the pull of the bow is forty (40) pounds or more, compound bow, crossbow, recurved bow, long bow, at a stationery target on the person's property, or upon property for which the person has the owner's permission to

practice, if the stationery target is set up in such a way that it poses no significant risk of harm to any person or property.

For purposes of this section, a weapon is defined as: (a) A firearm or anything manifestly designed, made or adapted for the purpose of inflicting death or serious physical injury; or (b) Anything that in the manner of its use or intended use is capable of causing death or serious physical injury.

For some reason, they also have one just for city parks. Apparently, the authorities do not think that a city park is within the city limits—go figure.

Sec. 22-40.—*Fireworks or firearms.*
No person shall discharge any firearms or fireworks in the city parks.

Furthermore, they take infractions seriously.
Sec. 1-9.—*Penalty for violations.*
(a)   *In this section 'violation of this Code' means:*
   (1)   Doing an act that is prohibited or made or declared unlawful, an offense or a misdemeanor by ordinance or by rule or regulation authorized by ordinance;
   (2)   Failure to perform an act that is required to be performed by ordinance or by rule or regulation authorized by ordinance; or
   (3)   Failure to perform an act if the failure is declared a misdemeanor or an offense or unlawful by ordinance or by rule or regulation authorized by ordinance.
(b)   *In this section 'violation of this Code' does not include the failure of a city officer or city employee to perform an official duty unless it is provided that failure to perform the duty is to be punished as provided in this section.*
(c)   *Except as otherwise provided, **a person convicted of a violation of this Code shall be punished by a fine not exceeding one thousand dollars ($1,000.00), or double such sum for each repetition thereof.** If the violation is, in its nature, continuous in respect to time, the penalty for allowing the continuance thereof is a fine not to exceed five hundred dollars ($500.00) for each day that the same is unlawfully continued.*

(d)   *If a violation of this Code is also a misdemeanor under state law, the penalty for the violation shall be as prescribed by state law for the state offense.*

(e)   *The imposition of a penalty does not prevent revocation or suspension of a license, permit or franchise.*

(f)   *Violations of this Code that are continuous with respect to time are a public nuisance and may be abated by injunctive or other equitable relief. **The imposition of a 'penalty' however does not prevent the simultaneous granting of equitable relief in appropriate cases.***

The City of North Little Rock was not to be left behind. They did their across the river neighbor one better.

NLR Sec. 66-156.—Discharging firearms.

Except as authorized by law, **it shall be unlawful for any person to discharge any firearm within the city.**

Sec. 66-157.—Discharging air guns.

It shall be unlawful for any person to discharge an air gun of any kind within the city, or for parents or guardians of minor children to permit such. In case of wilful destruction of property with an air gun, the air gun may be confiscated by the police.

It shall be unlawful for any person to shoot or 'flip shot' any slingshot or beanshooter.

In NLR, you will be "unlawful" if you shoot a "beanshooter!" Good thing my youth was lived in other locales, or I would still be paying off the fines. And my poor parents would still be in the jailhouse for allowing me to own and shoot a *Red Rider BB gun.* Their crime would have been especially reprehensible as they permitted my older brothers to actually own and fire a *Daisy BB gun.* It sort of makes me sad to realize that I come from a long line of "outlaws." But I perk up when I realize that we all circumvented arrest, have no resulting criminal records, plus did not have to pay any fines. (No wonder we all miss the good old days.)

Perhaps you remember the movie *To Kill a Mockingbird*. In one scene, Gregory Peck was alerted to a rabid dog coming down the street toward his house and daughter. He promptly retrieved his rifle and shot the rabid dog, thus preventing untold misery and potential death for some poor child. Had he done this within the city limits of LR or NLR, he would have committed an unlawful act, would have had to pay the fine, and then beg for some type of court leniency. When one city attorney was questioned about this, he did agree that there were no exceptions to the ordinance, but that if he were in such a situation, he would shoot the dog and pay the fine.

Hey, I don't like it either, but that's the law, as stupid as it may be. Maybe you should get involved and convince all those politicians that there should be some exceptions like: when protecting your life or the life of another.

CAVEAT: I am not a lawyer. I have zero legal training. Do not construe any of the bold font wording or my comments as legal opinion or advice. They are not. They are my opinion only. Consult your own attorney for legal advice or interpretation of laws and statutes.

Chapter 28

County Firearm Ordinances and Codes

Compared to the city codes, the counties do not even seem to be trying, at least if Pulaski County is any indication. Their firearm ordinance seems almost reasonable, probably due to the fact that much of the county controlled area is rural and not citified. Below is the only ordinance that I was able to dig up, but do not conclude that there may not be some other "gotchas" lurking out there. Here it is:

13-1—Discharging firearms restricted.

(a) **No person shall knowingly fire or discharge a firearm within one mile of any residence anywhere in the county**, *without first having obtained the written permission of the owner of the residence to fire such firearm;*
provided, that this section shall not apply to one shooting upon his own land or land which is legally in his possession,
nor shall this section apply to one shooting upon the land of another who has given written permission to such shooting.
No person shall discharge a firearm over a public road.

(b) *This section shall not apply within the limits of any incorporated city or town in the county, nor shall it apply to designated public hunting areas or to hunters while hunting on unposted private or public and/or federally owned lands during legal hunting seasons, as set by the state game and fish commission and/or federal authorities, except* **that the prohibition as to discharging firearms over public roads does apply to such** *public hunting areas, unposted private, public and federally owned lands. (Ord. No. 38, Art. 3, 4-26-77)*

What this tells me is to get someone's written permission before you drive out into the county, find a nice spot, get out, and start shooting at a bunch of tin cans or bottles. Well, yes, you could drive out first, stop, and then go get written permission from the property owner. What I was trying to communicate is that you are not legally alright to just drive out into the country, stop at some likely looking spot, and get out and start shooting. Either you own the property, or you get the owner's prior permission.

I think that part about shooting across a public road is also a state law "no-no." No need to take my word for any of this, go search it out for yourself.

1. On your computer's Internet search line enter: *www.co.pulaski. ar.us* and press "ENTER."
2. On the resulting screen, there will be a blue horizontal bar near the top. Put your "Cursor" over the option titled *County Government.* A drop down menu will pop up. Move your cursor down the menu and "CLICK" on *QUORUM COURT.*
3. On the next screen, along the left edge will be several options. Put your "Cursor" on the *PULASKI COUNTY CODES* option and "CLICK."
4. On the next screen, put "Firearms" in the "SEARCH" entry box and leave the next box with "ALL." "PRESS GO."

To find the county ordinances for other counties, call their local attorney's office. They may have a website or just tell you the law(s) over the phone.

CAVEAT: I am not a lawyer. I have zero legal training. Do not construe any of the bold font wording or my comments as legal opinion or advice. They are not. They are my opinion only. Consult your own attorney for legal advice or interpretation of laws and statutes.

Chapter 29

Some Interesting Miscellaneous Laws

There are some laws that are not directly related to carrying a concealed weapon or handguns, but just might be of interest to you.

I. Body Armor

Arkansas Statute 5-79-101. Criminal possession of body armor.
*(a)   No person may possess **body armor** if that person has been found guilty of or has pleaded guilty or nolo contendere to any of the following offenses:*

(1)   Capital murder, § 5-10-101;

(2)   Murder in the first degree, § 5-10-102;

(3)   Murder in the second degree, § 5-10-103;

(4)   Manslaughter, § 5-10-104;

(5)   Aggravated robbery, § 5-12-103;

(6)   Battery in the first degree, § 5-13-201; or

(7)   Aggravated assault, § 5-13-204.

(b)   As used in this section, 'body armor' means any material designed to be worn on the body and to provide bullet penetration resistance.

(c)   A violation of this section constitutes a Class A misdemeanor.

II. Tear Gas and Pepper Spray

Arkansas Statute: 5-73-124. Tear gas—Pepper spray.
*(a)   (1)   Except as otherwise provided in this section, any person who carries or has in his or her possession any tear gas or **pepper spray** in any form, or any person who knowingly carries or has in his or her possession any gun, bomb, grenade, cartridge, or other weapon designed for the discharge of tear gas or **pepper spray**, upon conviction is guilty of a Class A misdemeanor.*

(2)   (A)   **It is lawful for a person to possess or carry, and use, a container of tear gas or pepper spray to be used for self-defense purposes only.**

(B)   However, the capacity of **the container shall not exceed one hundred fifty cubic centimeters** (150 cc).

(b)   The provisions of this section do not apply to any:

(1)   Peace officer while engaged in the discharge of his or her official duties; or

(2)   Banking institution desiring to have possession of tear gas or **pepper spray** in any form for the purpose of securing funds in its custody from theft or robbery

III. Taser or Stun Gun

5-73-133. Possession of a taser stun gun.

(a)   As used in this section, "taser stun gun" means any device that:

(1)   Is powered by an electrical charging unit such as a battery; and

(2)   Either:

(A)   Emits an electrical charge in excess of twenty thousand (20,000) volts; or

(B)   Is otherwise capable of incapacitating a person by an electrical charge.

(b)   (1)   No person who is eighteen (18) years of age or under may purchase or possess a taser stun gun.

(2)   No person shall sell, barter, lease, give, rent, or otherwise furnish a taser stun gun to a person who is eighteen (18) years of age or under.

(c)   Any law enforcement officer using a taser stun gun shall be properly trained in the use of the taser stun gun and informed of any danger or risk of serious harm and injury that may be caused by the use of the taser stun gun on a person.

(d)   (1)   A person who violates subdivision (b)(1) of this section is deemed guilty of an unclassified misdemeanor punishable by a fine of not less than five hundred dollars ($500) nor more than one thousand dollars ($1,000).

(2)   *A person who violates subdivision (b)(2) of this section is deemed guilty of a Class B felony.*

So what do we learn from this section? Do not sell a Taser or stun gun to a kid 18 years or younger. Although the statute refers to Taser stun **gun,** I am quite confident that the D.A. would willingly include those stun devices that are hand-held and require you to actually touch the person with the prongs. I would not bet between $500.00 to a $1,000.00 on beating the charge by claiming that my stun device isn't a gun because it doesn't **fire** an attached barb. But,

"You makes your choices and you takes your chances."

IV. Miscellaneous Firearm Laws

A.   Certain Firearms are banned.

Under Arkansas law, it is **illegal to even possess** the following:

1.   *A rifle with a barrel length of less than 16 inches or an overall length of less than 26 inches. (Statute 5-1-102.)*
2.   *A shotgun with a barrel length of less than 18 inches or an overall length of less than 26 inches. (Statute: 5-1-102)*
3.   *Any firearm with the serial or registration number removed, defaced, or marred. (Possession of a defaced firearm is a Class D felony.)*

Why the first two are big deal laws is a mystery to me. By all reputes, a sawed off 12-gauge shotgun with "00" or "000" buckshot is the optimum home defense firearm. (Send me information if you have the good logic for this law).

B.   Do Not Drink and Carry.

The director shall revoke the license of any licensee who has pleaded guilty or nolo contendere to or been found guilty of an alcohol-related offense committed while carrying a handgun. (Statute 5-73-312.)

"If I'm carrying, isn't it OK to have one beer or one glass of wine? Is it OK to have two? Well what about three?" Well, imitator of Abraham, unfortunately, these are not uncommon questions. To my mind, it only takes one beer or glass of wine to put you on the slippery slope to jail. Two beers will have you underway. Three or more and, wait, can you hear the band playing, and the words to that old song wafting across the airways?

> *"He's in the jailhouse now!*
> *He's in the jailhouse now!*
> *I told him one or twice,*
> *Don't carry and drink, it isn't nice.*
> *But he rolled the dice,*
> *He drank more than twice.*
> *He's in the jailhouse now!*
> *He's in the jailhouse now!'"*

(Alright, I did mess with the words again.) Consider yourself the designated "sheepdog" for your companions, whether you are the driver or not! **If you are carrying, do not drink!**

Sure, one beer or one glass of wine may not push you up to the legal limit for a DUI. Maybe after two, you are still under that legal level for a DUI. But if some type of incident occurs and you are now explaining something to a policeman and he smells alcohol on your breath, and he already knows that you have a CHCL and are currently carrying, you may discover that he has less concern for your "breathalyzer" results and more for the safety of the community at large. You just do not know what type of day he has had. Maybe he has just come from an accident where an Escalade smashed a family of four into the "Great Beyond" and the Escalade's driver smelled similar to you, like a brewery. He decides that even though you successfully did the "toe-to-toe dance" and passed the math test by counting from 100-to-1 backwards; you are not in full control of your faculties. Sure, you might beat the charges after hiring a good attorney. You may even retain your CHCL. But please, do not set yourself up to be the "Poster Person" for all the media and anti-gun crowd by doing dumb things. For your consideration: **if you are armed, do not drink any alcoholic beverage.** I do not care whether you are driving or not.

C. **Shooting in the wild could become expensive.**
*The Mere **possession of a firearm** in fields, forests, along streams, or in any **location known to be game cover shall be considered prima facie evidence that the possessor is hunting.** (Statute: 15-43-105.)*

Be careful going out into the woods to just shoot; it might get expensive. A Game Warden is a Law Enforcement Officer and may be more heavily armed than the local cop on patrol in your neighborhood. Treat them with the same respect and submissive attitude that you would show to a policeman.

D. ***Furnishing a deadly weapon to a minor:*** *It is an offense to furnish a deadly weapon to a minor by selling, bartering, leasing, giving, renting, or otherwise furnishing a firearm or other deadly weapon to a minor without the consent of a parent, guardian, or other person responsible for general supervision of the minor's welfare. (1) Furnishing a deadly weapon to a minor is a Class A misdemeanor. (2) However, furnishing a deadly weapon to a minor is a **Class B felony if the deadly weapon is: (A) A handgun;** (Statute 5-73-109.)*

E. ***No person in this state under eighteen (18) years of age shall possess a handgun.*** *(Statute 5-73-119.)*

CAVEAT: I am not a lawyer. I have zero legal training. Do not construe any of the bold font wording or my comments as legal opinion or advice. They are not. They are my opinion only. Consult your own attorney for legal advice or interpretation of laws and statutes.

Chapter 30

Laws Needing
Your Help to Get Changed

In working on this *Companion*, there were some laws of which I became cognizant and decided they should be changed. I formed the opinion that these changes in our existing laws would better protect the licensed gun owner as well as the community. This list is by no means complete, but should you agree with any of them, contact your city, county, or state elected officials as appropriate and start pressuring them to make these changes. Enlist other friends with the same interest to get involved.

State Statutes:

1.   The Arkansas statutes should be modified **to clearly** provide indemnity from civil law suits to the shooter when the shooter is not convicted of a felony nor pleads "nolo contendere" for the incident involving the shooting.

    a.   This would prevent the perp, or the perp's family, from filing a lawsuit against you and making you their new IRA or retirement plan.

    b.   But, if you are convicted of a felony in a shooting incident, then the victim could file a lawsuit and seek damages.

    c.   It should also include, if a person is shot or harmed while committing a felony, that person cannot sue the other party(s).

    d.   For example, the law of the state of Ohio has the following, *Recovery on a claim for relief in a tort action is barred to any person or the person's legal representative if any of the following apply: the person has been convicted of or has pleaded guilty to a felony, or to a misdemeanor that is an offense of violence, arising out of a criminal conduct that was a proximate cause of the injury or loss for which relief is claimed in the tort action.* It goes on to list about five other actions from which a "victim" cannot claim relief.

Arkansas does have a "twisty worded" statute in this area. I found this statute one afternoon at the Bowen School of Law library. Not understanding it, I spied a young woman working on a terminal and accosted her for assistance in interpreting the law. She read it, and then she read it out loud. Then she stared at it again and finally turned to me and said, "I'm afraid that I can't help you. I don't practice criminal law." Give me a break! Not even a lawyer understood the thirty-six words. Read the law for yourself and tell me what you think it means.

Statute 5-2-621. Attempting to protect persons during commission of a felony.

No person is civilly liable for an action or omission intended to protect himself or herself or another from a personal injury during the commission of a felony unless the action or omission constitutes a felony.

This is my translation into everyday English of the following: *"No shooter is civilly liable for shooting to protect himself from a personal injury during the commission of a felony, unless the action constitutes a felony."* My questions:

    a.   Is the shooter committing the felony when the shooter acts to protect himself from harm by another felon?

    b.   Is the shooter committing a felony unrelated to the shooting, but shoots another engaged in a separate felonious act, and as long as the shooter is not personally engaged in the other felonious act, he is not liable?

    c.   Is the shooter engaged in a felonious act but intervenes and shoots another person to protect his own or someone else's life from another perp who was also trying to commit another felony? (See how confused I am?)

    d.   Perhaps this law is protecting the shooter, who is not engaged in a separate felony at the time of the shooting, from liability, if the shooting is determined to be a lawful shooting because the person shot was committing a felony?

If you understand what the law means, please send in a full report with case law examples.

2. The Arkansas statutes should be modified to clearly state that if a CHCL holder accidentally and inadvertently momentarily displays a concealed weapon, it should not be prosecuted as an unlawful act.

    a. This would protect the CHCL holder from being arrested and prosecuted in the situation of his concealed weapon being exposed by clothing being pulled back by whatever means.

    b. It would protect the CHCL holder should the weapon fall out of the holster and be displayed.

    c. It protects the CHCL holder from prosecution under any bans on open carry.

3. The Arkansas statutes should be modified to allow churches to make their individual decision about firearms being allowed on their premises.

    a. In the fall of 2011, there were at least two reported armed robberies of churches in the Little Rock area.

    b. Criminals are guided by self-preservation and thus attracted to targets that are, often by law, helpless to defend themselves.

    c. A recent occurrence of a church burglary was in Little Rock in September 2011.

    Two youths armed with 9mm handguns robbed the pastor and members of the Third Baptist Missionary Church on Sunday morning. The two gunmen barged into a Little Rock church Sunday morning and robbed 17 members of the congregation. (Arkansas Democrat Gazette).

    Good job all of you. This was modified February 11, 2013. (Refer to Chapter 15.)

4. The Arkansas statutes should be modified to allow school districts to make their individual decision about firearms being allowed on their school premises as well as who and what training would be required by those authorized to be armed on school property.

a. There have been a number of shooting incidents on school property by "nut cakes." It seems to be a very easy target.

b. Some number of school officials trained and armed just might be a deterrent, even against a "nut cake."

c. If not a deterrent, several armed administrators on campus just might limit the amount of misery the "nut cake" could mete out before being stopped. Administrators on site are faster responders than police somewhere else.

Good job all of you. This was modified March 1, 2013. (Refer to Chapter 15.)

5. Arkansas should permit CHCL holders to store firearms in a private vehicle anywhere the private vehicle is parked except in those places specified in Arkansas Statute **5-73-306.**

6. Local law enforcement organizations may resist voluntarily returning your handgun after some dispute in which you prevail. The Arkansas statutes should instruct the courts to award costs and reasonable attorney fees to any person, group, or entity that prevails in a challenge to an action, ordinance, rule, or regulation that is violation of the Second Amendment rights or the CHCL statutes.

City Ordinances:

1. The City Ordinances should be modified to allow the following defenses against violating the ban on firing a firearm within the city limits:

a. If the firearm is discharged while the shooter is protecting himself or another person from serious physical harm.

b. If the firearm is discharged while the shooter is protecting himself or another person from harm from an animal not under control.

c. If the firearm is discharged by a property owner attempting to rid his own property of varmint(s) causing destruction or unsanitary conditions; as long as the cartridge is of the "Shot-shell" variety and none of the pellets cross the property line into the property of an adjacent neighbor.

2. The crime status of BB guns, slingshots and bean shooters should be modified to be allowable as long as on the person's own property and as long as none of the pellets or projectiles cross into a neighbor's property.

Feel perfectly free to develop your own list or add to this list. Send me your ideas, and if there is another edition printed and I like and agree with your idea, I will include it. (I know, it does sound a little unfair, but after all, I am doing the writing.) Have I now proved beyond a reasonable doubt that I am not a lawyer?

Chapter 31

The Right of Jury Nullification

Jury Nullification is a very controversial area, to understate the debate. Nevertheless, there are many who firmly believe that a Jury has the right as well as the obligation to assure that the law under which someone is being tried is a good, valid, sensible, true law and that it is being applied judiciously.

To digress, in Scotland they have an interesting twist to their trial verdicts. A defendant can be found "Guilty," "Not Guilty," or "Not Proved," in which case the defendant can be retried later. Point being, just because you have not seen or heard of some twist to the law, does not mean that it does not exist. You, as a member of the Jury, have the ability and the responsibility to ensure that the person on trial is being prosecuted for a valid law as well as determining his guilt or innocence.

Below is a reprint from the *Fully Informed Jury Association*, (*www.fija.org*).

I am certain that if this were brought up under an Arkansas judge or lawyer, you would be instructed that it is not valid and not a correct interpretation of the law. A judge or lawyer would most likely say that a jury can not decide that a law just is not a good law and, therefore, find the defendant innocent even though the prosecution has met the burdens of proof for a bad law. But should you ever find yourself on a jury and you think that the government is prosecuting someone for a law that should not even be a law, read below.

Reprinted by Permission

State Language on Jury Nullification
Citizens Must Claim Rights: Founders Gave Juries the Right
to Determine Law
Spotlight March 20, 2000
Some say jury nullification is the most practical way to stop the
juggernaut police state.
By Tom Stahl

The *Washington Post* published a front page story entitled, *'In Jury Rooms, a Form of Civil Protest Grows,'* last year. According to the Post article, jurors are not always following judges' instructions to the letter. The article recounted that sometimes in jury trials, when those facts which the judge chooses to allow into evidence indicate that the defendant broke the law, jurors look at the facts quite differently from the way the judge instructed them to. The jurors do not say, *'On the basis of these facts the defendant is guilty."* Instead, the jurors say, *'On the basis of these facts the law is wrong,'* and they vote to acquit. Or, they may vote to acquit because they believe that the law is being unjustly applied, or because some government conduct in the case has been so egregious that they cannot reward it with a conviction.

In short, a passion for justice invades the jury room. The jurors begin judging the law and the government, as well as the facts, and they render their verdict according to conscience. This is called *jury nullification.*

Dr. Jack Kevorkian, recently convicted, was acquitted several times in the past, despite his admission of the government's facts, of assisting the suicide of terminally ill patients who wanted to die. Those acquittals were probably due to jury nullification. And Kevorkian might have been acquitted again if the trial judge had allowed him to present his evidence, testimony of the deceased's relatives, to the jury. A corollary of jury nullification is greater latitude for the jury to hear all of the evidence.

The Post took a dim view of this and suggested that jury nullification is an aberration, a kind of unintended and unwanted side-effect of our constitutional system of letting juries decide cases. But the Post couldn't be more wrong. Far from being an unintended side-effect, **jury nullification is explicitly authorized in the constitutions of 24 states.** (But Arkansas apparently is not one of them.)

ALL CRIMINAL CASES

The constitutions of Maryland, Indiana, Oregon, and Georgia currently have provisions guaranteeing the right of jurors to 'judge' or 'determine' the law in 'all criminal cases.'

Article 23 of Maryland's Constitution states:

In the trial of all criminal cases, the Jury shall be the Judges of Law, as well as of fact, except that the Court may pass upon the sufficiency of the evidence to sustain a conviction. The right of trial by Jury of all issues of fact in civil proceedings in the several Courts of Law in this State, where the amount in controversy exceeds the sum of five thousand dollars, shall be inviolably preserved.

Art. 1, Sec. 19, of Indiana's Constitution says:

In all criminal cases whatever, the jury shall have the right to determine the law and the facts.

Oregon's Constitution, Art. 1, Sec. 16, states:

Excessive bail shall not be required, nor excessive fines imposed. Cruel and unusual punishments shall not be inflicted, but all penalties shall be proportioned to the offense. In all criminal cases whatever, the jury shall have the right to determine the law, and the facts under the direction of the Court as to the law, and the right of new trial, as in civil cases.

Art. 1, Sec. 1 of Georgia's Constitution says:

The right to trial by jury shall remain inviolate, except that the court shall render judgment without the verdict of a jury in all civil cases where no issuable defense is filed and where a jury is not demanded in writing by either party. In criminal cases, the defendant shall have a public and speedy trial by an impartial jury; and the jury shall be judges of the law and the facts.

These constitutional jury nullification provisions endure despite decades of hostile judicial interpretation.

LIBEL CASES

Twenty other states currently include jury nullification provisions in their constitutions under their sections on freedom of speech, specifically with respect to libel cases. These provisions, listed below, typically state:

. . . in all indictments for libel, the jury shall have the right to determine the law and the facts under the direction of the court.

But New Jersey, New York, South Carolina, Utah and Wisconsin omit the phrase 'under the direction of the court.' South Carolina states: In all indictments or prosecutions for libel, the truth of the alleged libel may be given in evidence, and the jury shall be the judges of the law and facts.

Alabama (Article I, Sec. 12); Colorado (Article II, Sec. 10); Connecticut (Article First, Sec. 6); Delaware (Article I, Sec. 5); Kentucky (Bill of Rights, Sec. 9); Maine (Article I, Sec, 4); Mississippi (Article 3, Sec. 13);Missouri (Article I, Sec. 8); Montana (Article II, Sec. 7); New Jersey (Article I, Sec. 6); New York (Article I, Sec.8); North Dakota (Article I, Sec. 4); Pennsylvania (Article I, Sec. 7); South Carolina (Article I, Sec. 16); South Dakota (Article VI, Sec. 5); Tennessee (Article I, Sec. 19); Texas (Article 1, Sec. 8); Utah (Article I, Sec. 15); Wisconsin (Article I, Sec. 3); Wyoming (Article 1, Sec. 20).

Delaware, Kentucky, North Dakota, Pennsylvania and Texas add the phrase 'as in other cases.' Tennessee adds the phrase 'as in other criminal cases.'

These phrases suggest that the jury has a right to determine the law in more than just libel cases. The Tennessee Constitution, Art. I, Sec. 19, says: . . . and in all indictments for libel, the jury shall have a right to determine the law and the facts, under the direction of the court, as in other criminal cases.

The phrase 'under the direction of the court," omitted by five states, provides for the trial judge to give directions, like road directions which the jury may or may not choose to follow, to assist the jury in its deliberations.

Our forefathers did not intend by this phrase for the trial judge to infringe in any way upon the sole discretion of the jury in rendering its verdict. Although later courts have held otherwise, the Tennessee Supreme Court in Nelson v. State, 2 Swan 482 (1852), described the proper roles of the judge and jury as follows: The judge is a witness who testifies as to what the law is, and the jury is free to accept or reject his testimony like any other.

The Maine Constitution affirms these roles in its section on libel:

. . . and in all indictments for libels, the jury, after having received the direction of the court, shall have a right to determine, at their discretion, the law and the fact.

In addition, 40 state constitutions, like the Washington state Constitution in Article I, Section 1, declare that 'All political power is inherent in the people,' or words to similar effect.

And 34 state constitutions expound on the principle of all political power being inherent in the people by saying that 'the people . . . have at all times . . . a right to alter, reform, or abolish their government in such manner as they may think proper,' or words to similar effect.

For example, the Pennsylvania Constitution declares that: *All power is inherent in the people, and all free governments are founded on their authority and instituted for their peace, safety and happiness. For the advancement of these ends they have at all times an inalienable and indefeasible right to alter, reform or abolish their government in such manner as they may think proper.*

If the people have all power, and have at all times a right to alter, reform or abolish their government in such manner as they may think proper, then they certainly have the right of jury nullification, which is tantamount to altering or reforming their government when they come together on juries to decide cases.

A single nullification verdict against a particular law may or may not alter or reform the government, but thousands of such verdicts certainly do. Witness the decisive role of jury *nullification in establishing freedom of speech and press in the American Colonies, defeating the Fugitive Slave Act and ending alcohol prohibition.*

Of special note is the right of revolution in the New Hampshire Constitution.Government being instituted for the common benefit, protection, and security, of the whole community, and not for the private interest or emolument of any one man, family, or class of men; therefore, whenever the ends of government are perverted, and public liberty manifestly endangered, and all other means of redress are ineffectual, the people may, and of right ought to reform the old, or establish a new government. The doctrine of nonresistance against arbitrary power, and oppression, is absurd, slavish, and destructive of the good and happiness of mankind.

If the people have the ultimate right of revolution to protect their liberties, then they certainly also have the lesser included and more gentle right of jury nullification to protect their liberties. It should also be noted that New Hampshire declares an unalienable 'Right of Conscience': Among the natural rights, some are, in their very nature unalienable, because no equivalent can be given or received for them. Of this kind are the Rights of Conscience.

If the right of conscience is unalienable, then it can not be taken away from people when they enter the courthouse door to serve on juries. The people have an inherent and unalienable right to vote their conscience when rendering jury verdicts.

There is no doubt that jury nullification was one of the rights and powers that the people were exercising in 1791 when the Bill of Rights of the United States Constitution was adopted. As legal historian Lawrence Friedman has written:

In American legal theory, jury-power was enormous, and subject to few controls. There was a maxim of law that the jury was judge both of law and of fact in criminal cases. This idea was particularly strong in the first Revolutionary generation when memories of royal justice were fresh.

Jury nullification is therefore one of the 'rights . . . retained by the people' in the Ninth Amendment. And it is one of the 'powers . . . reserved . . . to the people' in the

> *Tenth Amendment. Jury nullification is decentralization of political power. It is the people's most important veto in our constitutional system. The jury vote is the only time the people ever vote on the application of a real law in real life. All other votes are for hypotheticals.*
>
> *Tom Stahl is a former FIJA Board member and practicing attorney from Waterville, Washington.*

While of lesser importance than other topics, I included this topic primarily because it intrigues me. It does reassert the right of individual citizens to override laws that the politicians have instituted which do not necessarily embody the will of the people. Obviously, we need laws to govern the conduct of society. But do we really need laws that outlaw *bean shooters?* More to the point, in the current political climate where gun ownership and your Second Amendment rights are under continuing assault, you just might find yourself on a jury to try some fellow gun owner over such rights. The above might give you confidence to do something different from the D.A.'s and Judge's instructions to protect those rights. Remember, our "unalienable rights" come from God, not our politicians.

Chapter 32

History Is to the Victor; Facts to the First Caller?

History is usually written by the victor, the winner, or the survivor. Only when a later historian or archeologist stumbles across some previously hidden scrap or artifact are the recordings of the victor's records or writings called into question. It would make sense that the same is true for firearm incidents. The first call to 911 sets the facts of the incident. All subsequent calls, statements, and evidence are probably weighed against the first 911 call. You are aware that those calls are recorded, are you not? There are some reasons for this. An obvious one is to protect the 911 operator from subsequent allegations of failure to respond appropriately. The second is to record what the caller, often the person involved, says actually occurred. This recording is used by the police and D.A. to assist in determining what crimes, if any, should be charged against you. Whether valid or not, it is accepted by law enforcement that the first statements are the most accurate, despite medical evidence questioning this.

Let us review a situation. A woman, Melissa Grey, having finished her after-work shopping, is walking out of the store across the parking lot carrying her purchases. Just as she opens her car door, a malevolent miscreant appears out of nowhere, pushes her into the car, brandishes a knife at her, and tells her to move over and give him the car keys. He will kill her if she screams or does not cooperate. (Melissa Grey had been told at her CHCL class that if you let a felon kidnap you and drive you away, your odds of survival have just plummeted.)

As the felon is hitting her and shoving her across the seat demanding the car keys, Melissa Grey manages to open her purse and pull out her .380 semi. She twists and fires three times at the felon. The miscreant falls out of the car back onto the pavement and is twitching and bleeding.

First Call—Option #1

Melissa Grey calls 911 and tells the operator, "I just shot a man who had a knife and was threatening to kill me. I was terrified for my life. He was threatening me with the knife and shoving and hitting me. I was terrified for my life. He was going to kidnap me and I feared he would kill me after all sorts of horrible things." Of course, the 911 operator is going to ask, "Who, what, where, when, and how," questions. Melissa Grey tells 911, "I am wearing a red coat and I am standing near the light pole with the A7 sign in the Mega Store parking lot on Main Street. I have my pistol pointed at the kidnapper. Please send an ambulance to help save the man's life. Send police, I am terrified."

First Call—Option #2

Melissa Grey is too shaken and distraught to think straight. She stares at the human whom she has just shot. She cannot remember how many times she fired. She feels sick and is shaking. Her pistol is pointing at the man on the ground but is unsteady and waving in circles.

Meanwhile, another person has heard the shot and looks over to see the cause. He observes Melissa Grey holding a gun pointing at a man on the pavement who appears to be wounded. The person calls 911 and reports, "There has been a shooting at the Mega Store parking lot on Main Street. A woman in a red coat has just shot a man and is standing over him waving her gun around. Better send the police before someone else is shot."

You are the responding police officer in Car #54. The basic facts are relayed to you by 911. You are speeding toward the scene of the shooting. When you arrive, do you respond differently?

1. To a kidnapped victim who defended herself and needs an ambulance and police?
2. To a woman in a red coat, who has just shot one man, and is waving her pistol around and threatening others.

There are differences of opinion as to whether you, the person who did the shooting, should be the one who actually calls 911. In the November/December, 2011, issue of *Concealed Carry Magazine*, there is an interesting article by K. L. Jamison critiquing a book titled *After You Shoot* by Alan Korwin. One of the arguments between the two was over the advice to call your lawyer first and have your lawyer call 911. Some other points debated were just what do you, the shooter, tell the 911 operator and what do you tell the police officers who arrive on the scene.

My own personal Criminal Defense Attorney said to me, when we first discussed if he would represent me should I ever have the misfortune to become embroiled in such a situation, *"I've never had a client talk himself **out** of being arrested. I've had several talk themselves into it."* His advice was to say as little as possible.

I have read several articles that discuss the physical and psychological changes that the human body experiences under the stress of a "kill or be killed" scenario. All expressed the opinion that your brain and body shut down some normal abilities while your whole being is discretely focused. Memory is not reliable within some period of time after this occurs. The advice given was to say as little as possible until you have had sufficient time to recompose your body and mind. Unfortunately, the 911 operator and the police on the scene do not operate that way. They want info fast, quick, and immediate.

In the October 2011 issue of *Concealed Carry Magazine* there was an article titled *The Stay Out of Jail Card*. In the article was represented a card reportedly distributed by *The Western Missouri Shooters Alliance* which not only summarizes Missouri weapons and self defense law, but supplies six statements to give to the 911 operator. They are:

1.   Location (of the shooting or incident).
2.   "He tried to kill me."
3.   "I was afraid for my life."
4.   "I defended myself."
5.   "Send an ambulance."
6.   "The scene is safe."

If you join the *U. S. Concealed Carry Association (USCCA)*, they will send you two wallet cards that have statement examples for you to use with both the 911 operator and the on-scene police. As the above, *USCCA* also advises very short, factual statements that assert, *"You were afraid for your life; he was going to kill me; I'm innocent; I'll sign a complaint; There's the evidence; please let me talk to my lawyer."*

I guess you explain to the cop that you are so upset and nervous that you do not really know what else to say or something. You have never been in this situation before. You are about to upchuck and wet your pants simultaneously, and please would the officer let you call your lawyer before you faint. Actually, that is something that you probably should have already done. (Call your lawyer, I mean.)

An example given in the *Stay out of Jail Card* article, also by K. L. Jamison, was the story of the statement made by a woman who had just shot her boyfriend. When asked by the police officer why she had killed him she replied, *"Well, he drank all my beer and smoked all my cigarettes."* Guess what the officer wrote down, verbatim? Guess what the D.A. decided to do? Guess who had to hire a lawyer?

Common sense and the tragic experience of others who have walked through this type of terrible situation would scream for you to go find a good criminal defense attorney **before** you need one. Ask his advice on how you should respond in your own locale. Regardless of that, it is wise advice from others to be very, very discrete and terse as to what you say to 911 and to the responding police. They are not on your side. They are on the side of law and order, as they have been trained to interpret it. They will quiz you for every detail that you will provide. Unfortunately, under such an ordeal, most of us are so grateful to be alive and to have the police there to maintain order and safety we blurt out just about anything. Even if you try to correct what you just said, the cop will write it down as you first uttered it. He may also write the retraction.

"Why did you shoot him?" Telling the police, *"The perp 'dissed' me by staring at me!"* is probably not a good start for your defense.

Have you ever heard of the "Miranda" warning? Are you aware that you are not "Mirandized" until it has been determined that you are a suspect in a crime? Are you aware that anything that you tell 911 or the police prior to their Miranda warning **can** and **will** be used against you? Your statements could be one of the best evidences against you at your trial unless you are very careful and terse under the most extreme circumstances that most of us would ever experience. A key point to support the argument that you, the shooter, should call 911 and establish the first call facts is the reliability, or not, of eye witnesses and their subsequent versions of what they think they saw.

Let us return to the Miss Melissa Grey "kidnapper shot in the parking lot" scenario reviewed earlier. Let us assume that the bystander was the one who first called 911. The police arrive and get his statement. He repeats that he *"heard a gunshot and saw this woman in a red coat standing over a man on the pavement who appeared to be shot. She was waving a gun in a threatening manner."*

Next, the local newspaper reporter, tuned into a police band radio, appears on the scene. She is an attractive young woman and asks the witness, who now realizes he is a key figure in this episode, to tell what he saw. *"Well, I saw this guy, shot by a woman in a red coat, fall onto the pavement. She then stood over him like a female 'Dirty Harry' and pointed the gun at him first, then began to wave it around at the rest of us. It was a little unnerving."* We all have this hidden desire for our own fifteen minutes of fame. That, plus adrenaline, attention, memory tricks, etc. can begin to push us further and further from what we really saw.

By this time, the local TV station crew drives up in a marked van and a crew of five tumbles out. After filming cops, a bleeding torso, and a handcuffed shooter, they come over to the witness. The TV reporter, a shapely blonde, exudes solicitous empathy as she emotes that the witness must have been terrified to see a shooting. She implores him to please tell the viewing audience what he saw; it will be on the 6 p.m. news.

"Well, I was walking to my car when I looked up at the sound of a gunshot and saw this woman in a red coat firing multiple shots into this guy. He fell to the pavement. I didn't know at the time that she had killed him. Boy, it happened so fast there was nothing that I could do to stop her. She just stood there over the guy's body like a hunter standing over her prey. It was a little unnerving, but I wasn't really scared or terrified. In fact, I called 911 right away. But there was nothing I could do to save the guy."

Guess what details the D.A. sees reported on TV? Guess what the D.A. pressures the police to pursue? If it goes to trial, guess which story the witness testifies to as "Truth, the whole truth, and nothing but the truth, so help me God?" Will it be his first report to 911, or will it be the TV recording played for the jury? Guess who has probably spent some time sleeping at the jailhouse? Guess who has hired an expensive criminal defense lawyer? Guess who has learned all the nuances of Bail Bondsmen financial requirements? Guess who wishes she had read this before all of that occurred? (I know, that sounds a little self-serving; sorry.)

There is good logic for you **not** being the one to call 911 after your shooting incident. But there is just as compelling a case for you **being** the one who calls 911. The one who sets the initial facts; who is recorded as a terrified, emotionally distraught victim of attempted murder; who is now concerned for police safety; and who asks for medical aid for the victim whom you were forced to shoot to defend your life. Still, you do not want him to die, etc., etc., etc.

Ken Hanson, Attorney at Law, authored a book *The Ohio Guide to Firearm Laws*. It is available through the *Buckeye State Firearms Organization* (see *Appendix F*). He has a chapter on *"What to do After a Shooting."* He begins his chapter with a checklist. He covers calling 911 telling: that you were forced to shoot in self-defense, to send medical aid, to send police, to identify yourself, and report if any other good or bad guys are present, etc. He then advises telling 911 that you are going to leave the call live but are putting down the phone. When they tell you "Do not put the phone down," do it anyway. In big, bold, underlined print he advises, *"after the police arrive and secure the scene, that you ask to call your attorney and any medical help you might need, and then to **Keep your mouth shut.**"* He goes on to state, *"keeping your mouth shut might mean you spend a night or a weekend in jail. That is a small price to pay."* And, oh yea, while in jail he advises that you do not discuss this with your cellmates; they will sell you out in a New York minute for their own benefit. He further advises, *"Ask any person thoroughly involved with hands-on criminal justice, and he/she will tell you that the majority of criminal cases depend on statements from the accused to obtain a conviction."*

Lacking knowledge of a similar book by an informed Arkansas author, and since he discusses some of the same stuff I have glossed over, albeit from an Ohio law perspective, Hanson's book is a worthwhile addition to your gun library. (No, it will not do you any good unless you read it.) Seek the advice of your own criminal defense attorney as to what you should, or should not do and say after an incident, is my best advice.

"Still you makes your choices and you takes your chances."

By the way, have I mentioned that I am not a lawyer and that my opinions should not be construed to be legal advice or counsel and that you should consult your own attorney?

Chapter 33

A Non-Shooting Incident Follow Up

I am of the belief that most of us have a far, far greater likelihood of experiencing a non-shooting episode than an actual shooting incident. This opinion is based on no real data, but consider the following math. In Arkansas, there are over 100,000 CHCL holders. If there was a shooting incident every day of the year involving a CHCL holder, it would require 273 years for every one of them to experience an actual shooting event. That is why I conclude that it is more likely that I would be involved in a non-shooting incident.

The question then becomes, what do you do afterwards? Well, that all depends. If the police were called and show up, call your criminal defense attorney, and then the legal process will determine what you do afterwards. Of course, you will follow the same type of common sense verbal interaction that you would employ as if it were a shooting incident, right? (Review *Chapter 32.*)

But what if the incident did not escalate to involving the police on site? Then what do you do? Breathe a deep sigh of relief and go home? Call your best friend and say, *"You won't believe what just happened to me?"*

The following is one of those Internet stories that one does not really know whether it is true or just another "Urban Legend Tale." According to this Internet story, it was taken from the *Police Log of Sarasota, Florida:*

> *An elderly Florida lady did her shopping and, upon returning to her car, found four males in the act of leaving with her vehicle.*
>
> *She dropped her shopping bags and drew her handgun, proceeding to scream at the top of her lungs, 'I have a gun, and I know how to use it! Get out of the car!'*
>
> *The four men didn't wait for a second threat. They got out and ran like mad.*
>
> *The lady, somewhat shaken, then proceeded to load her shopping bags into the back of the car and got into the driver's*

seat. She was so shaken that she could not get her key into the ignition.

She tried and tried, and then she realized why. It was for the same reason she had wondered why there was a football, a Frisbee and two 12-packs of beer in the front seat.

A few minutes later, she found her own car parked four or five spaces farther down.

She loaded her bags into the car and drove to the police station to report her mistake.

The sergeant to whom she told the story couldn't stop laughing.

He pointed to the other end of the counter, where four pale men were reporting a car-jacking by a mad, elderly woman described as white, less than five feet tall, glasses, curly white hair, and carrying a large handgun.

No charges were filed.

Moral of the story? If you're going to have a senior moment . . . make it memorable.

What makes me suspect the veracity of this story was the next to last line: *"No charges were filed."* The cops had her dead to right! Four witnesses, a confession, a clean case. There was a list of criminal offenses that would fill a whole page, an officer's delight. An arrest with only the paper work to complete! A slam-dunk for the D.A.! But the point of the tale is that there are times when you are better served by going ahead and alerting the local police to the non-shooting event.

For instance, as you approach your car in the convenience store parking space, a disheveled man approaches you and demands money. You decline. He comes closer and, in an even more menacing manner, demands that you give him some money. You quickly open your door, tumble in, lock the door, start the car, engage gears, and drive off. You should probably call the police and tell them that a man of menacing manner is operating around that store. After all, the next patron to drive up and park just might be your mother or daughter. He may not be so nice to them.

Let us play the above with a slight twist. After you decline his first offer to give him some of your money and he approaches you in what you perceive to be a threatening manner, you draw your pistol and holding it down at your side, you tell him to "Stop! Don't come any closer! I have a gun and I will defend myself." As he retreats and you drive off, do you call the police? Why not? Nothing has really changed concerning his behavior and the potential for the next "victim" to have a less happy ending to an encounter. You might wish to leave out the details about drawing your weapon unless it is really germane. For example, if there are twenty-three witnesses who saw you draw your pistol and "threaten" their own pet neighborhood tramp.

Another twist: you answer your doorbell and there is a tramp asking you for money. You decline and shut the door. He begins to bang on the door and shout. You go get your pistol and return and tell him that you are armed, etc. He persists with his banging, etc. You call 911 and the operator tells you that a car will be sent as soon as available, whatever that means. You open the door and point the pistol into the tramp's face and repeat your warning. Shocked, he turns and runs off.

The police never arrive because after 911 calls back and asks if you still need assistance, you decline. Do you just drop it? "NO!" is the correct answer. "Why," you ask? The answer: because the tramp may return a week later, break into your house, and you might shoot him. By having the prior incident on record at the police station, you have established a history of violence on this tramp's behalf that should go a long way in reducing the possibilities that you will face criminal charges. Plus, just maybe the local authorities would have reacted to your initial, formally written complaint and would have removed the tramp from the area or reduced his freedom to roam. Consequently, you are saved from the horrible experience of taking another human's life.

I guess the point of all of the above is that some incidents should be formally reported to police, even if nothing occurred to warrant their involvement. You just might prevent another citizen from experiencing a "bad day," or document an established pattern of behavior of an individual who thinks society owes him his next buck. That might also aid another citizen if this guy became violent with them and had to be "taken down."

"But, you makes your choices and you takes your chances."

You do understand that I'm not a lawyer and that my opinions should not be construed to be legal advice or counsel and that you should hire your own lawyer, right?

Chapter 34

Self-Defense Plea Rejected

Under the *lethal force* defense, what one is really claiming is *self-defense*. It would seem reasonable that *self-defense* refers to an imminent threat, not a *some-time-in-the-future* threat. Even if that *some-time-in-the-future* threat is only minutes away, it is still a *future*, not an imminent threat. Of course a threat in the past few seconds or minutes is even less *imminent*. An interesting case was reported in the *Arkansas Democrat Gazette* on Friday November 18, 2011, that reinforces this concept. A certain convicted felon (we will refer to him as "Mr. C.F.") had his conviction affirmed by the state Court of Appeals. Mr. C.F. claimed in his appeal *"he was justified in shooting to defend himself."*

The shooting saga apparently started in a bar and had a woman, some marijuana, and "foul" comments involved. An altercation ensued and a "Mr. Victim" ran from the bar and Mr. C.F. pursued him. Mr. Victim apparently tried to get into his truck to flee, but bad luck intervened—the door was locked. Mr. C.F. took this opportunity to fire several shots at Mr. Victim.

Mr. Victim was apparently *"struck in the arm,"* and deciding that flight was better than valor, took off running. Witnesses testified that Mr. Victim attempted to hide as Mr. C.F. *"drove around the neighborhood and found"* Mr. Victim. *"Shooting from the driver's side window,"* Mr. C.F. successfully placed several more rounds into Mr. Victim.

The police evidence reported that Mr. Victim's truck had six bullet holes and Mr. Victim had five bullet holes in him, four of which were apparently received while attempting to hide in the neighborhood. Mr. C.F. alleged that he took Mr. Victim's gun when it fell to the bar floor but thought that Mr. Victim *"might try to get another one from the truck."* Mr. C.F. alleged that he fired only after Mr. Victim *"rushed at him and threatened to kill him."* He denied chasing Mr. Victim down to continue shooting him.

So, what can we learn from this? Well first, it is not a wise move to go to a bar and get involved with marijuana, "foul" comments, and a woman. Secondly, do not drop your pistol on the floor. In fact, do not take your pistol into a bar. (You do remember that it is illegal to carry a concealed weapon into an establishment that serves alcohol, wine or beer?) So, Mr. Victim is guilty of placing himself in danger by breaking the law. Still, I will agree that infraction did not warrant a death penalty.

But back to the main point; Mr. C.F. was no longer in imminent danger after he picked up the pistol and Mr. Victim fled the premises. Following Mr. Victim outside made Mr. C.F. less a person needing to protect himself from imminent danger and placed him more in the role of a **hunter**. At least that appears to be the conclusion of the jury in the original trial and the judges in the Court of Appeals.

So what do we learn from this? Once imminent danger is past, call 911 and let the police handle the hunt for Mr. Victim. Pursuing a threatening individual makes you the hunter, not the hunted. I know, you are saying that I am stating the obvious. So why did we even discuss this, you ask?

Let us move the site from the bar to your house. There you are, facing "Mr. Potential Victim." We will refer to him as "Mr. P.V." There he is. Whether he broke in, crawled through a window, sneaked in through an unlocked door or whatever, he is there facing you, intent on doing you or "your'n" no good.

Suddenly, you have the only firearm. Whether his, yours, or the Preacher's is not the point. He turns and flees out the door. Even if he is leaving with your Aunt Harriet's tiara, you **do not** "pop off" a few rounds at him. Unless he is dragging your wife, child, or Aunt Harriet out the door with him, you have won! Let him go! Do not pursue Mr. P.V.! Do not follow him out the door and "pop off" a few rounds as Mr. P.V. attempts to open his vehicle door, or yours. Do not jump into your car and chase after him thinking that you have become a vigilante and you are going to catch the scumbag.

You won when he turned and fled. Yes, you should observe his retreat to ensure that he does not go to a vehicle and return fully armed with an AK-47 or augmented by thirteen friends. Call 911. Give a complete description of the perp, the vehicle, if any, and the direction of flight. Turn this over to the police. They are very good at tracking down miscreants by description, vehicles tags or description, similar crimes, etc.

My friend John smiled and explained that at his CHCL class someone opined that if you do shoot someone, make certain that you drag the body inside your house! People, you and I have watched sufficient *CSI* episodes on TV to know that *Gus Grissom* or someone will determine from blood splatter, scuff marks, body hair, body lividity, phase of the moon, shell striations or something else that you dragged the body inside.

You also know from the above TV viewings that messing with a crime scene is a "no-no." Once the perp has turned to flee, you cannot legally shoot the scumbag. However, if this event occurred outside your house on your "curtilage" and he was not fleeing, but coming after you, should you shoot him, leave the body lie. Do not attempt to drag it inside the house. You can protect yourself on your "curtilage" as well as inside your home. (Don't you just love the word "curtilage," whatever it means?)

CAVEAT: I am not a lawyer. I have zero legal training. Do not construe any of the bold font or my comments as legal opinion or advice. They are not. They are my opinion only. Consult your own attorney for legal advice or interpretation of laws and statutes!

Chapter 35

Shooting into the Air Is a Bad Thing

Most of us would heartily agree that we are quite happy to live here in the good old U.S.A. and not in some Middle Eastern locale where the firing of weapons randomly into the air is viewed as some type of celebratory action, with total disregard of where the bullets eventually come to ground. When we see such behavior we think that it is a pretty stupid act. However, the thought, if not the outright question that often arises, is "What about firing a warning shot?" One hundred percent of the experts will tell you this is a bad idea. There are many reasons for this position in addition to the main one—you have no clue where the bullet may come to ground and what damage it might inadvertently cause when it does. In the October, 2011 issue of *Concealed Carry Magazine*, George Harris wrote an article that addressed this very subject. He stated, *"I know of two people who have been hit, one fatally, by bullets shot into the air by people far away with no thought of where the bullet would actually come to rest."*

Not convinced? Then how about a few additional, recently reported real life episodes? Per the local press, on or about December 7, 2011,

> *Arkansas State University police arrested a student Wednesday after his gun was accidentally fired while he was showing it to a friend.* (We'll refer to the participants by initials.) *R.D., 22 . . . faces a felony charge of possession of a firearm on school property, according to the campus police report. K.G., 20 . . . accidentally fired R.D.'s .357-caliber revolver through an open window in the . . . dorm after he reloaded its cylinder, the arrest report said . . . Police charged K.G. with discharge of a firearm within city limits, a violation of a city ordinance.*

Not even accidental discharges are forgiven by the law. And note, the felony charge went to the owner/possessor, not to the shooter. Luckily, the bullet apparently came to ground without further repercussions, or the ordeal would have been much worse. (By the way, in Arkansas, a felony conviction sort of ends your right to own or carry a firearm.) It was reported on October 30, 2011, in Richardson, Texas,

> *Shots in the air break up fight at church. A 22-year-old man fired a gun inside a church to break up a fight, police said. No one was injured. The Dallas Morning News reported that a group of people had gathered Friday night at the church . . . when some others arrived about 10 p.m. Richardson police . . . said the groups began fighting and one man who had been at the church pulled out a gun and fired several times into the air. The groups dispersed.*

Rewarded for being a Good Samaritan, right? He used his pistol to prevent an altercation that might have resulted in severe injuries or even fatalities, right? Stopped all further problems; a hero, right? Think the police cut the man any slack? *"Officers **arrested the man who was charged** with discharging a weapon in a public place, a Class B misdemeanor. (Police) called the gunfire effective, but it was a poor decision."* Even the police called the action *"effective,"* but the law trumps good intentions. (In Arkansas, concealed firearms may or may not be prohibited in houses of worship. Refer to Chapter 15, paragraph 16.) It's my suspicion that the above D.A. cut the shooter some slack in this instance as they usually pile on the charges. (One does wonder what two groups were fighting about at a church. Perhaps they were fighting over the efficacy of grape juice versus wine?)

Another real incident from the December 23, 2011, *Arkansas Democrat Gazette:* the headline shouts, *"Mall fray started by stare, says man shot. **Bullet aimed in air**, ricocheted, pal says."* The article goes on to explain,

> *The 20-year-old shot outside a North Little Rock shopping center told police that the shooting started with an errant stare inside the mall. According to police reports, [victim], 20, was walking around the west wing of the mall with some friends about 6:55 pm when they came across a group of four unknown black males' who were 'staring' at them. 'What y'all looking at?' one of [victim's] friends asked. The two*

groups began arguing and [victim], [now referred to as the
loud mouthed victim], *asked them whether they wanted 'to
box'. . . . The two groups walked outside to fight . . . and as
soon as they were outside, one of the bigger unknown males
pulled out a handgun and fired at least one shot at* [victim].'
*The victim's friend, who was standing next to him recounts,
'Man, we didn't know them from a can of paint. They just
followed us out there . . . .' According to* [friend], *'the gunman
pointed in the air when he fired.'* [This witness], *'Doesn't
think that the shot was meant for his friend. It was a ricochet
because we all heard it ding off of something.*

That is all we know, but fantasize with me on this. Just suppose
that *"one of the bigger unknown males"* who pulled out the pistol was the
only intelligent guy in the two gangs. He understood that nothing good
was going to come out of a gang fight and maybe a bunch of bad—like
knives, lost teeth, etc. So he decides to calm down the whole scene by
firing his pistol into the air. Not trying to harm anyone, just trying to get
everyone's attention and to calm things down and get everyone to back
off. (Maybe he had heard about the Richardson, Texas church incident
where shooting in the air had dispersed those two groups.) Well the
"Law of Unintended Consequences" showed up at that very minute and
stood in front of the bullet, ricocheting it back into the "loud-mouthed
victim." (Forget any thought of poetic justice here.)

Now, humor me and trade places with the big dude shooter. You are
in a gang confrontation because you "stared" at one of them, and they
followed you outside and now are confronting you. You draw and fire
into the air as a warning. Your bullet ricochets and hits "loudmouth,"
who has been doing all the trash talking about what he's "going to do
with your butt."

Guess who gets arrested? Guess who goes to jail? Guess who gets to
hire a lawyer? Guess who loses his handgun and his CHCL? Guess who
gets sued in civil court by "loudmouth," alleging you caused him injuries
that prevent him from working for the rest of his life? Guess who gets
sued by "loudmouth's" girlfriend who alleges "loudmouth" can no longer
perform his conjugal duties? Guess who has an expensive criminal trial
coming up soon? Guess who wishes he had read this first? (Yeah, I know,
I've done it again, but you see my point.)

New Year's Celebrations seems to turn off the brain in many folks. It was reported that the Little Rock police received over two hundred-fifty "shots fired" calls on New Year's Eve, 2011. I hope that none of the intellectually challenged who were doing this shooting were also CHCL holders. Folks who have a CHCL need to be very law abiding. The woods are full of fuzzy minded, politically correct liberals who want nothing better than to end your right to own a gun and to carry a concealed weapon.

Firing into the air is not a harmless, victimless celebratory demonstration. You can harm or kill someone. A bullet leaves the barrel of a handgun traveling at speeds from about 800 fps (feet per second) to 1,300 fps. A bullet descends at the speed of around 600 fps. At 200 fps, a bullet can penetrate the skin. At 600 fps, it not only penetrates skin, but also organs; think lung, heart, liver, etc. It is traveling at about half its original speed and at that reduced speed will not "pass through," therefore all of its kinetic energy impacts the unintended target. Example: a .45-caliber ACP FMJ round leaves the muzzle at approximately 850 fps. That is its full kill speed. It would return to earth at about 75% of its initial kill speed—600 fps. That is still sufficiently fast to penetrate, wound, maim, and kill an unintended victim.

Speaking of kinetic energy, bullets travel a long distance. From the local paper on Sunday January 15, 2012:

> *Edinburg, Texas—Doctors have removed a bullet from the back of a 13-year-old Texas boy shot while trying out for his middle school basketball team in December.* (the boy) *still does not have feeling in his legs. On Jan.6, authorities charged Dustin Wesley Cook with aggravated assault in the shooting. Cook was target shooting with a sniper rifle on ranchland nearly a mile away but in line with the school.*

My point is this: Do **NOT** fire warning shots to diffuse a situation; **bad things WILL happen.** You can book this and take it to the bank—or to the jailhouse! And PLEASE don't shoot to WOUND to diffuse a bad situation. The cops, the D.A., your lawyer, all your friends, and even your mother will assume that you were just a poor shot! In the same *Concealed Carry Magazine* article mentioned above was this admonition against shooting to wound.

Once the trigger is pulled and the projectile launched, you have no control over the damage the projectile inflicts on the target. (Regardless of what you intentions were.) The article goes on to say, *For example, there are just a few millimeters of difference between a painful flesh wound that would in all likelihood heal without complications and a breach of the femoral artery of the upper leg, which often results in death.*

Consider this: it is generally reported that 80% of all law enforcement shots fired in a gunfight miss the target. Of the 20% that do hit the target, more than 80% of those hits are non-lethal. These statistics will support the D.A.'s argument that if a trained policeman is that poor a shot under duress, your marksmanship is also just as suspect, if not more suspect. No, your "warning shot" or "shoot-to-wound shot" will be charged as an intentional act to kill; it was just fired by a very poor shot.

A Concealed Handgun Carry License only affords you one legal right: to carry a concealed handgun. It does NOT provide the legal right to draw, threaten, shoot into the air or the ground, or to wound. You can lawfully use lethal force only to save your life or the life of another. Nothing is said about a handgun in that statute. You could just as well use an axe, a knife, a baseball bat, a brick, a bow and arrow, a black iron skillet, a rock, or if not in North Little Rock, a bean-shooter. Carrying a concealed weapon gives you no additional authority to do something dumb.

"But, you makes your choices and you takes your chances."

(Sometimes I get a little "preachy" but I come by it naturally—I'm married with children.)

CAVEAT: I am not a lawyer. I have zero legal training. Do not construe any of the bold font or my comments as legal opinion or advice. They are not. They are my opinion only. Consult your own attorney for legal advice or interpretation of laws and statutes!

Chapter 36

Airports Are Dangerous Places for CHCL Holders

Statistics reported by various states substantiate the fact that CHCL holders as a group are very responsible and safe citizens. The number of concealed carry licenses revoked is very few, less than one-tenth of one percent. (Would that most groups were as reliable as CHCL holders are.) Nevertheless, there are those situations where the CHCL holder runs afoul of the law.

There is evidence available to substantiate this claim of concealed carry license holders being very responsible citizens. In his book, John Lott recounts the following:

> *Between October 1, 1987, when Florida's 'concealed carry' law took effect, and the end of 1996, over 380,000 licenses had been issued, and only 72 [0.00019%] had been revoked because of crimes committed by the license holders (most of which did not involve the permitted gun). Dade County records indicate that four crimes involving a permitted handgun took place there between September, 1987, and August, 1992, and none of those cases resulted in injury. Multnomah County, Oregon, issued 11,140 permits over the period from January, 1990, to October, 1994; only five permit holders were involved in shootings, [0.0004%], three of which were considered justified by the grand juries.*

There have been very few revocations of permits from crime related incidents and few have to do with misuse of a firearm by an honest CHCL citizen. But the one area that continues to make the newspaper headlines is the arrest of CHCL holders attempting to board an airplane with a concealed weapon. (No, I'm not implying that you lose your CHCL. This offense is usually a misdemeanor and that **may** protect you from revocation of your CHCL unless you make a habit of it. Call the state police to verify this; they won't return my calls.)

In the past two years, about twenty people have been stopped by airport security at Little Rock's Adam's Field for having a concealed weapon on their person or in their carry-on baggage. Not in one single incident was it determined that the "miscreant" had any type of illegal intent. To a woman (OK, to a man too) they were all innocent, forgetful, stupid, dumb, very costly, and embarrassing mistakes.

As reported in our faithful *Arkansas Democrat Gazette:* on Christmas Day, 2011,

> *Gun found in bag at airport security. Two days after a woman was arrested for taking a handgun through security at Little Rock National Airport, Adams Field, a Murfreesboro man was arrested on the same offense police say.* [The man] *was arrested about 6:45 a.m. Saturday and charged with carrying a weapon, a misdemeanor.* [He] *was moving through a Transportation Security Administration checkpoint when a .22-caliber Beretta handgun was found in his carry-on bag, police said. The report did not specify whether the gun was loaded.* [He] *was booked into the Pulaski County jail. He received a citation to appear in court and was released from custody. At least eleven people have been arrested at the airport this year for attempting to carry handguns onto planes. The most recent arrest was Thursday, when a loaded .38-caliber Taurus handgun was found in a carry-on bag belonging to a Little Rock woman.*

What can we learn from this report? First, what a miserable way to start Christmas Day. This should prove to any of you who may have doubted, Airport Security has no sense of Christmas spirit and no sense of humor. Second, he was carrying a Beretta .22-caliber. The woman has more gun-sense as she had been carrying, prior to its confiscation, a .38-caliber Taurus. What was the man planning to do—shoot mice? To his credit, a Beretta is a very fine weapon; at least he was "small-calibered" in a non-cheap weapon.

More important, there is no, "Oh, gee, I'm so sorry, I forgot," accepted. You get caught with a weapon entering a government or other prohibited building or location with guards and detection devices, there is no, none, nada, zero forgiveness and second chances. You are de-armed, handcuffed, arrested, taken to the pokey, booked, charged (apparently with a misdemeanor, the only lucky break in the entire miserable experience), given a court date, and if lucky, released on your own recognizance. Next, you call your lawyer and you both show up at court. (I am not certain when the lawyer's meter starts running, but think of something in the neighborhood of $1,500.00 to $2,500.00 for this experience, plus fine and the cost of parking.)

Apparently, whether the weapon is loaded or not may make some difference with the judge. In one newspaper article, a woman, guilty of this same forgetfulness, was blessed to have emptied her gun into an armadillo the night before and tossed it (the emptied gun, not the armadillo) back into her purse. When found at the airport, she underwent all the above indignities and embarrassment, but at the court hearing was only fined $1,500.00. For that amount of money, you can buy at least three nice handguns or go shooting at an indoor pistol range weekly for one year.

Why pick out just these airport instances when there are over twenty places that are prohibited to carry, you ask? Well, first of all, I bet that if you ask every CHCL holder, they would confess to you of entering some prohibited establishment fully armed only to be blessed by the absence of armed security guards and detection devices. You see, if you finally select a carry method that is comfy for you and you carry very, very frequently, it becomes a part of your daily attire. Sort of like your underwear or pants belt, you just forget about wearing it. But bet your bottom dollar, if a situation dangerous to your life suddenly confronts you, your memory will instantly remember where "Mr. Boom" is hiding. My point is that concealed carry becomes a habit and becomes so unnoticeable to you that it is easy to arrive at the school to pick up your kids or go to the Post Office to buy stamps and suddenly realize you have just committed a very stupid "No-No!" Fortunately, you can usually beat a hasty retreat and either disarm or wait on safer turf. (It is wise to avoid having a mild myocardial infarction at these times; the paramedics would just as soon turn you in as not.)

Also, purse, briefcase, and hand-baggage are even easier carry locations to forget. You don't even need to put them on each day as you would a holster. Of course, just how you intend to ask the perp to wait while you open up your briefcase, carry-on, or handbag is a mystery to me. (Please send written descriptions of your plan for this occurrence.)

Concealed Carry Will Become Second Nature, unless you seldom carry or you have some gizmo that is so uncomfortable that it reminds you of "Mr. Boom" with each step. **Therefore PLEASE be vigilant and mindful of those places that "Mr. Boom" should not go! Failure to do so is not only embarrassing, it can ruin your plans for the day, and your budget for the year!**

Chapter 37

Car Jacked!

Car jacking, more often than not, includes the driver also being kidnapped. Therefore, this crime is one of those criminal events for which prior consideration as to one's actions seems to be particularly beneficial and worthwhile. This focus was the result of the following news story as reported in the *Arkansas Democrat Gazette* on Saturday, December 31, 2011. "*Hijacked car used to rob LR bank!*" [This was the headline. It initially caught my attention because I wondered just how one uses a car to rob a bank. I have heard of using a gun, a bomb, a note, but never a car.]

> *Little Rock police were looking for a man Friday night who they say stole a woman's car at gunpoint and then robbed a nearby bank.*
>
> *Police spokesman Lt. Terry Hastings said a man approached a woman and two teenage girls who were getting out of their car at Breckenridge Village shopping center at North Rodney Parham Road and Interstate 40 about 4:40 p.m. He displayed a handgun and demanded the keys to the woman's car, which she surrendered to the gunman.*
>
> *The man drove a short distance to the Regions Bank branch at 800 S. Shackelford Road. He entered and 'indicated that he was armed' to bank employees, Hastings said.*
>
> *The man then left the bank with an undisclosed amount of money.*
>
> *Police said he was last seen driving south on Shackelford Road in the woman's white Chevrolet Impala.*
>
> *The gunman was described as white, about 5 feet 9 inches tall and weighing around 180 pounds.*

This woman and her two daughters (?) had a very, very fortunate day. Per the above report, the felon was interested only in her car, not in her, or her daughters, or all three. He told her *"Give me the keys to the car."* No demand that the woman, her daughters, or all of them get into the car also. This was a quick, clean car jacking with minimum threat, violence, intimidation and decision making on Mom's part. Hand over the keys and "get out of Dodge," so to speak.

I am under the belief that most car jackings are not so quick and minimally traumatic. (Yes, I understand that this Mom and her two daughters (?) were scared to death and terrified. But this was minimally threatening to them personally for this type of crime). Most car jacking reports involve the theft of the vehicle as well as the abduction of the driver, often of the female variety. So here is my point; faced with a similar situation, what would you, should you, do?

The Scenario: You are alone, and as you approach your vehicle and unlock the door, a perp comes up behind you and says:

1. "Give me the keys to your car;" or
2. "Get in and drive," as he climbs into the back seat or comes around the car keeping a handgun pointed at you the entire time; or
3. "Give me the keys and get in and move over to the passenger seat;" or
4. Grabs you and hits you and struggles to push you into the car. "Don't make me kill you!' he screams into your ear.

What do you do? Frankly, I do not know what an expert would advise in this scenario. What I do believe is that your odds of being physically assaulted increase dramatically and your odds of survival diminish a whole bunch, if you get into the car and you and the perp drive off.

Let us talk logic for a minute. If the perp threatens to kill you right then and there in the parking lot if you do not comply with his shouted demand, well, he just might. But consider the type of perp with which you are dealing. If this felon is so consumed with evil that he will shoot and kill you right there in the parking lot, guess what he will probably do to you when you reach his final destination. If he is so evil that he will shoot you in the parking lot, I think he is even more likely to shoot you at the end of the ride. And should you be female, I am surmising that your death might be subsequent to even more terror, torture, and probably rape.

If the perp is not that evil and is merely threatening an action that he probably will not follow through—shooting you in the parking lot, then he might not shoot you at the end of the ride. But things can happen on a terror filled trip. You cannot be certain what he might do to you at the final destination. Will he really willingly leave living eyewitnesses?

Of course, you do not know which level of evil is facing you with the largest pistol you have ever seen. So, do you risk being shot here in the parking lot where there are potential witnesses or folks who might run over and, if the wound is not fatal, quickly call for medical aid. Or do you risk the actions at the end of the ride, maybe twenty miles out in the country under the trees and among the weeds, where no one will know the outcome any time soon.

The following is what I have decided would be my actions or reactions. Of course, it is easy to make up some scenario response when you are not facing a screaming perp armed with knife or pistol, your mind closing down, logic fleeing, nerves fraying, limbs shaking, and the body functions needed are not performing, and the body functions not needed start performing. I understand that. That is why I am making up my mind on my course of action while I can still calmly sort through the options. So, to sort through the four options listed above let us take them starting with the easiest ones first. (Yeah, I know that most folks go in numerical order.)

Option #4: If hit, slugged, "tasered," etc., I will drop as a dead weight until able to offer some type of resistance. I weigh over 160 pounds, and a perp will have some difficulty lifting me up and into a car while maintaining his grip and control on his weapon. He might get me into the car, but it will not be quick and easy. It might take sufficient time and effort to permit others to see what is happening, or maybe the perp becomes so concerned, frightened, or frustrated he just gives up trying to load me into the car. If he shoots me, my conclusion is that he would have done so at the end of the trip anyway. My hope: he gives up tugging at me, takes the keys, and leaves in my beloved automobile.

If not beaten, bludgeoned, or otherwise incapacitated to some degree or another and I am standing facing this excited, weapon waving, screaming antagonist, then what?

Option #1: "Give me your keys!"—will result in my giving him my keys. I love my car. It has been a reliable servant for seventeen years. It is the best car that I have ever owned, but I am not going to die over it.

254

I am with "Mom" in the earlier report. If all he asks for is my keys, the keys he gets.

Options #2/3: "Get in and . . ." Here is where I start what I hope will be a dialog with the miscreant and not a lone soliloquy ending with an abrupt, loud boom.

Me:	"Here are my keys. You can take the car!"
Perp:	(Screaming threateningly) "Get in the car or I'll shoot you!"
Me:	"Sir, here are my keys. Please just take my car."
Perp:	(Voice tone and decibel level ascending as he threatens) "Get in the car or I'll kill you right here."
Me:	"Sir, you've won! Take the car. I'm not resisting you. You are in control. But I am not getting into the car with you."
Perp:	"Yous wanna die right here? Get in the car!"
Me:	"No, I do not want to die here, or anywhere. But if you are so consumed with evil that you would shoot me here, then you would shoot me when you are finished with the car and me. Please, just take the car and go."
Perp:	"Get in the car now or you'll die! Move! Get in!"
Me:	"I don't believe that you are that evil. Here!" (Reaching out with the keys held in my left hand, I attempt to drop them into his hand, whether extended or not.) "Take my car and please do not hurt me. You have won!"

Now as his eyes follow the falling keys, I have three options, maybe four:

1. Lunge for his pistol and attempt to wrestle it from him. Bad choice—for me. The pistol may still point in my direction. Should he pull the trigger, the bullet will more than likely follow the direction in which the barrel is pointing—at me. Not having been trained in defensive techniques of hand-to-hand combat to remove a pistol from a perp's hand, this has very, very, very long odds for success. Plus, whatever hesitancy the perp may have had about shooting me has just been ripped away like a two-day old band-aid off a raw sore.

2. Stand there and watch what he does next is a strong possibility as a course of action. However, there are two possible results:

he will pick up the keys and drive off as hoped, or he will demand that I pick them up and the dialog continues.

3.   If his eyes follow the direction of the car keys descending toward the pavement, I quickly sweep back the flap of my coat and draw my snub-nosed Smith and Wesson *Bodyguard* .38 Special revolver from my strong side OWB holster and fire two shots into his upper torso. If he is not yet neutralized (on the pavement with his pistol no longer a threat) I fire two more, saving the last rounds for headshots if he is still a threat to fire back. Yeah, sure, in your dreams "Ramboette."

4.   As he watches, grabs for, or stoops for the keys and his attention and reflexes are elsewhere employed, turn and run like a scared rabbit toward the end of the car. (Unless you are wearing a slim-line long skirt and three inch spiked heels, you can cover about 20 feet in 2-3 seconds.) Distraction and surprise are your hope with this maneuver. Turn at the end of the car and run as fast as you can, screaming as you run, toward the nearest shop door, moving vehicle, or crowd of people. In five seconds, you will have traveled about 40-50 feet. At that range, the perp will need to be very good or very lucky with his aim to hit you. Good odds. Hopefully the perp will not fire as you turn and flee and will accept the gift of your automobile. Will he? No one knows. But this is my choice when I have one of those incredibly bad days such as the Mom and her two daughters experienced.

"You makes your choices and you takes your chances."

OK, "Ramboette," let us do it your way. Here is another real life example, but this one is from John Lott's book *More Guns Less Crime* on page 3 in the *Introduction*.

> *A College Park woman shot and killed an armed man she says was trying to car jack her van with her and her 1-year-old daughter inside, police said Monday . . .*
>
> *Jackson told police that the gunman accosted her as she drove into the parking lot of an apartment complex on Camp Creek Parkway. She had planned to watch* [a movie?] *. . . with friends at the complex.*

She fired after the man pointed a revolver at her and
ordered her to 'move over,' she told police. She offered to take
her daughter and give up the van, but the man refused, police
said.

'She was pleading with the guy to let her take the baby
and leave the van, but he blocked the door,' said College Park
Detective Reed Pollard. 'She was protecting herself and the
baby.'

Jackson, who told the police she bought the .44-caliber
handgun in September after her home was burglarized, she
fired several shots from the gun, which she kept concealed in
a canvas bag beside her car seat. 'She didn't try to remove it,'
Pollard said. 'She just fired'.

This was an example of shooting the perp in an attempted car jacking, but with several differences between this one and the "Mom's" options above. In the Mom's options, Mom did not have a gun, as far as we know. Mom was outside the car and thus had the ability to flee. Mom did not have a 1-year-old in the car. Jackson had a pistol, readily available, and apparently could access the weapon without alerting the perp. Jackson was trapped inside the car. The perp was insistent that he wanted Jackson along for the ride.

But are there some lessons from the Jackson shooting? First of all, she had taken steps to protect herself and had already purchased a handgun; although I am amazed at her choice of a .44-caliber cannon. Second, she had it with her, not locked up at home. Third, it was not in the glove compartment or center console where an effort to access it might have alerted the perp. Fourth, it was concealed from the perp's, or anyone else's, eyes. Fifth, she did not hesitate by trying to "get the drop" on the gunman. She did not try a "citizen's arrest." Her responsibility was to survive, to get out alive. However, she fired with the pistol inside the bag. Fortunately, it was a revolver. If it had been a semiautomatic, one shot might have been all that she could get off if the slide's recoil or the ejecting shell were too confined to operate successfully. Also, a canvas bag is not my first choice for concealed carry holster. In her purse would probably have resulted in the same successful defense and not had the pistol available for a 1-year-old to climb across one day. All that said, let us continue with Mr. Lott and read what an expert has to say about this incident.

> *Although the mother (Jackson) saved herself and her baby by her quick actions, it was a risky situation that might have ended differently. Even though there was no police officer to help protect her or her child, defending herself was not necessarily the only alternative. She could have behaved passively, and the criminal might have changed his mind and simply taken the van, letting the mother and child go. Even if he had taken the child, he might later have let the baby go unharmed. Indeed, some conventional wisdom claims that the best approach is not to resist an attack. According to a recent Los Angeles Times article, 'active compliance is the surest way to survive a robbery. Victims who engage in active resistance . . . have the best odds of hanging onto their property. Unfortunately, they also have much better odds of winding up dead'.*
>
> *Yet the evidence suggests that the College Park woman probably engaged in the correct action. While resistance is generally associated with higher probabilities of serious injury to the victim, not all types of resistance are equally risky. By examining the data provided from 1979 to 1987 by the Department of Justice's National Crime Victimization Survey, Lawrence Southwick . . . **found that the probability of serious injury from an attack is 2.5 times greater for women offering no resistance than for women resisting with a gun. In contrast, the probability of women being seriously injured was almost FOUR times greater when resisting without a gun than when resisting with a gun.***
>
> *In other words, the best advice is to resist with a gun, but if no gun is available, it is better to offer no resistance than to fight.*

The way I understood the above was this: if a female has a gun available for resistance to an attack, her odds of escaping injury are 400% better than a resisting, unarmed female. The above advice from the L.A. Times was to "comply." DOJ statistics suggest that if you do not have a gun, do not resist. Well, that may be what the statistics say, but as for me—I am not getting into the car!

But, "You makes your choices and you takes your chances."

One last live example that is a semi-fit to this subject, as reported in the *Arkansas Democrat Gazette* on January 6, 2012:

> *According to an arrest affidavit,* [Victim's] *girlfriend told detectives she was with her boyfriend at a North Little Rock apartment when he got a phone call late that night from a man named 'Big Mike'* . . . *and he asked* [Victim] *to meet him* . . . *to buy some marijuana* . . .
>
> *Her account said that* [Victim] *showed the man the marijuana and 'Big Mike' stepped back out of the car, saying he had to speak with his 'brother' inside the other car.*
>
> *A moment later the three men, including 'Big Mike,' stepped out and approached the passenger side window of her Jeep, and the driver of the Dodge Charger pulled out a handgun, pushed her aside, and pointed it at* [Victim.]
>
> *The woman told police she leaped out of the car and started running away when she heard several gunshots, the affidavit said.*
>
> *When she reached the 3800 block of* [street name] . . . *she called police.*
>
> *Officers found* [Victim] *in the Jeep* . . . *where he had crashed into a light pole.*
>
> [Victim] *was shot once in the left upper back* . . . *he was pronounced dead at 11:10 p.m.*

OK, so it was not exactly a car jacking, but there are several lessons that we might glean from this tragedy. First, "she" violated all three of the "Don't Do Stupid Things" rules. She was with a person who was doing a stupid thing; she went to a stupid rendezvous; she was involved in a stupid activity. All that said, did you note that she jumped out of her Jeep and ran off? By so doing, she lived to call 911 and eat breakfast the next day. Sure, I will agree that she was not the target, like in a car jacking. But do you think that the three "brothers" would have left her alive? Would they have just asked her pleasantly, "Please, pretty please, do not tell the police that we shot your boyfriend?" Perhaps they would even have asked her to join them for a late night snack? You know what I think? I think that she jumped and ran while the three "brothers" were distracted and that saved her life.

What would you have advised? Tell her to just stay there by her man and hope for the best? What would you advise your wife to do if three "brothers" came up to your car and the same scenario went down? (No, I do not mean that you were there selling marijuana; just that you were somewhere in the wrong place at the wrong time.)

Honestly, I do not know what the "experts" would advise you to do under these circumstances. But as for me, I am not getting into the car with the perp, and I am telling my wife to run like a fleet deer! But,

"You makes your choices and you takes your chances."

By the way, have I advised you that I am not yet an expert in any of this self-defense stuff. Have I advised you that my opinions are just that, my opinions? These scenarios are not sanctioned by the "International Defense Scenario Institute;" they lack three levels of management sign-off; they have not been proved in laboratory experimentation, much less in real life. It bothers me not one whit if you think one of my ideas is not optimum for survival; just as long as you develop a superior response. (Please submit suggestions should you desire.)

Chapter 38

"Thou Shall Not Murder"

Most of us have serious reservations when it comes to even thinking about shooting another human and even greater reservations about actually taking the life of another human being. Whatever the genesis of this feeling of reservation and doubt, it exists for most of us. In the Western world's culture there is the overriding influence of the Judeo-Christian tradition of Biblical teachings of "Thou Shall Not Kill." It is one of the *Ten Commandments* memorized by many from childhood Sunday School classes. For those who take the word "Commandment" at face value, rather than assume it is actually just the "Ten Suggestions," that admonition weighs very heavily.

Yet we send our young men, and now women, into combat with direct orders to kill the enemy. We expect our law enforcement officers to kill criminals when absolutely necessary. We even execute criminals whose crimes were so egregious that society is best served by sending them back to their Maker. How do we reconcile these actions with the ingrained admonition "Thou Shall Not Kill?"

It was a tremendous relief for me during my years in the military to have been presented with a scholarly exposition of both the Biblical books of *Exodus* and *Deuteronomy.* As it was explained to me, there are several Hebrew words for "kill" or "murder." The Hebrew word used in both *Exodus 20.13* and *Deuteronomy 5.17* is "ratsach." According to *Young's Analytical Concordance to the Bible* (page 563) this Hebrew word "ratsach" is best translated into English as "murder." If one then looks up the word "murder" in the *Random House Webster's College Dictionary* (copyrighted 1991) the definition of murder is, *"the unlawful killing of a person, esp. when done with deliberation or premeditation, or occurring during the commission of another serious crime."* That same reference defines "kill" as, *"to deprive of life; cause the death of."*

You might argue that I am splitting hairs, but "murder" is an "unlawful" act; "kill" may not be. Thus the *Ten Commandments* actually state *"Thou shall not murder."* That is also the manner in which the *New American Standard Bible* translates the sixth commandment, *"You shall not murder."* (I am not just making this stuff up.)

261

To me, if someone is trying to take my life or threatening severe physical danger, then under the laws of Arkansas I am **lawfully** permitted to use deadly force in defense to prevent my own death or the death of another innocent.

Arkansas Statue: 5-2-607. Use of deadly physical force in defense of a person.

(a) *A person is justified in using deadly physical force upon another person if the person reasonably believes that the other person is:*

    (1) *Committing or about to commit a **felony involving force or violence**;*

    (2) *Using or about to use **unlawful deadly physical force**;*

Therefore, if I am lawfully permitted to use deadly force under very extreme and unusual circumstances, then I am not committing "murder." Yes, I might kill another human-being in self-defense, but I am not committing murder, and thus, in my mind, not violating God's *Sixth*. To you, this may all be rationalization. To me, it helps clarify. It also makes the burden on me very difficult. Yes, I can carry a weapon. Yes, I can use it to defend myself. But are the circumstances under which I use the weapon in self-defense deserving of the killing of another human being? That is sort of why I decided to carry "Mr. Pepper" also. I wanted an option that will provide me some protection other than just shooting. But remember:

"When violence is the answer, it's the only answer."

Or to make it more germane to the above discussion:

"When shooting someone is the answer, it is the only answer."

It is with great hope and trembling that I pray that neither you nor I ever have to make that quick, two-second decision. But other than the obvious, why bring this up? The world in which we live has become very dangerous. From an article by the *Buckeye Firearms* organization:

1. *In a typical week in the United States there are about 300 murders,*

2. *15,000 violent assaults,*

3. *1,700 rapes, and*

4. *7,800 robberies. (These numbers come from FBI statistics.)*

The article goes on to state, "*But in a typical week 20,000 or more acts of violence are* **prevented** *because the prospective victim is protected by a firearm. In at least 90 to 95 percent of these cases the gun is not fired.*"

Assuming that the above is accurate (and I have no reason to doubt it), then the act of carrying a concealed firearm may prevent additional murders, rapes, assaults, and robberies. For me, that is sufficient deterrent to encourage me to carry. The odds are better than twenty to one that the encounter will not require me to fire the weapon in order to prevent this crime. And per the article, if I do shoot, "*about twenty percent of the rounds fired at a person in a violent encounter actually hit the person. In about twenty percent of the cases where the person is hit by one or more rounds, the person ultimately dies.*" So even if forced to shoot to save my life or that of another person, the odds of actually killing the perp are about 20% even if I hit him.

To my mind, defending myself is justified and not a grave risk of violating the *Sixth Commandment's* threshold of obedience. That said, "May God have mercy on my soul!" should I be in error.

Chapter 39

Gun Control—Some Perspectives

Do Guns Kill People?

> *"Lizzy Borden took an axe*
> *And gave her Mother forty whacks.*
> *When she saw what she had done,*
> *She gave her Father forty-one."*

What do we learn from this? Well at least two things. First, do not live with a Lizzy Borden. But more broadly, it is intuitively obvious that **axes kill people**. A greater perspective would include that **both hatchets and axes should be placed into the same category** as weapons that kill people. They should, therefore, be made illegal for all but law enforcement, public safety, and a few very restrictive, legally designated institutions. Of course, there may be those few "woods dwellers" who still find utilitarian need for them, but most of modern society has no need for either of these dangerous weapons and thus they should be outlawed for the general good.

Auto Deaths

Despite the fact that traffic fatalities in 2010 were the lowest in 62 years, there were over **32,700 automobile fatalities** in the U.S. alone. This is a terrible and completely unnecessary slaughter of human life with resultant high misery and loss of potential for mankind. Despite tens-of-thousands of lines of legal codes, growing police manpower, traffic control devices, divided highways, and continued implementation of car safety devices, the slaughter continues each year. Over one third of a million Americans have been killed since 1999. On average in 2009, 93 people were killed on the roadways of the U.S. **each day**.

What can we learn from this? It is intuitively obvious that **cars kill people**. It is also obvious that despite all of society's efforts, the carnage continues without abatement. The only reasonable solution, cars should be outlawed from the general population for societal good. Oh sure, there are instances where there is some utilitarian value, but we must consider the broader good for society. Society's transportation needs can be addressed by buses, taxis, trains, and other professionally licensed entities. People should not own cars, except under very restrictive circumstances.

Smoking Deaths

The CDC reports that smoking is the cause of:

- **443,000 deaths annually** (including deaths from secondhand smoke),
- 49,400 deaths per year from secondhand smoke exposure,
- 269,655 deaths annually among men, and
- 173,940 deaths annually among women.

Further, it relates that "*More deaths are caused each year by tobacco use than by all deaths from human immunodeficiency virus (HIV), illegal drug use, alcohol use, motor vehicle injuries, suicides, and murders combined.*" So what can we learn from this? It is intuitively obvious that **cigarettes cause death**. Therefore, they should be totally outlawed and the mere possession made a criminal offense. At the very least, outlawing them for males would save over 269,000 deaths a year. There is zero utilitarian benefit from smoking a cigarette. Soaring health care costs demand that this drain (smoking) on all of our resources be exorcized from society.

Deaths by Poisoning

The CDC reports that over 40,000 U. S. residents died from poisoning in the year 2007. This is a complete waste of human life and a loss to all of society. Despite all the warning labels, childproof caps, "skull and cross bones" label icons, restriction on certain poisons, and continued FDA and EPA vigilance; we keep losing citizens to this pernicious killer. It is intuitively obvious that without quick and drastic action we will continue to fill our cemeteries with the bodies of these poor souls. It is intuitively obvious that poisons kill people. All poisons must be banned and the mere possession of one be made a crime. Well, of course there are some utilitarian values to some poisons when used in the correct manner by experienced handlers, but a complete ban is the only sure way to protect society.

Deaths by Firearms

The CDC reports that out of our total population of over 300,000,000 there were more than **31,224 deaths** in 2007 from firearms. Of that number a distressing 3,067 gun deaths occurred in the 0 through 19 age groups. We are killing over 3,000 children a year! What? You question that 18 and 19 year olds are children? Well if you exclude those two years, then there were 1,520 gun deaths in the 0 through 17 age groups (out of 74,340,127 children). This is still a tragedy and a complete waste of human potential, not to mention the heartache of grieving families. It is intuitively obvious that **guns kill people** and should be banned and the mere possession of one made a crime. "Wait! What? What article? A report from MSNBC in 2010 said what?"

> *Americans overall are far less likely to be killed with a firearm than they were when it was much more difficult to obtain a concealed-weapons permit, according **to statistics collected by the federal Centers for Disease Control.** But researchers have not been able to establish a cause-and-effect relationship.*
>
> *In the 1980s and '90s, as the concealed-carry movement gained steam, Americans were killed by others with guns at the rate of about 5.66 per 100,000 population. In this decade, the rate has fallen to just over 4.07 per 100,000, **a 28 percent drop.** The decline follows a **five-fold increase** in the number of 'shall-issue' and unrestricted concealed-carry states from 1986 to 2006.*
>
> *The highest gun homicide rate is in Washington, D.C., which has had the nation's strictest gun-control laws for years and bans concealed carry: 20.50 deaths per 100,000 population, five times the general rate. The lowest rate, 1.12 deaths per 100,000, is in Utah, which has such a liberal*

concealed weapons policy that most American adults can get a
permit to carry a gun in Utah without even visiting the state.

The decline in gun homicides also comes as U.S. firearm
sales are skyrocketing, according to federal background checks
that are required for most gun sales. After holding stable at 8.5
to 9 million checks from 1999 to 2005, the FBI reported a
surge to 10 million in 2006, 11 million in 2007, nearly 13
million in 2008 and more than 14 million last year [2009], *a*
55 percent increase in just four years.

CNNews's Joe Schoffstall elaborated: **In this decade,**
the gun-homicide rate has fallen to 4.07 *per 100,000,*
which equates to a 28 percent reduction in homicides with the
use of firearms. This decline in homicides follows a five-fold
increase in a 'shall-issue' (requirement of a permit to carry a
concealed handgun, but where the granting of the permit is
subject only to meeting certain criteria laid out in the law)
and unrestricted concealed-carry laws in states from 1986 to
2006, reported MSNBC.com.

According to federal background checks conducted on the
sale of most firearms, the decline in homicides comes as U.S.
firearm sales are skyrocketing.'

All in all a very surprising piece from one of the nation's
most liberal news outlets . . .

"What? More Guns Equals Less Crime? Are you out of your mind?"

No, I am not. That is exactly what John R. Lott, Jr. determined and reported in his book *More Guns Less Crime* which was published in 2000. He compared crimes in all 3,054 counties in the U.S. based on the individual state's concealed handgun carry law ("shall issue, non-discretionary" law) or lack thereof ("discretionary" law) from 1977 to 1992. His work resulted in dispelling the fact that banning guns would reduce crime; in fact, just the opposite is true. **The more concealed handgun permits issued by a state, the less violent crime in that state.** (The term "shall issue" means that the authority that actually issues the license "shall issue" the license, if the applicant meets the statutory requirements without employing other non-statutory reasons to deny the license. "Non-shall issue" states often leave the decision of issuing the licenses up to some local authority which may or may not issue, regardless of the applicant meeting the statutory requirements.) Page 47 states:

> *The difference is quite striking: violent crimes are 81% higher in states without non-discretionary laws.* (I.E., 'discretionary'—the state strictly controls or does not allow concealed carry). *For murder, states that ban the concealed carrying of guns have a murder rate 127 % higher than states with the most liberal concealed carry laws. The states with non-discretionary laws have less crime, but the primary difference appears in terms of violent crimes.*

Page 20 states,

> *Guns also appear to be the great equalizer among the sexes. Murder rates decline when either more women or more men carry concealed handguns, but the effect is especially pronounced for women. One additional woman carrying a concealed handgun reduces the murder rate for women by about 3-4 times more than on additional man carrying a concealed handgun reduces the murder rate for men.*

Page 5 answers the question that puzzled MSNBC above as to why this should be so, that more guns equal less crime.

> *Criminals are motivated by self-preservation, and handguns can therefore be a deterrent. The potential defensive nature of guns is further evidenced by the different rates of so-called 'hot burglaries,' where a resident is at home when a criminal strikes. In Canada and Britain, both with tough gun-control laws, almost half of all burglaries are 'hot burglaries.' In contrast, the United States, with fewer restrictions, has a 'hot burglary' rate of only 13 percent. Criminals are not just behaving differently by accident. Convicted American felons reveal in surveys that they are much more worried about armed victims than about running*

into the police. The fear of potentially armed victims causes American burglars to ensure that nobody is home. Felons frequently comment in these interviews that they avoid late-night burglaries because 'that's the way to get shot.'

So what can we learn from this? First, if you carry a concealed weapon you have a better chance to survive an encounter than if you are unarmed. Second, the more citizens who carry concealed weapons, the greater is the decline in the rates of murder, rape, and armed robbery. Third, the more women who carry a concealed weapon, the greater the reduction of all women murdered and raped in the state. Fourth, by carrying a concealed weapon, you create a "Halo Effect" by which the general felon is less likely to commit a violent crime on anyone else in your specific state.

FBI Statistics

Still not convinced? In the NRA's August, 2011, *America's 1ˢᵗ Freedom Magazine*, it was reported on page 56:

> *In May the FBI reported preliminary data indicating that in 2010 the nation's total violent crime rate decreased more than six percent, to a 37-year low, and the nation's murder rate decreased more than five percent, to a 47-year low.*

So, while more states have become "shall issue" for concealed carry and several hundred thousand to several million more citizens are now licensed to carry concealed weapons, both the violent crime rates and the murder rates are down. Just a coincidence? Probably not.

National Safety Council Statistics

The NRA's October, 2011, issue of *America's 1ˢᵗ Freedom Magazine*, on page 23, states: "*Today less than 1 percent of fatalities in the home are caused by firearm accidents, according to the National Safety Council. While gun ownership in the United States has risen to an all-time high, accidental firearm deaths are at an all-time low.*" These statistics would support the argument that the more responsible citizens who are armed, the lower the crime rates for murder and other violent crimes and that home firearm accidents do not rise proportionately.

So do guns kill? They can and do when in the wrong hands. But in the right hands they sure do bring down the murder, rape, armed robbery, and aggravated assault rates for all of us. Therefore, Go! Get Trained! Get Armed! Get Legal! Carry!

> *"I'm in favor of gun control—I think every citizen should have control of a gun."*

The Battle for the Right to Bear Arms seems to never end

The longsuffering citizens of Washington, D. C. must still deal with fuzzy-logic-minded leaders. That city has had one of the strictest gun control laws in the country and one of the highest violent crime rates. There just might be a connection.

Despite losing the lawsuit brought by one Mr. Dick Heller over the city's ban on handgun ownership, D.C. is up to its old tricks. But to review, in 2003 Mr. Heller sued the city over their ban on handgun ownership. The Supreme Court of the old U. S. of A. overturned that ban in June 2008, saying that it violated the Second Amendment. (Only took them five years to read a one-line sentence in the Constitution and reach that opinion. OK, maybe two lines.)

After that, the city rewrote their gun control laws, and for the first time in over thirty years, the embattled citizens of our nation's capitol were permitted to own handguns. Although defeated, the city leaders were unbowed and instituted new requirements that are at the least very numerous and to some degree restrictive. Not to be out-foxed by the foxes, Mr. Heller sued again over the new restrictions. Although that case is still speeding through the courts at a snail's pace, the Federal Appeals court this last October did request that the city fathers provide evidence justifying what it called "novel" handgun registration requirements—for example, requiring vision tests.

The city is considering changes to their new laws which, if implemented, could impact the current court case. Why are they suddenly trying to be so reasonable and responsive? A federal judge just this past Thursday, December 29, 2011, ordered the city of Washington, D. C. to pay $1,137,072.27 in lawyer fees and expenses to Mr. Heller's attorneys, and that was only for the first law suit. So, you have two guesses: either they have had a change of heart, or the fear of further litigation costs has changed their attitude, and maybe their laws. Which do you think, common sense or pocketbook necessity?

Fewer Arms, More Crime?

Mr. Lott provides the following incident on page 12 of his book.

> *Less than a year ago, James Edward Scott shot and wounded an intruder in the back yard* [curtilage] *of his West Baltimore home, and according to neighbors, authorities took away his gun.*
>
> *Tuesday night, someone apparently broke into his three-story row house again. But this time the 83-year-old Scott didn't have his .22-caliber rifle, and police said he was strangled when he confronted the burglar.*
>
> *'If he would have had the gun, he would be OK,' said one neighbor who declined to give his name, fearing retribution from the attacker, who had not been arrested as of yesterday . . .*
>
> *Neighbors said that burglars repeatedly broke into Scott's house . . . a neighbor said Scott often talked about 'the people who would harass him because he worked out back by himself.'*

The states that issue concealed carry licenses under "shall issue" laws without discretionary interference have less violent crime than do the states that use "discretionary" police or administrative rules to limit citizen access to carry concealed weapons. "Shall Issue" means just that; the state "shall issue" the concealed carry license if the applicant passes the background check and other lawfully defined requirements. "Discretionary" means it is up to the discretion of some individual to decide if you should receive the permit, even though you meet all the statute requirements.

Criminals may, as a group, have a lower intelligence than society as a whole, plus other severe psychological abnormalities. But overall, they do seem to behave rationally. When certain types of crime become more difficult or dangerous for them to commit, they commit less of those types of crimes. Ergo, armed citizens are more dangerous to them, so they will revert to other types of crime less likely to confront an armed citizen.

More Recent Evidence that More Guns Equal Less Violent Crime

"Media Silence Is Deafening About Important Gun News"
By John Lott | Published September 30, 2011 | FoxNews.com

> *Murder and violent crime rates were supposed to soar after the Supreme Court struck down gun control laws in Chicago and Washington, D.C. Politicians predicted disaster. 'More handguns in the District of Columbia will only lead to more handgun violence,' Washington's Mayor Adrian Fenty warned the day the court made its decision. Chicago's Mayor Daley predicted that we would 'go back to the Old West, you have a gun and I have a gun and we'll settle it in the streets . . .'*
>
> *The New York Times even editorialized this month about the Supreme Court's 'unwise' decision that there is a right for people 'to keep guns in the home.' But Armageddon never happened. Newly released data for Chicago shows that, as in Washington, murder and gun crime rates didn't rise after the bans were eliminated—they plummeted. They have fallen much more than the national crime rate.*
>
> *Not surprisingly, the national media have been completely silent about this news. One can only imagine the coverage if crime rates had risen. In the first six months of this year, there were 14% fewer murders in Chicago compared to the first six months of last year—back when owning handguns was illegal. It was the largest drop in Chicago's murder rate since the handgun ban went into effect in 1982. Meanwhile, the other four most populous cities saw a total drop at the same time of only 6 percent.*
>
> *Similarly, in the year after the 2008 'Heller' decision, the murder rate fell two-and-a-half times faster in Washington than in the rest of the country. It also fell more than three times as fast as in other cities that are close to Washington's size. And*

murders in Washington have continued to fall. If you compare
the first six months of this year to the first six months of 2008,
the same time immediately preceding the Supreme Court's late
June 'Heller' decision, murders have now fallen by thirty-four
percent.

Gun crimes also fell more than non-gun crimes. Robberies
with guns fell by 25%, while robberies without guns have
fallen by eight percent. Assaults with guns fell by 37%, while
assaults without guns fell by 12%.

Just as with right-to-carry laws, when law-abiding
citizens have guns some criminals stop carrying theirs.

So what do you think? I would bet that you favor citizens having the right to carry concealed weapons, or you would not be reading this. But the real question is, "What are you doing to ensure that we retain that right?" Some items for your consideration:

1. Support the NRA; it lobbies nationally for gun rights.
2. Join some state, regional, or local group that supports these rights.
3. Query your campaigning politicians and vote with your donations, as well as your cast ballot, for those who share your gun views.
4. Money to the organizations that support your causes is a very powerful tool to maintain the protection of your rights.

Appendix A

A Review of the Complete Journey

The following is a broad, high level review from the first twelve chapters with a little stuff added. You may have already read the entire book or just skimmed through to here to help with your purchase decision. Regardless, the following should reinforce what you have read or encourage you to become even more knowledgeable. Whether you already own a handgun and seek some additional information, or are now convinced to purchase a weapon, please read the following and take what pertains to you into your mind and work it over.

If you have made the decision to "get armed" and your choice is a handgun, then there are several things that I have learned through that old, revered but hard "school of experience." Learn from my experience where you can. Some is covered in the sections below, but most is covered in the complete chapters. If you already own your weapon of choice, then you can skip #1 and perhaps a few other sections, depending on just where you are in your own personal journey of being a responsible owner of a handgun. Otherwise, dig right in at #1; it is a quick read.

1. Purchase a Handgun

A. First, before you purchase a handgun, learn something about them. Some suggestions:

1. Write out what you think are your reasons for needing a handgun and specifically what you need it to do for you when you are so terrified that you cannot talk, spit, or see straight. (See *Chapter 2: Define Your Specific Requirements BEFORE You Purchase a Handgun.*)

2. Go to a gun store and explain what you are thinking of acquiring (See *Chapter 3: Handgun Selection*) and what you want your weapon to accomplish.

3. Locate a shooting range that rents guns and go there. Tell the gentleman in charge what type of handgun you are thinking of acquiring and what you want your weapon to accomplish.

4. Rent his best recommendation as well as your own handgun of choice, and have him show you the basics of shooting and fire fifty rounds with each pistol.

5. Return time and again to the gun range and fire fifty rounds from every single gun that you are considering. I would only fire one or two different handguns per trip. When you rent a pistol, they will require that you buy the ammo to fire in it; therefore, rent only the same caliber guns on each trip.

6. Go onto the Internet and sign up on a Web-chat and ask for help from anyone who has experience with the handgun you are now zeroed in on. (See *Appendix F: Some Sources and Resources*).

7. Only after you have listened to a bunch of advice and opinions from experienced shooters and gun owners and after you have zeroed in and fired your handgun of choice at least two different times for fifty rounds each, sit down and take a deep breath. All of the opinions of others are just that, their opinion. Consider them, but they are not you.

8. You now have fired one or more types, models, and calibers of handguns and have zeroed in on the one that seems to best accomplish your goals. One that you can control and fire with accuracy without fear and flinching.

9. You must finally, after all the advice, articles, books, Internet help, gun shops and friendly input make a decision and purchase your own personal handgun. Pick the handgun that feels right **to you,** one which you can fire without flinching and that will meet your requirements.

B. Do not buy a cheap gun to save money. Buy a very good handgun with a great reputation and hopefully with a manufacturer's lifetime guarantee; your life may depend on it. As the old proverb states, "*Buy the best and you only cry once.*"

To mangle a quote from John Ruskin:

Any one can make a product a little cheaper, a little inferior, and sell it for less. If you buy the best, you are out some money; but that is all as it performs the function for which it was acquired. If you buy a cheaper, poorer quality item and it doesn't do the job, then you have lost everything.

2. Go to School

Second, now that you own a handgun that meets your needs, you can fire with ease, and not be afraid to shoot, **go to school**. Whether you desire to carry your handgun or you will only leave it at home for protection there, go to a Concealed Handgun Carry License Class!!! In case you are speed reading and missed the previous, **go to a Concealed Handgun Carry License (CHCL) Class!!!**

"Why," you ask? Well, there are about a hundred reasons, but let me just give you two.

1. You will be instructed on the primary Arkansas Laws that pertain to concealed carry as well as the one and only SINGLE time that you are LEGALLY justified in shooting someone. All other instances will most likely result in your going to the jailhouse for an extended period of time.

2. If you have a CHCL and are ever stopped while transporting a weapon, or if confronted in a home invasion or robbery and have had to shoot a perp, it is prima facie evidence that you are somewhat of a responsible gun owner. That just might go a long way with the D.A.'s office.

At the Arkansas CHCL class, be sure that you qualify with a semiautomatic regardless of your personal handgun type. (They may rent them. If not, borrow a semiautomatic.) This permits you to carry all types of legal handguns—you never know what type you may desire to carry in the future. If you qualify with a revolver, you are not authorized to carry a semiautomatic and should you do so and be caught, you lose your CHCL. I know, that seems strange to me too, but it is the law. And as a gun owner and possibly a gun carrier, obeying the laws is a brand new discipline that you now should become dedicated to following to the point of being anally retentive.

3. Find a good Criminal Defense Attorney before you need him

Now that you own a handgun and have been to school and have a CHCL, personally meet **and make tentative arrangements with a good criminal defense lawyer whom you can call for representation should you ever draw your weapon in public, much less fire and shoot someone.** "What! You did not realize that if you draw your handgun in public that it is at the very minimum a serious misdemeanor and might even be charged as a felonious armed assault depending on who, what, and where you did such an imprudent act?" **See, you do need to go to class and to talk with a criminal defense attorney.** Remember to carry his office phone number, his home phone number, his cell phone number, and his Mother's phone number. Chances are that when you really, really need to talk to him, it will not be during normal office hours.

4. Safe Keeping

You are now a proud owner of a moderately priced but excellent handgun, you attended and hopefully passed a CHCL class, you are licensed, and you have legal back-up if and whenever needed. Now, where do you keep this new thing that goes bang? **Buy a Safe!**

"What? First I need to rent and fire a bunch of handguns, then buy one that costs more than I planned, then spend hundreds of bucks on a class and CHCL, fuss with a lawyer, and now you want me to go out and buy a safe to put the thing in? Who do you think I am, King Midas?"

Sorry dear reader, but you sound just like my Significant Other who says: "I'm insensitive, don't listen, have too many rules, and just don't understand reality." Alas, that is probably accurate, but not in this instance. If you have children, grandchildren, neighbor kids, domestic help, friends, or if you are likely to be the victim of a burglary at some time, you are responsible for that handgun. You are MORALLY, if not CIVILLY and LEGALLY, responsible for what it does in the hands of others.

But let us make it personal. How would you feel if some child found your handgun and accidentally shot himself or someone else? How do you think the D.A. would feel toward you for having allowed such "an attractive nuisance" to be readily available to a minor? What if your handgun were stolen and ended up being used in a robbery or killing? How would you feel if your negligence and "cheapness" resulted in harm to another one of God's children? I suspect you would feel pretty bad, and I am surmising those feelings of guilt and regret would never go away. So, give up lattes, or "Frosties," or movies for a few months and buy a safe that is sufficient to protect your handgun(s) from others' unauthorized access and use. Sure, a "perp" can still steal the whole safe and get your handgun that way, but at least you will not be guilty of negligence!

5. Decide IF you will Carry Concealed

Now for one of those big decisions; **do you desire to actually carry your weapon on your body as a concealed carry?** All of the above has been necessary preparation if you desire to actually tote a handgun around on your body every day for the rest of your life or some other undefined length of time.

A piece of personal experience: my "Significant Other" did not favor my carrying a concealed weapon outside of the house. This sort of defeats the purpose if you can only carry it inside your own home. Anyway, she proposed the Barney of Mayberry compromise. I could carry the handgun; she would carry the bullet (magazine). Fellow citizens, it just does not work well that way. Why?

As Tyler Olsen was listed as stating in the Aug/Sept, 2012, issue of *Concealed Carry Magazine*: *"Always remember that having an unloaded gun is like having a dead guard dog . . . it doesn't do anything."*

Most personal defense experts aver that if and when you need a handgun for defense, you are not given five minutes prior notice. It is also stated that most gunfire exchanges involving handguns occur within nine feet of the participants. A healthy individual can cover a distance of twenty-one feet in under two seconds.

"Wow, more statistics, I'm impressed? Why do I care?" Well, if you have only two-to-three seconds to draw, aim, and fire a handgun to protect your life, your "Significant Other" cannot be carrying the bullet (magazine). Your weapon must be loaded, chambered, and ready to be fired.

"Ouch! That sounds dangerous!"

"Yes Shirley, it is dangerous." Therefore, the decision to actually tote a handgun around all day, day after day, comes with some real introspective, "belly-button lint" contemplation, "think about your psyche" time. Are you ready to carry a loaded, chambered, and ready to fire handgun? One slight little accident can either shoot you, or someone else, plus land you in the jailhouse.

Remember Plaxico Burress, the professional football player who, while at a bar, grabbed for his own handgun as it was sliding down the inside of his pant's leg. He accidentally pulled the trigger as he grabbed it, shooting himself in the leg. The result was a year in jail, tens of thousands of dollars in legal fees, and the loss of several millions of dollars income for the football season he missed. On top of that, the *Giants* traded him to the *Jets*. But as the experts say:

"Stupidity should be painful."

Yes, you have the license that legally allows you to carry the weapon **concealed**, but it also makes you 100% responsible for your actions: intended or accidental. Being legally armed does not empower you to legally wound or kill except in one very rare specific situation. You have not suddenly been "knighted" as a law enforcement officer or "Dirty Harry" to apprehend miscreants and set the world straight according to your beliefs. A CHCL only affords you one lawful activity: to carry a concealed weapon. No more, no less; you are not empowered to show, flash, draw, threaten, shoot in the air, or anything else. You can only carry—**concealed!**

6. Get Holstered up

OK "Rambo," so you have decided to "carry." Well, just how do you plan to carry this new armed, loaded, cocked, and ready to fire weapon? Plaxico Burress must have decided to do it "on the cheap" because at the time of the above referenced event he did not have his handgun (a nice, expensive, excellent-choice handgun, by the way) in a holster. Reportedly, he was carrying it "Mexican Style." It was just loose, tucked inside his pants at the belt line. **Think about your lifestyle and how you want to carry your handgun, but always carry your weapon in a holster, not loose.** Go back to the first item, handgun selection, and follow some of those steps as appropriate regarding holsters.

There are eight general on-body holster types, all based on where/ how they are positioned on the body. A short list: Ankle holster; Inside the Waistband holster (IWB); Outside the Waistband holster (OWB); Shoulder holster (think private eye in old Humphrey Bogart movies); Bra holsters (generally only applicable to females); a "Crotch" holster (it actually hangs down inside and behind the front zipper area of your pants); Pocket Holsters (yes, carried inside your pants' pocket or coat pocket). All are a better solution than the one employed by poor Plaxico Burress. In addition, there are "off-body" methods of concealed carry: purse, fanny pack, briefcase, pack, carry-on, etc. These offer their own series of concerns and responsibilities. And it is the "off-body" carry that is the most likely to land you in jail and cost you some money.

Whatever holster type you select, it is strongly recommended that it cover the trigger guard area. Without the trigger being covered, you can still accidentally fire the weapon even in the holster. Our war cry is "Remember the Plaxico Burress!"

I can personally attest that almost every type of holster is uncomfortable to some degree; does not feel natural; takes some getting used to; and in general a pain in the . . . well, in the part of the body where you are wearing it. (OK, there are a few that I have not tried to wear, but you get my point.) You can spend a lot of money on holsters looking for the perfect one. Ergo, talk to others, go "on-line" and read some of the "Chat sites." Apparently, some folks spend as much or more on holsters as on handguns. Most likely, they were trying to find the perfect one for their perceived needs.

But be advised, some folks want a "quick draw" release holster, and some want a "suspenders and belt," overly safe holster. Most folks probably can feel comfortable somewhere in between. I Can Not! "Why," you ask? My carry weapon has a thumb safety. Yes, it does increase the time for me to draw, flick off the thumb safety, aim, and fire. I am willing to make this trade-off because my first concern is to avoid accidentally shooting myself during those hundreds or thousands of days when I will not need to execute a quick draw to shoot at an aggressive, violent felon attempting to maim or murder me or one of my family. Plus, I try to avoid stupid places and activities.

My carry holster has a thumb strap release. Again, this lengthens the time for me to release the thumb strap, draw, flick off the thumb safety, aim and fire. Again, this is a personal trade-off decision to fit my psyche. First, I want to prevent two potential problems. One is my handgun falling out of my holster because of some body movement, a quick jerk, bending over, or a sudden turn on my part. Second, I want to make it more difficult for some perp or fool to jerk the handgun out of my holster during a struggle or more likely because he has noticed a "Printing," "Brandishing," or stupid remark on my part and knows that I am carrying.

Your lifestyle and your environment may help you decide, if not dictate, what type of holster you select. For example, if you never wear a coat at work, then a shoulder holster would only be useful on Sundays when you dress up to go to church, but in Arkansas you may or may not legally carry into a church. (Refer to Chapter 15, paragraph 16.) If you always wear a skirt at work, unless it drags the floor, an ankle holster will not work for you. If you are pregnant and/or have little kids, then a Bra holster just might be a good compromise.

There are many holster manufacturers who actually mold their holster to your exact handgun make, model, and caliber. These have excellent "Retention," and many gun aficionados swear that your handgun will not fall out accidentally from such a design-specific holster. Demonstrations prove this to be true time and time again. If and when my holster is such a one, I will ask the maker to add the thumb strap. (I am a "suspenders and belt" kind of gun guy. The day-to-day responsibilities weigh more heavily on me than the potential need to draw, aim, and fire in under two-to-three seconds. Hopefully, I will never have to test my "Casper Milk Toast" gun toting persona versus a malicious miscreant intent on doing me or mine harm.) You see, for me to be comfortable carrying a handgun, I just need all these safety things; otherwise, I would probably leave the handgun in my car or at home. And as a wise gun person once said:

"It is better to have your gun and not need it, than to need it and not have it."

For me to have "it" (my firearm) with me, then "it" comes with all these "Draw, Aim, Fire" impediments to quick draw and firing. You might well be more comfortable, better trained, and more competent than I and not feel the need to require them. Nevertheless, I strongly endorse the following advice:

"Don't do things you don't want to explain to the Paramedics."

Continue getting educated. There are excellent books/pamphlets and videos on holsters. Plus, the Internet is a valuable tool to review individual manufacturers' offerings. Take some time and do the following:

1.   Write down your daily lifestyle major environment: where do you go; what do you wear, etc.
2.   Write down which type of holster seems best to fit your daily lifestyle.
3.   Now, by visits to gun stores, gun shows, the Internet, etc. evaluate, and if possible, actually put on the holsters that seem to offer the best solution for the buck. Again, don't go cheap. You do not want the seams to come unglued or unraveled on you. However, you also do not have to have an exotic skin with fancy design. Cowhide can work just fine.

Carry your concealed weapon in a holster, even if it is not the perfect one!

7. Practice

"I've acquired a handgun of good repute, attended a class, have a CHCL, consulted a legal representative, have become disgruntled about pouring even more money into a gun safe, decided to 'carry,' and purchased a holster; now please just leave me alone!" Not quite yet, my fellow armed and responsible citizen. There is one last responsibility for you to commit to doing rather frequently.

> *"To own a gun and assume that you are armed is like owning a piano and assuming that you are a musician."*

You must make a commitment to practice shooting the weapon you carry as well as the weapon that will be your primary home defense handgun. Hopefully, they will be one in the same, but I must confess, it is not so in my case. An obvious question then is "How much?" or "How frequently must I practice?" The first question is easily answered. ***Practice as frequently as required to maintain your accuracy,*** *proficiency, and confidence.* A suggestion is about one-hundred rounds monthly as long as 80% hit within a six-inch circle.

"How did you come up with that criterion?"

OK, so I made it up. But after all, do you want to miss the perp trying to slice up your wife or girlfriend with a "Ninja Knife" **more** than 20% of the time? If you want, practice till all one-hundred rounds hit the six-inch circle. As an old gunfighter once said:

"Only hits count. You can't miss fast enough to catch up in a gunfight."

But the absolute best answer to the question of "how much practice" is one I copied off a gun site:

"Do it until you get it right? Or train until you can't get it wrong."

As Wyatt Earp advised:

"Fast is fine. Accuracy is final. You need to learn to shoot slow, real fast."

8. Dry Fire

"But I can't afford to go and shoot two or three times a month until I become good," you say. Then there is an option, a very good totally free and quick option. Simulate shooting at home.

If you have any caliber handgun of modern manufacture other than a .22 caliber, .17-caliber, or other rim-fire handguns, you can "Dry Fire" the weapon at home. Dry firing is the act of pulling the trigger on an empty, unloaded, weapon. How do you know that it is empty or unloaded, you ask? Well, if the pistol is a revolver, swing out the cylinder, push the cartridge extractor thing, and push ALL the cartridges out. Next, eyeball each cartridge firing chamber several times to ensure the weapon is empty. Next, check it again. Remember:

"You never want to do anything that you don't want to explain to the paramedics."

The number of shooting accidents from "empty" handguns runs in the hundreds every year. In 1986 there were 1,695 accidental firearms' deaths in the U.S. There are probably even more today.

If you own a semiautomatic, then you have several steps to perform to "empty" the weapon. (1). First, press the magazine release and drop it completely out of the weapon and place it somewhere safe in the next room. (2). Next, rack the slide and eject the cartridge in the firing chamber. Go place it with the magazine in the next room. (3). Next, rack the slide back and eyeball the firing chamber; if empty, put your finger into the empty firing chamber; if still convinced that weapon is empty, eyeball the space in the grip where the magazine is inserted. (4). If you are now completely confident and convinced that weapon is unloaded and safe, repeat step #3.

Again, it is **not** a good idea to "dry fire" a .22-caliber pistol or other rim-fire pistols. If that is the only handgun you own, then consider using an empty cartridge casing as a substitute for a live round by inserting it into the barrel bore or cylinder chamber. (Before doing this option, please call the manufacturer and determine if that will damage your weapon.)

It is perfectly acceptable to dry fire other modern, high quality center-fire handguns. In fact, the practice is encouraged to acquire familiarity with the handling and aiming of one's gun. My LEO reviewer had this to say, *"The main goal of dry firing is to focus on the sight picture with each trigger press. The sight picture should not be disturbed as the trigger is pressed and the trigger 'breaks'."* Dry firing an inexpensive, poorly made firearm is not a good idea. Some advice from the *Front Sight Company*:

> *"In the category of Dry Practice: Only perfect practice makes perfect."*

> *"Shooting doesn't make you good. Dry practice makes you good. Shooting is merely a validation of your dry practice."*

> *"When it comes to your life, how good is good enough? We are never good enough!"*

> *"You don't want to be good. You want to be perfect!"*

Get the point? Good! Commit to practice "Dry Firing" for 10 minutes a day for the first three months. After that you should have the habit.

9. Insurance, or do you want to Pledge your fortune?

Do you have car insurance? Do you have homeowner or renter's insurance? Do you have life insurance? Do you have health insurance? On how many of these do you make money? **Do you need special insurance just in case you are arrested for a weapons violation; or even worse, charged and brought to trial and faced with legal bills?** Probably just as much as you need insurance for those other needs listed above; but coverage for this is not required by law, only by common sense. There are several organizations who offer insurance of some type or another. None are perfect and none are cheap. The NRA and the US Concealed Carry Association are just two of which I am familiar.

I will not endorse any offerings nor will I go into their coverages and details. You can chase that rabbit, should you feel that protecting all of your life's saving is important. I do have some insurance. I hate it; I totally loathe the cost. But in the world in which we live today, there is a mentality to sue even if the perp you shot was inside your own house, with his sack full of your silver and jewels, his hand bristling with weapons, and a "rap" sheet longer than your arm. Even if the perp is "dead as a doornail," his family just might view you as their retirement plan. Plus the D.A. might not see your actions in the same light as you see them.

10. Develop some Home Defense Plans, or plan for your worst nightmare

One final thought. Your spouse or significant other should also be trained to fire the handgun. I know, that is not always an easy sell, but "man-up" and make it happen. Why? Consider the following scenario: Your spouse shakes you awake at 2 a.m. and says that she heard some strange noise go "bump in the night." You grumble that you did not hear anything. She insists that you get up and go check it out. You tumble out of bed and cross the room, shut the door muttering something, and exit partially awake into the upstairs hall as she whispers after you, "Be careful Grumpy." She waits patiently for your return to report that all is well.

Minutes pass; you do not return. She may hear what sounds to her like another "bump in the night." Now she really begins to worry. Her alert flag goes from "orange" to "red." What should she do? What would you want her to do?

Obviously, she should pick up her cell phone and call 911. What? Her cell phone is in her purse downstairs in the kitchen? OK, then have her pick up the land-line phone and call 911. Uh oh, the land-line is dead. OK, then have her pick up your cell phone and dial 911. What, your cell phone is where? Never mind, for this scenario let us pretend that one of the cell phones is in your bedroom where you should ensure that you have one each and every night.

Responsively, 911 answers on the second ring and your spouse reports that you have disappeared inside the house. "No, I don't know where inside the house, but I heard a strange noise and he went to investigate and it's been, well several minutes, and he's not come back!" Again, 911 asks how long you've been gone. What? Your spouse did not look at the clock to establish the time you departed? Oh well, tell her to do so next time. She tells 911 she does not know exactly how long you have been gone, but it sure seems like a long time. Now, do you think this is going to be treated as a "code one" or high priority by the police? Will they come quickly, or at all? Will they suggest that she go look for you; perhaps to find you in the kitchen eating a snack?

It might have been a good idea for you to have previously insisted that she also know how to handle the handgun as well as shoot it. She can hold it while she stays on the phone with the 911 operator. What, she does not have a handgun? You took the one and only weapon with you on your late night patrol? Oh my, that is bad news. OK, for this scenario let us pretend that you have two guns; one for you and one for her and she knows how to load, rack, drop the safety, aim, and fire. (No, Shirley, it is **not** a good idea for her to go wandering around the house looking for him. What if that really was a "Stranger's noise" that she heard? Besides that chance, they might shoot each other.)

Your spouse has the phone to her ear with 911 still on the call and has positioned herself at the room's "safe point" and is hidden, waiting. What? What's a "safe point?" That is a predetermined location in your bedroom where she can hide with maximum protection while still aiming her handgun at the door opening into the bedroom from the hall. You do not have one? Sure you do. She should at least take cover behind your king size bed or an overstuffed chair. What? You do not think she knows that she is supposed to do that? Well, you should cover that with her when we are done.

She is crouched behind one side or end of the bed with the bulk of her body protected by the "Sleepy Tyme" mattress and springs. She has the high lumens mini-light trained on the door. It is at one end or side of the bed opposite from her. What? Oh, you took the only flash light with you. I see, well for this scenario let us pretend that you had the forethought to have two high-beam handheld flashlights in the bedroom for just such an occasion, batteries included.

Several minutes pass and still no "Grumpy" returns. She hears something in the hallway. She thinks the noise is approaching the bedroom door. She tells the 911 operator that she hears someone approaching the door and, being in fear of her life, is now putting down the phone so she can aim her pistol with both hands, but will not hang up. She ensures the magazine is "seated" in the grip, racks a round into the chamber, flips the thumb safety off and holds the semi in both hands, aimed at the door, **with her finger off the trigger**. After all, it just might be you that comes through the door.

The noise is now just outside the bedroom door. She shouts, **"I have a gun! I will use it to defend myself! The police are on the way!"** (Whether they are or not, the "noise maker" in the hall will not know and may well believe her.) **"Don't come any closer; I'll defend myself! I have a gun and a license to use it!"** What? Oh my, I do not want to hear that. Let us pretend that you were sufficiently smart and wise and made certain that she too went through CHCL class. **"Identify yourself or I'll shoot you!"**

If it is you—sleepy, Grumpy spouse—who left to go check out strange noises in the night, now responding in terror at your wife's threats, she should make you identify yourself by: your mother's middle name, your first pet's name, the city in which you were born, or something. (Experts advise that it is wise to have two password exchange scenarios. One password is to identify and to indicate the coast is clear. The other password also identifies, but indicates the coast is **not clear** and that the miscreant is right behind Mr. Grumpy holding him captive with knife, gun, or something. It is always good to have come up with a password exchange in advance of these situations.) If the approaching person fails all the tests she can dream up, she should ensure that the flashlight remains fixed on the door and that she holds the handgun pointed there also. What the perp's weapon is, is not the most critical item to know at the moment. What is critical is that your spouse understands that coming through the door is you, or you plus one armed bad guy, or one armed bad guy and no you.

Your spouse is probably shaking all over, terrified, and wondering why the 911 operator is muttering all kinds of words and questions that are not helping immediately. "Where are the police?" runs through her mind. Tell her to relax a little; she has a 7 to 1 advantage over the "Noise Maker" approaching your bedroom door.

First, the perp has no idea where she is inside the bedroom. She knows exactly where he will be when he steps inside. (In fact, doorways are often referred to as "death funnels" as they funnel those entering into a very narrow, predetermined space.)

Second, the perp has a high beam mini light of 200 lumens or more shining in his face. That will partially blind him.

Third, the perp has no idea how the furniture is laid out in the room or that your wife has placed a chair on the floor just beyond the opening door's swing to force him to step over if he sees it, or stumble and fall if he cannot. What? You did not discuss "booby-trapping" the doorway? Oh my, well, let us pretend that you discussed this when you practiced this self-defense scenario. What? No, I am well aware that you never practiced a self-defense scenario. It might be a good idea to do so in the future, don't you agree?

Fourth, the perp will assume that she is holding the flashlight and if he fires, it will naturally be toward the light. Since the flashlight is at the other end of the bed, his first shot will be a certain miss and be heard by the 911 operator. Your spouse now has no reason to hesitate; he has declared himself to be a killer—intent on her death. (It is extremely advantageous to any future legal entanglements your wife might face from this event that all of this has been recorded by 911.)

Fifth, she is crouched behind cover; the perp is in the open.

Sixth, because she has practiced firing her weapon, she is twice as effective a marksman as the average night time "Noise Maker."

Seventh, the perp is concerned that the police may actually be on their way. He knows that he has less than five or ten minutes before they arrive. Therefore, he is distracted and nervous about getting away. Nervousness causes carelessness.

Eighth, your spouse can rest her firing hands on the bed for support, providing her with a solid shooting platform. The perp will have to attempt to locate her in the dark with his gun hand moving and jerking.

Ninth, wait, since I said only seven advantages earlier, I will stop here and let you continue to come up with additional advantages to having a plan.

What was the price paid in this scenario **for failure** to plan and prepare? The failure to have a second weapon in the bedroom; to have a spouse trained in its use; to have a second flash light; to have a cell phone just in case the land line had been cut; to have an identified safe point for her to hide behind; to have a set of exchange passwords; and to have mindset readiness to take the life of a malevolent miscreant to protect her own life?

The price? There are at least two outcomes, but with extreme differences. In the first outcome, "Grumpy" returns to report that canine, cat, canary, or some other innocuous noise-knocker has kicked over the ficus tree and all is well. Both "Grumpy" and spouse return to sleep with an unwarranted sense of security that the next "noise in the night" will be just as benign. Yes, I will admit that the overwhelming majority of "noises in the night" are concluded with such innocent outcomes, but there are those rare occasions when that is not the case.

The Price paid in this scenario? After two days of failure to come to work, and no answer to repeated phone calls, concerned co-workers convinced the police to break into the house. The husband had been "tasered" and his throat cut. The wife had been raped repeatedly and murdered. The police taped off the crime scene, collected forensic evidence, interviewed suspects, and handled the case per their standard operating procedures. Maybe the miscreants will be identified, charged, tried, convicted, and punished. That would be a good outcome to a horrible incident. Well, good for all but the husband and wife.

Could this have been prevented? Yes, possibly, probably. How? Yes, you guessed what my answer would be. Get armed, get trained, get legal, be alert, and have a PLAN for home defense.

Brutal? Yes. Could it happen? Certainly. What? Oh, you do not think it would happen to you, not where you live, and not in your neighborhood? Well, statistics support your confidence, but may I remind you:

"Lightning and violence have one thing in common, they both strike somewhere."

More important, could, would you let it happen to you and your family if there were some way to prevent or reduce the likelihood? Then, what is your plan when a sound goes "bump in the night?"

"Better to be prepared and have a plan never needed, than to have a need for which you've never planned nor prepared."

In the above scenario, as *doctored* by the author's assumptions, the odds were seven to one in favor of the spouse. Without the plan and preparation, the odds switch to an insurmountable advantage in favor of the miscreant.

The cost for her preparation (ignoring CHCL class and CHCL license fees): an additional, excellent 9mm semi, a box of JHP cartridges, a spare cell phone, and hi-lumen flashlight (with batteries); in total, probably less than $800.00, maybe even less than $700.00 total cost. The cost for discussion and walk-through of various home invasion and robbery scenarios—no charge. The benefit of the above—life! Life as you have lived it and come to love it.

Give it some thought. Could this or something similar happen to your family? If so, are you just going to read this and then through inaction, potentially let it happen? If not, then what do you plan to do?

"You makes your choices and you takes your chances."

I am certain that there are many other things that we should discuss that are also very, very important. Luckily, or unluckily, I have not yet made their acquaintance. But PLEASE do not assume that the above covers all the things that you need to know, do, or heed. But I hope that it is a good first start. You can find further help and advice from the book, *Intruder in Your Home*, see *Appendix F*.

Appendix B

Lethal Force Scenario Solutions

Oh, so you do want some discussion of potential solutions to the Lethal Force scenarios? These are not legally approved, nor even condoned by anyone in authority or with experience and lack three levels of management signoff. They are just my thoughts of what you or I might do to remain safe as well as to keep out of jail.

Scenario #1: The guy climbing over the back fence screaming that he will beat your . . .

Suggested response: As you turn toward your house, **shout** and tell the gentleman that you carry a pistol and are licensed to use it to protect yourself. If he does not stop, you will be forced to defend yourself. Shout "**Stop**!" Then, turn and run as fast as you can to your house one hundred yards away. Lock the doors and call 911. "I'm John Scaredy Pants and am inside my house at 123 Main Street. There is a man outside threatening to maim or kill me. I have locked my doors. I have a CHCL and a gun. I do not know if the man who is threatening my life is armed, and if so, with what. Send police ASAP. I will stay on the line until they arrive."

Of course the 911 folks will ask why the man wants to maim or kill you. "He was not coherent. He just kept screaming that he was going to maim or kill me. I told him that I had a pistol and was licensed to carry it to defend myself. I shouted at him to stop. I ran into my house and locked the doors before he could grab me. Please send help ASAP. I'm afraid for my life."

911: "Why does he want to harm you?"

Folks, they are recording the call. All you want to tell them is your name, address, that you are a CHCL holder, armed, and that some crazy has threatened to maim or kill you, and that you fear for your life. And in this situation you have retreated into your house (from your curtilage?). Hopefully, the police will arrive before one of your doors or windows is smashed and you have shot both rounds from your *Kimber Pepper BlasterII* followed up by several rounds from your handgun should the Kimber thing not keep him down until the police arrive. (Go back and read the legal statutes.)

293

The D.A. will have difficulty bringing this to trial even though the guy was his cousin. After all, you warned the gentleman; you told him to stop; you told him you were armed; you told him you were authorized to use a pistol in self-defense; you retreated into your house; and you were fearful for your life or of grievous bodily harm, and he broke into your house to harm and kill you.

Scenario #2: The gentleman burst through the door and screams for you to return his property in front of the five church deacons.

Suggested Response: Draw and hit the fool with a blast from the *Kimber Pepper Blaster*. Ask the five witnesses to sit on him while you call the police. Call 911. "Hello, the is Jeremiah Nonlethal Jones at 123 Main Street. A man has just intruded into my house, screaming wild things and threatening me with grave bodily harm. I am a CHCL holder and have a gun. I have not had to use it—yet. Currently, I have subdued him with pepper spray. Send the police ASAP. I am fearful for my life. I will stay on the line as long as I safely can."

911: "Why is he shouting at you? What did he say?"

"I could not really understand him. I was shocked and frightened. It all happened so quickly and I am still shaking. Hurry and send the police. I do not want to have to shoot him to save my life." You do not want to mention or bring up any reference to his claim that you have his property. Whether that is true or false, this is not the time to discus it. What is germane is the threat to your life requiring immediate police presence. However, if you did take the gentleman's property, you just might have been wise to initially inform him that you are sending out two church deacons with his stuff before he breaks in and you respond with "Mr. Boom."

You have what the British call "a sticky wicket" in this scenario. If you did purloin the gentleman's property, you are not legally authorized to take lethal force. The fact that this was alleged in front of witnesses places you under suspicion from the "get-go." Be careful and be wise. At this point, you might offer the five church deacons something to drink—water, juice.

Scenario #3: The gorilla outlining your ancestral lineage is approaching your car with a tire iron held in a very angry hand.

Suggested solution: Maneuver your car and get the heck out of there. Go to the nearest police station or fire station and file a formal report. Report as much as you can remember as to description of man, vehicle, license, etc. This is no time to be a hero in a hospital bed. You have a family to protect. Even if you have to bump a few fenders to get the heck out of there—GO! No pepper spray, no handgun, no heroics. Be a responsible husband and Dad. Do not place your family in harm's way if you can avoid it, and drive more carefully in the future. And remember, **do** report it to the police. The nut may have your license plate number and attempt to make a non-social call at a future date of his choosing. If forced to use your handgun on the gorilla at that future date, it would serve you well to have already entered a police report referencing his attempted violence. Compare the cost of a few fender dings versus hospital bills or legal expenses. Yes, tell the police that you dinged a few fenders and left the scene of an accident—ran, fearing for your life. You were fearful for the lives of your family and are more than willing to pay for the damages when reported.

Scenario #4: The disheveled man crosses the street and hits you on the left shoulder with a bottle.

Suggested solutions: If it got this far, you are in very deep trouble. Even if you were sufficiently alert to have Mr. *Kimber Pepper Blaster* in your hand, it is not recommended within two feet, so you have a real dilemma. By the way, the small pepper spray that hangs from the keychain in your pocket **is** very effective within three feet.

You do not know whether he is drunk, mentally impaired, on "meth," or has confused you for the bozo having a love affair with his wife. What you do know is that you are face to face in a non-social encounter of the worst kind and you are hurt, probably in a lot of pain. Your left arm/shoulder may be weakened, numb, temporarily unusable, or broken. You cannot fumble for your handgun since you must do everything in your power to stop the second bottle-blow hitting your skull. You cannot fumble at the thumb strap, draw, flick off the thumb safety, point, and shoot. You must ward off the next blow with your good arm/hand.

Although he is armed with an improvised weapon, at least the man is not armed with a gun or knife. If you can incapacitate him or break away, you can try to outrun him. If successful, now start fumbling to draw and be prepared to fire as he just might well beat your brains out if he catches you.

If he is holding onto you with one hand and swinging the bottle with the other, you must do whatever you can with the one good arm to keep that bottle off your noggin. One blow could render you unconscious at the least. You are already under a violent unlawful attack, a felony. You had better be in fear for your life. If you defend yourself and gain sufficient time/space, draw and fire.

However, you were pretty dumb to get to the bottle blow on the shoulder point in the first place. When you first appraised the appearance of the individual, you should have increased your worry ratio up to the 50% "yellow" alert level. When he crossed over to your side of the street in the middle of the block, you should have been thinking that he is up to no good and has identified you as his next meal source or personal ATM. Your Alert Level goes to 75%: *Code Orange!*

Three options seem reasonable at this point:

Option #1: When you observe his suspicious crossing in the middle of the block to reach your side of the street, then you cross over to the side that he just left. If you both continue walking in opposite directions, well and good. You were just overly cautious and your left arm is not screaming out in pain.

Option #2: If, after you execute Option #1, the gentleman with the long necked bottle re-crosses to get back on the same side of the street as you, go into **Code Red** high alert self-defense mode! Put up your hand and shout to him "That is close enough; **STOP!**" Meanwhile draw Mr. Pepper. If he does not stop, repeat your command to stop and tell him you are legally armed and authorized to defend yourself. No reaction, then hurry and re-cross the street back to your original side. (a) If he follows, then you either retreat back to the closest location where there are people (my choice, but I am a wimp), or (b) you raise up Mr. Pepper and again shout loudly at the rascal that you are armed and legally authorized to defend yourself. If he comes one step closer, you will shoot. If he does, then shoot and while he is screaming and rubbing his face, run to your car and "get out of Dodge."

*"Violence is seldom the answer, but when it is the answer, it is the **only** answer."*

Option #3: When you observe the gentleman cross in the middle of the block to your side of the street, turn and immediately return to civilization where you have other adults around you.

No, you do not have to agree with any of my suggested solutions. But if you do not agree, then come up with your own solutions and then go back and read the laws. **One thing you should really consider is to acquire some type of less lethal deterrent and carry that even as much or more than your handgun. Why more? Because you can carry Mr. Pepper into places where guns cannot go, legally that is.**

You may have noticed that none of the above scenarios were of a miscreant armed with a knife or pistol obviously bent on doing you or yours serious harm. Those types of armed, malevolent situations are probably fairly straight forward, quickly identified, and potentially deadly. If the perp has a gun, you can safely make several immediate (without further hem-hawing) decisions that should hold up in a legal surrounding:

1.   The gun is real.
2.   The gun is loaded.
3.   The perp has reasonable knowledge of how the gun works. You know, pull the trigger and it goes bang.
4.   The perp is prepared to use the pistol to obtain his desire.
5.   Your life is of little consequence or value to him in his current state of mind.

As a matter of fact, make those decisions now. If that fearful, dreaded situation ever arises, you will already be five mental decisions ahead and can concentrate on what, if anything, you can or should do at that moment.

As the Arkansas law states:

A person is justified in using deadly physical force upon another person if the person reasonably believes that the other person is:

*(1)   Committing or about to commit a **felony involving force or violence;***

*(2)   Using or about to use **unlawful deadly physical force; or***

*(3)   **Imminently endangering the person's life**.*

There are many scenarios that can be built to describe an armed encounter. Read your local paper; chances are that you will have a scenario reported daily. Not all of the details may be reported to allow you to understand the exact situation, but you can hypothesize and build your own scenario and then visualize several responses. Just remember, statistics would indicate that most shooting encounters are within ten-to-twenty feet and happen fast, very fast—two or three seconds.

To use the "Old West" term, if someone has the "drop" on you, initial compliance becomes a very tough decision. For example, FBI statistics that I have read indicate that getting into a car with an armed perp increases your chance for harm by two or three times. But if the perp is pointing a pistol at your face . . ., a tough decision environment. But, in your favor, the perp is feeling very much in control and not overly worried about your causing a problem. He is probably nervous, shouting, acting very mad and malevolent, and commanding your immediate compliance with his demands.

What you have to quickly determine is how you can seem to be in compliance and at the same time put your body into a position that you can draw your handgun without the perp seeing you do so. Then, point and fire before the perp can visually comprehend what you are doing and sends the instruction to his trigger finger to pull. You are not a policeman or a bounty hunter. You are not worried about disarming or arresting him. You are worried about getting out alive. "Shoot" would seem to be the only prudent action. You probably will not survive a standoff by asking the perp to put down his pistol as you point yours at him. But can you shoot him? Boy, that is the question for all of us who are basically law-abiding citizens. Let us hope and pray that it will never come to that; but if it does, you may have less than 2-3 seconds to react, so decide now.

Or you comply, and hope that this perp "leaves eye witnesses alive."

Further considerations: who else might be in jeopardy if you try to draw and fire? Is your wife and/or kids standing there with you as the armed perp points the pistol and demands your money, your wife's jewelry, and your kid's *iPad*? If you start to draw and the perp reacts fast, how many of you will be harmed? But what if he is demanding that all of you get into the car with him, or that all of you go back into the house with him? Well, you just might have that discussion with your family now, before it ever happens; not when the perp is pointing a pistol in their faces.

The best advice is avoidance, vigilance, and having your weapon in your hand—but concealed—when in any place where such situations might likely occur. The best advice I have read for daily avoidance is also off the Internet:

If you avoid *The Three Stupids:*

1). *hanging with stupid people,*
2). *going to stupid places,*
3). *and doing stupid things, then none of this may ever even be an issue.*

Let us hope, but conduct ourselves accordingly and be alert and observant.

CAVEAT: I am not a lawyer. I have zero legal training. Do not construe any of the bold font or my comments as legal opinion or advice. They are not. They are my opinion only. Consult your own attorney for legal advice or interpretation of laws and statutes! Nor am I a self-defense or defensive handgun expert. You can go to schools to learn their suggested solutions.

Appendix C

Did You Know?

These are a few items of interest that didn't seem to fit into other chapters.

1. **911 calls can be made from a discontinued cell phone.** For example if you have an ATT *Go-Phone* that is no longer active, you can charge the phone and dial 911 and it will connect. (Tested October, 2011, in Little Rock, AR.)

    A. Consider placing an old cell phone by your bedside and keep it on the charger. It is there 24/7 should your hear something go "creak or bang" in the middle of the night and your "in-service" cell phone is in your purse out on the hall table, or in the kitchen, or in your briefcase in the car and some miscreant has cut your land-line phone's cable prior to breaking through your door or window.

    B. If you have more than one, consider putting the additional ones in your kids' rooms with training and instruction on when and how to use, and threats of "you know what" if they misuse the 911 phone.

2. **A 911 call made from a cell phone will ring in the closest 911 exchange**, not in the 911 exchange in which your cell phone's telephone number is located. For example, consider that you have a Dallas area cell phone with a 902 area code number and you are visiting in Little Rock, AR. Your Dallas neighbor calls to tell you there is a very loud, rowdy party going on in your house. Frantically you dial 911; you will be connected with the Little Rock area 911 office. (Tested October, 2011, in Little Rock, AR.)

    A. The good news is that if you are traveling and really need 911assistance where you are currently visiting, it will be the 911 office nearest you at that time, not back home several hundreds of miles away.

B. The bad news is that you will have to ask your Dallas neighbor to call 911 for you and have the police visit your house party there.

3. If you leave your home Alarm system in "Test" mode, it may announce to you every time there is a breach of security at a monitored entrance into your house. Most home alarm systems have a "Test" mode used by the technician to assist him during installation. He can open a door to test if the detection switch is working without having to set off the alarm. The control unit will merely announce, for example: "Fault, back door open." By leaving your system in "Test" mode continually, you will be told each and every time someone enters or leaves through a monitored egress. Few people arm the alarm when at home during the day. The "Test" mode would give you an early warning that someone, unannounced, has just entered by the front door, back door, or bedroom window. Rather than the first indication that someone has entered your house being when you turn around and see a perp standing behind you, the "Test" mode alert gives you valuable seconds or minutes to react. Another advantage, if you have little children and "Billy Be-Bad" loves to sneak outside, you will hear the alarm alert that a door has been opened. When armed, the alarm will still function and sound with the loud claxon noise we all love, when a security breach occurs.

4. Definition of a "person" (Statute 5-1-102)

Actually this has no direct bearing on handguns or firearms; I just find it very interesting that in the state of Arkansas a person is defined as,

(13) (A) *'Person,' 'actor,' 'defendant,' 'he,' 'she,' 'her,' or 'him' includes:*
    (i) *Any natural person; and*
    (ii) *When appropriate, an 'organization' as defined in § 5-2-501.*
(B) (i) (a) *As used in §§ 5-10-101-5-10-105, **'person' also includes an unborn child in utero at any stage of development.***
      (b) *'Unborn child' means a living fetus of twelve (12) weeks or greater gestation.*

I find it a curious paradox that a citizen can be charged with murder if that citizen causes the death of an unborn child. However, a pregnant woman can abort her fetus (to the resounding support of various organizations) and have no legal entanglements. See what happens when one is turned loose in a law library and has no clue how to look up laws about firearms; all kinds of strange things are found.

You might wish to add some of your own discoveries. Please share them.

5. _____

6. _____

Appendix D

Could You Benefit from Reading This Book? Some Answers

1. What occurs when you fire a handgun straight up into the air?
    The bullet will reach its ultimate altitude and then proceeds, under the power of gravity, to fall back toward earth at over 600 fps. If it hits a person, it will injure or kill him.

2. Name the three general categories of handguns.
    Revolver, Semiautomatic, and Derringer.

3. Of the eight most common styles of on-body holsters, how many can you describe?
    1. Cowboy; 2. Waist band-outside; 3. Waist band-inside; 4. Bra; 5. Crotch, 6. Ankle, 7. Shoulder, 8. Pocket.

4. What are the two major concerns that dictate the type of gun safe that you should consider?
    Opportunistic theft or misuse and professional burglary with time to empty the house.

5. What is the primary distinction between the crimes of "Assault" and the crimes of "Battery?"
    A charge of Battery is made when you actually physically harmed a person. Assault is only a threatened action or an action that is a threat.

6. Between the crimes of "Assault" and the crimes of "Battery," which type of crime is the typical handgun owner most likely to commit?
    Assault is the most likely, as it can be stumbled into by merely showing or drawing your handgun. Firing is not required.

7. Do you understand the **legal** concept "Choice of Evils?" Please explain.
    (d)   Conduct that would otherwise constitute an offense is justifiable when:

305

> ***(1) The conduct is necessary as an emergency measure to avoid an imminent public or private injury; and***
>
> *(2) According to ordinary standards of reasonableness, the desirability and urgency of avoiding the imminent public or private injury outweigh the injury sought to be prevented by the law proscribing the conduct.*
>
> *(e) Justification under this section shall not rest upon a consideration pertaining to the morality or advisability of the statute defining the offense charged.*
>
> *(f) If the actor is reckless or negligent in bringing about the situation requiring a choice of evils or in appraising the necessity for his or her conduct, the justification afforded by this section is unavailable in a prosecution for any offense for which recklessness or negligence, as the case may be, suffices to establish a culpable mental state.*

8. What actions are you **lawfully** authorized to perform with a CHCL, which a non-CHCL holder cannot do?
   You are authorized to carry a handgun CONCEALED. Nothing more.

9. If you **have** a CHCL, can you lawfully make a "Citizen's Arrest?" *Yes.*

10. If you **do not have** a CHCL, can you lawfully make a "Citizen's Arrest?"
    Yes, a citizen's arrest power is not related to having a fire arm or a CHCL.

11. Under what circumstances can you lawfully fire a warning shot to diffuse a dangerous situation?
    Never.

12. Explain the difference to a shooter between a SA and a DA handgun.
    A SA must be manually cocked. If a semi, this is usually accomplished by racking the slide to load a round into the firing chamber. If a revolver, this is accomplished by manually pulling the hammer back to a fully cocked position. A DA is cocked by the trigger squeeze.

13. Explain why "mushrooming" is an important characteristic you should consider?

Ammunition like a JHP will spread upon hitting the target. This will reduce the risk of "pass through" as well as place more kinetic energy onto the target.

14. How often should you clean your handgun?

    Best if done after every use, whenever exposed to the elements, and at least once a year or so if firing is never anticipated.

15. You are fighting with a criminal who has grabbed onto your semiautomatic pistol. In the struggle the magazine gets ejected. You successfully wrench the handgun free and press the trigger. What happens? Explain three scenarios.

    If the semi has a magazine safety, it will not fire. Lacking that safety, it will fire if there is a round in the firing chamber. Of course if no round was "racked" into the firing chamber, the gun will not fire.

16. You have finished loading your six shot Ruger *Bear Cat* .22-caliber revolver with .22-caliber long rifle ammunition. You close the cylinder's loading aperture. You aim at your target and you squeeze the trigger, but nothing happens. Please explain.

    Most likely you have SA revolver that requires you to manually cock the hammer back before firing each round.

17. Explain the following two terms: RN-FMJ and JHP.

    RN-FMJ = Round Nose-Full Metal Jacket round, which has a copper skin over a lead core and is shaped with a round nose. JHP = Jacketed Hollow Point round, which has a copper skin over a lead core with a hole in the end of the bullet.

18. What is one of the benefits of a semi having a "tang?"

    Helps secure a proper grip on the handgun and will assist in keeping your thumb and first finger "Y" from requiring stitches from a slicing by the slide.

19. If you have a CHCL, can you lawfully carry your weapon into a restaurant (in Arkansas) that sells alcohol and/or beer for consumption on premises?

    If it is open 5 days a week, serves 1 meal a day, has a kitchen, and can seat 50+ people.

20. If you are involved in a shooting incident, what is the common legal advice concerning what you tell the police?

> *To tell the police the absolute minimum that you can possibly say; preferably nothing more than name, address, I'm a CHCL holder, there's my gun, and I was frightened for my life. He was trying to kill me. There is the evidence. May I now call my lawyer? I will answer all of your other questions once my lawyer is present.*

21. Name two of the most inexpensive handgun ammos to use for target shooting.
    .22-caliber long rifle and 9mm Luger are generally the least expensive.

22. Can you list three reasons that support your obtaining a CHCL?
    1. *You can lawfully carry a concealed weapon. 2. You can lawfully carry a loaded weapon in your car. 3. You will have received at least some exposure to the laws related to firearms. 4. You will have shot at least twenty rounds with a handgun. 5. You might be encouraged to become even more knowledgeable. 6. You will have received some instruction on handgun safety.*

23. Does it make a difference if you qualify at your CHCL class (in Arkansas) by firing a revolver rather than a semiautomatic?
    Yes. If you qualify with a revolver, you are not authorized to carry a semiautomatic and should you do so and be caught, you lose your CHCL. If you qualify with a semiautomatic, you can carry any type legal handgun.

24. What is the key difference between "Aggravated Assault" and "Assault in the First Degree" with a firearm per Arkansas statutes? *Intent.*

25. Can you describe the circumstances under which you can lawfully shoot another human being under Arkansas statutes?

Arkansas Statue: 5-2-607. Use of deadly physical force in defense of a person.

(a) A person is justified in using deadly physical force upon another person if the person reasonably believes that the other person is:

    (1) Committing or about to commit a **felony involving force or violence;**

(Review *Chapter 13* for definitions of "crimes of violence.")

(2) Using or about to use **unlawful deadly physical force**; or

(3) **Imminently endangering the person's life or imminently about to victimize the person as described in 9-15-103 from the continuation of a pattern of domestic abuse.**

(b) A person **may not use deadly physical force** in self-defense if the person knows that he or she can avoid the necessity of using deadly physical force **with complete safety:**

   (1) **(A)** **By retreating.**

      (B) However, a person is not required to retreat if the person is:

        (i) In the person's dwelling or on the curtilage surrounding the person's dwelling and was not the original aggressor; or

        (ii) A law enforcement officer or a person assisting at the direction of a law enforcement officer; or

   (2) **By surrendering possession** of property to a person claiming a lawful right to possession of the property.

Thank you for your patience in taking the above exercise. Hopefully, it was helpful in assisting you in determining your level of knowledge of handgun and handgun related concerns. Twenty out of twenty-five correct answers are a score of 80%. Is that knowledge level sufficient for your mental comfort and for the safety of your family and friends?

If you are not an experienced "shootist" or handgun owner, the following definitions may assist you:

1. CHCL = Concealed Handgun Carry License
2. DA = Double Action
3. JHP = Jacketed Hollow Point
4. RN-FMJ = Round Nose-Full Metal Jacket
5. SA = Single Action

Appendix E

Some Actions You Might Term "Dumb Stunts"

Some news stories did not seem to fit well under any of the other chapters. However, they do demonstrate how to execute a dumb stunt with a firearm. I decided to place their unfortunate sagas here.

Stunt #1

Friday, December 30, 2011: *Gunshots from car lead to arrest of 2,* screamed the headline in the *Arkansas Democrat Gazette.*

> *Two Little Rock men were arrested Friday afternoon after officers witnessed one of the men firing a handgun out the window of a car.*
>
> *Officers waiting on a tow truck to remove a stolen vehicle near Base Line and Rock roads in southwest Little Rock heard gunshots in the area and drove toward the noise. They soon located a green Pontiac Grand Am traveling north on Base Line Road with a man hanging out the window firing a handgun, police said.*
>
> *The officers stopped the car about 3:30 p.m. and found a .40-caliber Smith and Wesson handgun under the passenger seat.*
>
> *The man the police said fired the gun,* [a Dumb Act], *was charged with unlawful discharge of a firearm from a vehicle. The driver,* [an Even Dumber Act,] *29, was charged with driving while intoxicated.*
>
> *Police said no one was injured during the shooting.*

A couple of observations: One, they were firing a pistol of good reputation: a Smith and Wesson. Second, should their vehicle ever be chased or attacked by a lion, or tiger, or bear, the .40-caliber sized handgun would give them a fighting chance for survival. This is their only plea and probably their best defense, in my opinion. They were practicing firing from a moving vehicle just in case an incredibly frightening beast attacked their Pontiac Grand Am while they were driving through the neighborhood.

Stunt #2

On Wednesday, February 22, 2012 in that same paper the small headline read, *"Gun seen in bank; woman charged."* The article continued,

> *A . . . woman was arrested Tuesday, four days after walking into a bank with a gun and demanding help with her bank account, according to a . . . police report.*
>
> *At 10:20 a.m., [we'll use her stage name 'LH'], 61, was arrested for terroristic threatening after employees at the Bank . . . called police to report that [LH] was the woman who previously had threatened employees.*
>
> *At 2:45 p.m. Friday, [LH] was discussing her bank account with employees when she became angry . . . The employees told officers that [LH] claimed that someone had withdrawn funds from her account and 'whoever it is, she's going to bust a cap in their ass' . . . [LH] pulled up her shirt to reveal a handgun in her waistband and left the bank. The incident was reported to police and when [LH] came back Tuesday, she was arrested . . .*
>
> *Police retrieved a .38 special revolver and a .22-caliber revolver from [LH's] home, . . .*
>
> *[LH] posted $2,000.00 bail Tuesday through a bondsman at the . . . Jail.*

There are several interesting things we can learn from this incident. She was armed with a .38 Special revolver, appropriate for protection, displaying good knowledge of required handgun power for protection. The police confiscated that one plus her .22-caliber revolver from her home. "LH" probably used the .22-caliber for less expensive target practice, another indication of good judgment. Why did they invade her home? The whole incident took place at the branch bank. No sense of fair play here. Why did the reporter think it necessary to give us the exact time of day on both days?

I can almost assure you that "LH" had tried on several occasions to resolve this via phone, with an "English as a second language" person stationed overseas, only in desperation to have finally decided to go to the bank in person. Having met with a person evidencing about as much interest in her situation as a terrorist does in your peace and quiet; No, wait, she was arrested for terrorism.

So far, the bail bond has her out about $200.00, plus the cost of two revolvers, plus her lawyer's clock has just started running. I bet you that she will spend far more money on this arrest than the amount of funds missing from her account.

You are probably thinking that I could have thrown this under the chapter on *Assault*. Well, perhaps, except what she did was so . . . well, there is no other term for it; such a dumb stunt that it deserved its own chapter. And besides that, she was not arrested for assault; she was arrested for "terroristic threatening." She also violated the "Remember the Plaxico Burress" by wearing her handgun in her waistband, not in a holster. (I probably should include laws on terroristic threatening in the next edition; what do you think?)

People, a Concealed Handgun Carry License only lawfully permits you to carry a handgun—**CONCEALED!** If you flash it, you can be arrested. Did you notice, per the above report, she never even drew her pistol, much less pointed it. She merely flashed it, intentionally, with some threatening remarks. And speaking of remarks, a refined woman of sixty-one should know better than use a word such as "ass," don't you agree?

Stunt #3

March 1, 2012, *Arkansas Democrat Gazette:*

> *CSP [we will protect the name], 27, of Taylorsville, Utah, has been charged with one felony count of discharging a firearm with injury and one misdemeanor count of possessing drug paraphernalia after police say he tried to shoot a mouse in his pantry and ended up wounding his roommate.*

It is patently apparent that in Utah, being attacked by a mouse does not justify a response of self-defense. Other things that we can learn from the above incident: a roommate should not live in a pantry. Also, keep your drug paraphernalia out of the reach of mice. (OK, I confess that there was no insinuation that the mouse was running off with the drug paraphernalia; I made that part up.) Drugs and drinking do not mix well with firearm ownership. Give up one or the other, or risk the chance of living at tax-payer expense for some period of time.

At the time of the publishing deadline, this was all that the editor had time to include. Unfortunately, there are probably more to come.

Appendix F

Some Sources and Resources

This will not be all-inclusive, but if you avail yourself of all of these, you will be a much better educated and knowledgeable Handgun Owner than most. Despite all best efforts, organizations do change their Internet addresses and web site designs. Should any of these suffer such a fate, let me apologize for having sent you down the wrong path. I would suggest if you discover that is the case, try a general search for the organization's new address, or figure out a changed web site's organization.

A. Associations:
    1. National Rifle Association (NRA): *www.nrahq.org*; 800-672-3888; non-profit organization promoting 2nd amendment rights for citizens to bear arms.
    2. U.S. Concealed Carry Association (USCCA): A for-profit company with lots of handgun related materials for members. *usconcealedcarry.com*; 877-677-1919
    3. Buckeye State: *buckeyefirearms.org*: general info on Ohio issues as well as national issues.
    4. Arkansas Rifle and Pistol Association: *davidj@specent.com*. David Joyner, Pres. 479-263-6665. Interface to sanction Rifle and pistol matches with NRA.
    5. The Right of Jury Nullification Association. *www.fija.org*

B. Books
    1. *The Samurai, The Mountie, and The Cowboy* by David B. Kopel. A Cato Institute book from Prometheus Books.
    2. *More Guns, Less Crime. Understanding Crime and Gun-Control Laws* by John R. Lott, Jr. Second Edition, 2000, the University of Chicago Press, Chicago.

3. *The Ohio Guide to Firearms Laws,* 4th edition, Oct 2011 by Ken Hanson, Attorney at Law.

4. *Intruder In Your Home—How to Defend Yourself Legally with a Firearm,* by Ronald L. Cruit, STEIN AND DAY publishers, Briarcliff Manor NY, 1983 edition

C. Websites

1. LexisNexis via one of two state sites. Go to *Arkansas State Police web site* (see below.) On the ASP main screen SCROLL to the very bottom to "Helpful Links," and CLICK on "Other Resources." On next screen titled "Other Resources," under *Arkansas Government—General,* cursor down to second line and "Click" on *Arkansas Code.* "Click" on *OK—Close* and you are in *LexisNexis* and you can search Arkansas law. (Good luck.)

2. *defensivecarry.com*

3. *USCCA.com*

4. *Stevespages.com* Contains among other stuff hundreds of owner manuals: "Manuals for Every Gun on Earth". Try this link to get directly to the gun manuals*: http:// stevespages.com/page7b.htm*

5. Ark Statutes on line; select *LexisNexis.*

6. *Shootingtimes.com*

7. *Handgunsmag.com*

8. *Laserlyte.com* (Sales site for their handgun laser lights and practice shooting tools)

D. Specific Internet sites for laws, ordinances, etc.

1. CDC Mortality Rates for Firearms: *http://webapp.cdc. gov/sasweb/ncipc/mortrate10_sy.html*

2. Arkansas State Police for Concealed Handgun Carry Licenses General Info: *http://www.asp.state.ar.us/*

3. Arkansas licensed CHCL Class Instructor search: *http:// www.asp.state.ar.us/asplicense/chcl_instructor_search/find. aspx*

Select your county on the Drop Down list and then press "Search." Will list all licensed instructors for that county.

4. City Ordinances: *www.municode.com*

5. Shooting Ranges in Arkansas: on internet: *www.huntingnavigator.com*. Scroll to "A" and find on right column near bottom "Arkansas Shooting Weapons Firing Ranges." Click on that. Lists in excess of 30.

6. Pulaski County Ordinances*: www.co.pulaski.ar.us*